Stefano Benvenuti
Gianni Rizzoni

the WHODUNIT

an informal history of detective fiction

Translated by Anthony Eyre

With "A Report on the Current Scene,"
by Edward D. Hoch

COLLIER BOOKS

A Division of Macmillan Publishing Co., Inc.
New York

COLLIER MACMILLAN PUBLISHERS
London

Frontispiece: *Roman mosaic from a dining-room floor.* NATIONAL MUSEUM, NAPLES

Copyright © 1979 by Arnoldo
Mondadori Editore S.p.A., Milano
English translation © 1980 by
Arnoldo Mondadori Editore S.p.A.,
Milano

The Italian edition of this book was
prepared in consultation with Alberto
Tedeschi.

Macmillan Publishing Co., Inc.
866 Third Avenue, New York, N.Y.
10022
Collier Macmillan Canada, Inc.

Library of Congress Cataloging in Publication Data
Benvenuti, Stefano, 1948–
    The whodunit.
    Translation of: Il romanzo giallo.
    Includes index.
    1. Detective and mystery stories — History and
criticism.   I. Rizzoni, Gianni.   II. Title.
PN3448.D4B4713   1981   809.3'872   81-38455
ISBN 0-02-048620-0 (pbk.)   AACR2

First Collier Books Edition 1981
10 9 8 7 6 5 4 3 2 1

The Whodunit is also published in a
hardcover edition by Macmillan
Publishing Co., Inc.

Printed in the United States of America

CONTENTS

THE WHODUNIT

1 | THE ROOTS

... I have heard
That guilty creatures sitting at a play
Have by the very cunning of the scene
Been struck so to the soul, that presently
They have proclaim'd their malefactions;
For murder, though it have no tongue, will speak
With most miraculous organ. ...

Hamlet, act 2, scene 2

Crime, mystery, and investigation have always played an important part in man's life and its faithful mirror, literature. From the Bible to Herodotus's *Histories*, from Greek tragedy to Elizabethan, from Gothic to Romantic novels, violent and mysterious death, the discovery, and Divine or human punishment of the guilty have furnished successful literary themes, demanding the emotional involvement of the reader. Yet not until the second half of the nineteenth century did a literary form that specialized exclusively in crime, investigation, and detection of the guilty party appear.

No literary form is born spontaneously. In its roots one can always find a subtle and often indecipherable mixture of sources and forerunners. Like other literary genres, the detective novel has been credited with illustrious antecedents that more or less provide the form's origins. Some, for instance, find the genre's prototype in Sophocles's *Oedipus Rex*, and, in fact, many of the elements in this tragedy invite comparison with the characteristics of the detective novel.

There has been a brutal murder: Laius, the king of Thebes, has been beaten to death during a journey. Many years pass. In Thebes a new king, Oedipus, has risen to the throne; a foreigner, he has freed the city from the curse of the Sphinx and married Laius's widow, Jocasta. But Laius's unpunished murder calls to the heavens for vengeance, and the gods make the city expiate the sin, letting loose a terrible plague on the people. To placate the gods, the murderer must be found and punished. Determined to save his city, Oedipus offers to investigate the crime and bring the truth to light. He questions the dead man's widow, the leading citizens of Thebes, the seer Tiresias, and an old shepherd. And he discovers the murderer: the least suspect person, himself.

Oedipus and the Sphinx, *or rather the meeting between human intelligence and the blind and brutal forces of destiny. (Painting by J. C. Ingress, 1808). The danger of the Sphinx can be avoided only by answering the riddle the monster puts to each passerby. According to some, including the Frenchmen Boileau and Narcejac, the oracle and the riddle form the ancient type of detective novel.* Opposite page: *an illustration by Aubrey Beardsley for "The Murders in the Rue Morgue" by Edgar Allan Poe, the true creator of criminal fiction.*

Voltaire (1694–1778). The character of Zadig, protagonist of the short novel Zadig, or Destiny *by the famous French polymath, is often seen as the modern detective's prototype, with his ability to see the significance in signs and to discover the unknown through clues. Zadig had predecessors in other literary traditions, such as the brother* Princes of Serendip *created by Cristoforo Armeno (Venice 1557), inspired by Arab and Persian tales.*

The basic elements are all here: the crime, the detective, the investigation, and discovery of the culprit. However, hundreds of similar stories can be found in the Bible, in *Herodotus*, in the *Arabian Nights*, in Persian stories, and in the ancient legends of China and Japan. Obviously a crime, a mystery, and a carefully worked-out solution are not enough to turn such a story—dealing essentially with the vicissitudes of fortune—into a detective *novel*. A basic element is still missing, and it arrived only in the nineteenth century: the professional criminal investigator, the police force, public or private. It has been said that Chaucer never wrote about airplanes because he had never seen one, and it is equally true that one could not possibly expect a detective novel to have been written until the police and professional detection had come into existence.

This does not mean, however, that the various extensive studies into the literary and historical sources of the detective novel are useless or meaningless. They inspired a literary genre that many, because of its popular appeal, underrate: Some of the novel's characteristic motifs—the detective, the mystery, the discovery of the culprit—are inherited from other types of novels and have merely been moved, without any major changes, into a new genre. This genre reflects both the new society in which it was born—the modern cities of an industrial age—and a new philosophy: nineteenth-century positivism. So let us take a look at the essential elements of the detective novel.

The Detective. Aesop's fox, who refused to go into the lion's den after he had noticed that there were many animal tracks entering the cave but no signs of any tracks coming out, might be considered one of the first true detectives. The most famous forerunner remains, however, Voltaire's Zadig, who was borrowed from Persian tradition. When the first Eunuch asks him whether he has seen the queen's dog, Zadig replies, "It's not a dog, it's a bitch." "That's so," the first Eunuch admits. "It's a very small spaniel," adds Zadig, "that has had puppies recently. Her left forefoot is lame, and she has very long ears." "You have seen her then?" "Oh no! I have not seen the animal, and I never knew the queen had a bitch."

Here is Zadig's explanation of the mystery:

I saw an animal's tracks on the sand, and I judged without difficulty they were the tracks of a small dog. The long, shallow furrows printed on the little ridges of sand between the tracks of the paws informed me that the animal was a bitch with pendent dugs, who thus had had puppies recently. Other tracks in a different direction, which seemed all along to have scraped the surface of the sand beside the forepaws, gave me the idea that the bitch had very long ears; and as I remarked that the sand was always less hollowed by one paw than by the three others, I concluded that our august queen's bitch was somewhat lame, if I dare say so.

This talented display of the art of deduction must be seen as the model for the most famous characters in the detective novel, from Dupin to Sherlock Holmes.

Mystery. Of all mysteries, the crime committed in a locked room is the most complex and demanding, and for these reasons few detective novelists are able to resist the appeal of its potential. Among the numerous forerunners of this category, many critics have noted a story found in the Bible (from Daniel 14). Daniel sought to show that the priests of the god Baal were lying when they claimed he ate thirty-two bushels of fine flour and forty sheep with thirty-six gallons of wine every night. In order to prove to the king that he was being fooled by the priests—that, although he himself locked up the temple every night the food was being taken away by them and their families through a secret entrance—Daniel sprinkled the floor with ashes. Next morning he showed the king the footprints of the priests, their wives, and their children. As a result, the king "fell into a rage; priest and priest's wife and priest's children must be taken into custody. . . ." Later "he put the whole company of them to death."

The unmasking of the culprit. Hamlet has a play performed before the Danish Court in which a murder occurs that bears many similarities to the circumstances of his father's death. The play is the vehicle through which Hamlet makes his father's mur-

The publishing success of the richly embroidered biographies of famous criminals influenced even Daniel Defoe. To make some quick money—a constant concern among novelists—he wrote the lives of such highwaymen as Jonathan Wild and John Sheppard. Left: Wild being conducted to his execution. Far left: Title page of the life of John Sheppard.

The detective novel's most direct predecessor is the Gothic novel. Above: One of Holst's illustrations for Frankenstein *(1818) by Mary Wollstonecraft Shelly (1797–1851), Shelley's second wife and the daughter of William Godwin, whose* Caleb Williams *(1794) anticipated modern criminal fiction.*

The condemned of Newgate Gaol (Thompson). The published confessions or last words of famous criminals condemned to death in this prison developed into the Newgate School of fiction which greatly influenced the growth of criminal fiction.

derer—his uncle Claudius—reveal himself by his agitated reactions. This is the classic finale to a detective novel, where all the protagonists are brought together and the detective reveals who the culprit is and how the crime was committed.

However, more immediate forerunners of the detective novel can be found. Perhaps the most important is the Gothic novel, from Horace Walpole's *Castle of Otranto* (1764) to Mary Wollstonecraft Shelley's *Frankenstein* (1818), and including the novels of Clara Reeve, Ann Radcliffe, Matthew Gregory Lewis, Charles Robert Maturin, and the American Charles Brocden Brown. From these the detective novel derives its popular appeal, its elements of fear and suspense, and its narrative structure.

Criminal fiction also bears a close relation to law reports, very popular in England as in France during the eighteenth and nineteenth centuries. In fact, as early as 1698 the chaplain of Newgate Prison published a very successful collection of confessions of prisoners condemned to death. This success was quickly repeated by other publishers who, in order to satisfy the public's morbid interest in criminals and crime, brought out such pamphlets as *The Newgate Calendar* or *The Malefactor's Register*, based on the official proceedings at the Old Bailey and heavily embroidered with particularly gruesome details. From these developed romanticized biographies of famous criminals, which were often recounted in the first person, such as those on highwaymen John Sheppard and Jonathan Wild (1724) and the Frenchman Mandrin by Daniel Defoe. In the first half of the nineteenth century, a taste for retired policemen's memoirs developed. William Russel's *Recollections of a Detective Police-Officer* (1856) is a good example.

However, the most important memoirs in the history of criminal fiction are those of Eugène-François Vidocq (1775–1857), published in 1828. He began as a deserter, forger, thief, pimp; he escaped innumerable times from France's grimmest prisons to become a police spy, then an officer, and (in 1811) the head of the Sûreté—the first large modern police force—which he himself had created.

Vidocq's police methods were relatively simple. When he had to carry out an investigation, he set all his men, mostly former criminals like himself, on the trail. He himself took on the disguise of a scoundrel— disguise playing an important part in the detective novel, from Nick Carter to Arsène Lupin—and made the rounds of seedy taverns where he won the sympathies of murderers and thieves and persuaded them to confide useful information to him. This he would later use against them.

Vidocq's *Mémoires* enjoyed a tremendous success and were translated all over the world—in the United States Poe read them with particular attention. Above all, they had the merit of inspiring immortal characters, such as Jean Valjean, the twisted convict in Victor Hugo's *Les Misérables*—but not, as is argued by many, the sadistic Javert who torments him. Most important of all was Vautrin (alias Jacques Collin, alias the Abbot Herrera) of Balzac's *Human Comedy*. It was Balzac who, in turn, first applied the characteristics of detective fiction to a novel, *A Murky Business* (1841).

Finally, an exotic note. According to the Dutch diplomat, sinologist, and author Robert Hans Van Gulik

(1910–1967), criminal fiction was born in China between the years 630 and 700. The basis of this claim lies in the law reports of the trials conducted by Li Jen-tse, a young judge who settled many criminal cases. These were the source of many anonymous stories, and as late as the eighteenth century he was the protagonist of a long crime novel, *Dee Goong An* (*The Trials of Judge Dee*).

Van Gulik translated—or rather rewrote, when he was not in fact inventing—a large number of Judge Dee's investigations. In his modern version Dee is a tall, well-built young man (he was in fact rather fat), a rational intellectual, as well as an expert in the martial arts. He is blessed with three wives and three lieutenants, two of whom are ex-criminals who are given the dirtier jobs—illegal searches, forced interrogations, contacts with informers. In practice, Van Gulick's Judge Dee is a cross between Vidocq and Edgar Allan Poe's Dupin.

THE FATHER: EDGAR ALLAN POE

It all began with a violent murder in Paris. One night in 1841, at three in the morning, the inhabitants of the rue Morgue were awakened by terrifying screams coming from an apartment on the fourth floor of an old building occupied by old Madame L'Espanaye and her daughter Camille. Those first to answer these screams had to break the door down—it had been securely bolted on the inside—in order to enter. The sight that greeted their eyes was horrifying.

The apartment was in the wildest disorder—the furniture broken and thrown about in all directions. There was only one bedstead, and from this the mattress had been removed and thrown into the middle of the floor. On a chair lay a razor smeared with blood. On the hearth were two or three long and thick tresses of gray human hair, also dabbled in blood and seeming to have been pulled out by the roots. . . . Of Madame L'Espanaye no traces were here seen. But an unusual quantity of soot being observed in the fireplace, a search was made in the chimney, and (horrible to relate!) the corpse of the daughter, head downward, was dragged therefrom, it having been thus forced up the narrow aperture for a considerable distance. . . .

After a thorough search of the apartment the neighbors went out into the small paved yard at the back where they found the old lady's corpse, her throat cut so viciously that when they tried to pick her up the head fell completely from the body. Both the head and the body were so horribly mutilated that they could

Above left: *The original manuscript of* The Murders in the Rue Morgue *by Edgar Allan Poe, widely regarded as the first detective story. In this short story Poe created the characters and situations that are fundamental to criminal fiction: the dilettante detective, his biographer-friend, the crime in a locked room.* Right: *Auguste Dupin and his friend (the figure on the left, who looks like Poe) in a drawing by Macauley (1904).*

hardly be recognized as human, as the Parisian daily papers reported with relish the next morning.

The police groped blindly for clues: the apartment had been found completely sealed, and it seemed that no one would have been able to leave it after committing the murders. The doors were bolted, the windows shut fast. The neighbors came up the staircase. They had heard the shouts and curses of the murderers, spoken in a strange language nobody could agree on—English? Italian? French? Spanish? Russian? To find a possible secret exit the police began pulling up the floorboards and knocking holes in the ceilings and walls, but all their efforts were in vain.

The whole case would probably have been filed as unsolved were it not for the unexpected appearance of the cavalier Auguste Dupin. A young gentleman of an old and illustrious family, which, through a series of misfortunes, now found itself impoverished, Dupin lived on the generosity of his creditors. The small part of his inheritance that they allowed him made it possible, in his own words, to provide, with strict economies, for the necessities of life.

At the time of the crime in the rue Morgue Dupin was living in a small old house, number 33 rue Dunot, with a young foreigner whom he had met in an obscure library in the rue Montmartre. This nameless friend was, in fact, to narrate the extraordinary investigative exploits of Auguste Dupin.

Armed with an authorization from the Prefect of Police, Dupin and his unnamed friend went to the scene of the crime. The police had already searched the apartment from top to bottom, but Dupin was not interested in their efforts—he wanted to see for himself. As it turned out there were no secret exits, and the

chimney was too narrow for anyone to climb up. There was no way in which the murderer or murderers could have come out of the first room without being seen by the neighbors who were watching from above or coming up the staircase to help the victims.

"The murderers must have passed, then, through [the windows] of the back room," Dupin explained. (Exactly those windows that had been found shut fast!) "Now, brought to this conclusion in so unequivocal a manner as we have been, it is not for us, as rational men, to reject it on account of apparent impossibilities. It is only for us to prove that these apparent impossibilities are, in reality not such."

So he began to search for proof that would show the validity of his argument. He soon found it: a broken nail, which appeared to be intact; and a spring that closed the window automatically. The picture was complete. But outside the window there was a sheer drop of many feet. No matter: The lightning rod was located about six feet from the window. Someone gifted with an extraordinary, almost supernatural, strength and agility—only such a person would have been able to push Camille up the chimney—could have easily swung from the wire to the chimney and back by grabbing the heavy wooden shutters and swinging off from them. And Dupin in fact found, at the bottom of the lightning rod, a piece of ribbon tied in a knot after the fashion of Maltese sailors.

Thus, he had discovered the vital clue to the mystery. It was easy to complete the puzzle by filling in those apparently contradictory pieces that had baffled the police: the ferocious and gratuitous nature of the crime; the murderer's superhuman strength; the strange, tawny hair found in one of the victims' hands; the incomprehensible shouts heard by the neighbors.

The murderer—for it could not be otherwise—was an enormous orangutang that escaped from a Maltese sailor who had brought it to Paris to sell to the Jardin des Plantes.

This, in short, is the plot of "The Murders in the Rue Morgue" by Edgar Allan Poe (1809–1849), first published in *Graham's Magazine* in April 1841. One does not have to be an avid reader of the detective novel to see grouped here all the motifs and characters that led to its international success. First and foremost there is the character of Auguste Dupin, the eccentric detective, philosopher, and rational thinker *par excellence*; as such, he is the immediate forerunner of Gaboriau's Père Tabaret and Monsieur Lecoq, Conan Doyle's Sherlock Holmes, S. S. Van Dine's Philo Vance, Agatha Christie's Hercule Poirot, Rex Stout's Nero Wolfe, and many others. Like Dupin, all are accompanied by a constant companion, often the narrator: Sherlock Holmes's Dr. Watson and Nero Wolfe's Archie Goodwin share the basic characteristics with which Poe endowed his "spectator."

Then there is the mystery of the locked room, the archetypal problem that can be solved only through the detective's intellectual virtuosity. In "The Murders in the Rue Morgue" this talent is contrasted with the gullibility and flat-footed approach of the police—("... This functionary, however well disposed to my friend, could not altogether conceal his chagrin at the turn which affairs had taken, and was fain to indulge in a sarcasm or two about the propriety of every person minding his own business. ....")—their search for a culprit, the arrest of an innocent party, and the detective's clumsy efforts to extract a confession from him.

A year later Dupin reappeared, with renewed hon-

SIX RULES FOR CONSTRUCTING A DETECTIVE NOVEL, DRAWN FROM POE'S WORKS.

1. The event providing the basis of the narrative is an apparently inexplicable mystery.

2. One or two characters, successively or simultaneously, mistakenly come under suspicion because some superficial clues seem to implicate them.

3. A minute examination of the facts, clues, and motives, followed by an examination of the witnesses and, above all, a rational deductive process, will always win out over any hurried theorizing. Whoever analyzes does not guess: he observes and reasons.

4. The solution, which fits the facts perfectly, is completely unexpected.

5. The more extraordinary a case seems, the easier it is to solve.

6. When all the impossible solutions have been discarded, the remaining one, even if it seems incredible at first, is the right one.

ors, in the news, solving the mystery of the disappearance of a pretty drugstore clerk, Marie Rogêt. He accomplished this without even leaving his house, basing his deductions on the facts reported in the press. The inspiration for this rather boring story ("The Mystery of Marie Rogêt," 1842–43) came from a real event: the 1841 disappearance in New York of a seamstress named Mary Rogers. In a note in the 1845 edition of his collected works, *Tales*, Poe claimed to have effectively solved this case quite a time before the police were able to. This was generally believed for over a century although recent American studies have shown that the case remains a mystery, despite Poe's brilliant deductions.

Four years after Poe published his first detective story, he returned Dupin to Paris and cast him as the main character in the short but perfectly contrived story "The Purloined Letter" (1845).

A compromising letter has been stolen from a lady of the royal family by an intriguing government minister. The minister's house has been searched numerous times by police agents but in vain, and finally the head of police, G., goes to Dupin as a last and desperate means of help. Dupin, on some invented pretext, goes to visit the minister and uses the occasion to look around the room and pick out possible hiding places for the letter. The next morning he returns to the thief's house, and when his host is distracted by a shot outside the window—a disturbance organized by Dupin himself—the detective pockets the letter. Where had it been? Propped up in a card rack on the mantelpiece, the most obvious place in the room. Poe had inherited this idea from Vidocq, who comments in his *Mémoires* that the most obvious places are usually those where one does not think of looking.

"The Purloined Letter" marks the end of Auguste Dupin's short but spectacular career, but Poe wrote other stories that can be considered detective tales. One such is "The Gold Bug" (1843), which tells of the discovery of buried treasure with the help of a complicated code—detection without crime, in a sense. And then there is "Thou Art the Man" (1844), the story of old Charley—pleasant, jovial and liked by all—who murders the rich Shuttleworthy in order to inherit his fortune. To put the police off his scent, Charley loads the evidence against the dead man's nephew, who is arrested and condemned to death. The narrator of the story discovers the plot, however, and confronts Charley with the coffin out of which, almost as if alive, the victim's corpse rises, forcing him into a public confession.

During his third case Dupin recovers a dangerous letter which has been stolen from the Royal Palace by an intriguing Minister (illustration by Frederick Simpson Coburn, 1902). "The Purloined Letter" is Poe's most popularly studied work: Freud and Marie Bonaparte (one of Poe's biographers) have psychoanalyzed it.

When he wrote his three detective stories, Poe had no idea that he was creating a literary genre that was destined to win a widespread following. Poet, critic, philospher, and novelist, Poe remains one of the most inventive and accomplished storytellers of all times. His life was sad and disordered, as suggested when his "spiritual brother" and translator Baudelaire commented that for him the United States was a vast prison through which he ranged with the feverish agitation of a person born to live in a world vastly different from the barbarian one illuminated by gaslight.

Thanks to Baudelaire's translations, Poe's works had their greatest influence in France; via French translation, they contributed importantly to the formulation of modern literary style. In the United States, meanwhile, he remained misunderstood and underrated for another century.

Above left: Edgar Allan Poe, a portrait by Osgood, husband of one of the women loved by Poe, the poet Frances Osgood. Right: An illustration by Harry Clarke for "The Mystery of Marie Roget," Poe's second detective story. In his essay "The Philosophy of Composition" Poe outlined the approach that every writer of criminal fiction has adopted: "Nothing is more clear than that any plot worth the name must be elaborated to its denouement before anything be attempted with the pen. It is only with the denouement constantly in view that we can give a plot its indispensable air of consequence, or causation, by making the incidents, and especially the tone at all points, tend to the development of the intention."

THE FIRST DISCIPLE: EMILE GABORIAU

Chosen by Poe as the fantastic setting for his criminal intrigues, Paris was to become the soil in which the new popular form of the detective novel would flourish. This ground had been prepared not only by Balzac, Victor Hugo, and Vidocq, but also by an opportune and successful innovation in the popular press, the *feuilleton*: realistic novels full of passion, murder, vengeance, flight, and capture that were published in installments. All the greatest writers of the period, from Bal-

Emile Gaboriau was Poe's main French follower, making a decisive contribution to the development of the detective novel. Joining Poe's intellectual rationalism to the feuilleton's melodrama, Gaboriau created a genre with wide public appeal. It is in his works that the focus of interest shifts from the criminal to the detective, to the characters of Père Tabaret and Lecoq, who arrogantly challenge the criminal world to provide them with a crime that would exceed their talents.

zac to Alexandre Dumas (for instance the "detective" passages in *The Count of Monte Cristo*) resorted to these pot-boilers to earn money, although the most successful practitioner of them all was the much praised Eugène Sue, author of *Les mystères de Paris* (1842–1843).

Among the principal *feuilleton* novelists, two of the most prolific mystery writers were Paul Feval (1817–1887), who wrote more than a hundred novels, and the Vicomte Pierre Alexis de Pouson (1829–1871). Under the pseudonym Ponson de Terrail, he created the delinquent Rocambole, a type of character destined to have a long line of followers and imitators such as Allain and Souvestre's Fantômas. Rocambole is the very embodiment of evil in a long series of stories from *Les drames de Paris* to *Les exploits de Rocambole* (1859), in which the feared criminal died, his face horribly distorted with rage. Later, in *La résurrection de Rocambole* (1863), he was brought back as a detective devoted to the cause of good.

However, the real French successor to Poe was Emile Gaboriau (1832–1873). After a fairly unsettled youth, Gaboriau arrived in Paris to become Paul Feveral's secretary and launch a career in journalism. While reporting for *Le pays* in Paris's Porte d'Italie area he struck up a friendship with an ex-inspector of the Sûreté, Tirabot (nicknamed Tirauclair, or Bring-to-Light), and was inspired to write a detective novel in the style of Poe, whose work he had admired greatly in Baudelaire's translations.

Thus was born *The Lerouge Case* (*L'affaire Lerouge*). Serialized in *Le pays* in 1863, the story excited practically no interest, although its reprinting in *Le Soleil* two years later brought great popular acclaim. In this first novel, Gaboriau stayed close to the example of "The Murders in the Rue Morgue": "Everything in the first room pointed with a sad eloquence to the presence of a malefactor. The furniture—a bureau and two large trunks—were forced and broken open. In the inner room, the disorder was even greater. It seemed as if some furious hand had taken a fiendish pleasure in creating frightful disorder. . . . Near the chimney was found extended upon the hearth the dead body of Widow Lerouge. She was lying with her face in the ashes. One side of her face and a portion of her hair were burned. . . ."

Three characters are called upon to solve the murder: Gevrol, the chief of police, a punctilious civil servant and rather typically unimaginative policeman; the elderly dilettante Père Tabaret (nicknamed Tirauclair); and, playing a smaller role, the young up-and-coming Inspector Lecoq (a name recalling that of Vidocq). It is Père Tabaret who solves the mystery of Widow Lerouge's killing, after the police have failed and arrested an innocent man. Discovered, the murderer commits suicide.

In the next novels, *Le dossier 113, Le crime d'Orcival* (both 1867), *Monsieur Lecoq* (1869), and *La corde au cou* (1873), the focus of attention moves from Gevrol and Tabaret to Lecoq.

This change begins in *Le crime d'Orcival*, the story of a mysterious double murder, which takes place in the castle of the Counts of Trémorel. The local police imagine that they have solved this bloody crime, and have arrested the supposed culprits when Lecoq arrives from Paris to shatter their illusions. Using his own methods, Lecoq begins his investigation: he examines all the circumstances of the crime; he collects the details, identifies the motives, assigning them to the various characters and the sequence of events, and finally discovers the guilty party.

Lecoq is an exceptional detective because he is gifted with a criminal brain, which would, under different circumstances, allow him to commit the perfect crime—and also, therefore, to solve it. A petty thief before being reconciled with the law, Lecoq worked as an assistant to a famous astronomer, Baron Moser, before joining the police. It was the baron who, when shown a perfect plan for robbing a bank, discovered Lecoq's vocation as a policeman and told him to choose between making his fortune as a thief or as a famous detective. Lecoq chose to join the Sûreté.

The use of the "criminal brain" is not chosen by Gaboriau without reason: it explains the method of "psychological identification" that is his main character's specialty. During his various investigations, Lecoq sheds his own personality and forces himself into the mentality and circumstances of the criminal. In this he is Dupin's spiritual heir, although unlike Poe's hero he does not isolate himself in abstract thought. Dupin, through his intellectually rational approach, avoids stooping to dirty his hands with particular details, gaining a rather morbid satisfaction out of being able to solve crimes without moving from his study. He is attracted by the crime itself rather than by the people caught up in it.

Lecoq, on the other hand, goes out, picks up trails, follows them until they peter out, and renews his investigations in other directions. Instead of proposing bold theories which the facts will eventually corroborate, Lecoq expresses an opinion only after a minute examination of the clues. Lecoq is a man, not a human

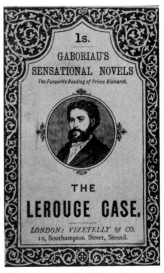

The success of L'Affaire Lerouge *was so great that it was soon translated into English (above, the 1881 English edition). Among Gaboriau's admirers was a young medical student, Arthur Conan Doyle.*

calculator; he prefers investigation to intuitive reasoning. The criminologist Edmond Locard noted this difference between Poe and Gaboriau, pointing out how Poe's hero adopts an intuitive approach while Gaboriau's detective tackles his problems with practical knowledge, wisdom, and experience.

Thus, Poe and Gaboriau created the two key personalities of the detective novel, the dilettante private eye and the police inspector, and in doing so they established two different schools of writing, the French and the Anglo-American. As the French novelist Thomas Narcejac commented, writers concentrate on either the investigation or the criminal drama, linking themselves with one of the two schools. The English are generally interested in the progress of the investigation, seen as a sophisticated sort of chess game the detective is called upon to play. The French, on the other hand, are attracted by the romantic and melodramatic possibilities of criminal fiction—the atmosphere of a particular place, the use of colorful characters, and the mastery of a dramatic narrative.

Among Gaboriau's numerous successors and imitators, some are still remembered: Constant Guéroult (*L'affaire de la rue du Temple*, 1880, and *La bande à Fifi Vollard*, 1881); Eugène Chavette, who created the detective Patapon (*La chambre du crime*, 1875—one of the many mysteries revolving around a locked room—and *La belle Aliette*); Pierre Zaccone (*L'inconnu du Belleville*); and Fortuné du Boisgobey, a prolific author who, in *La vieillesse de Monsieur Lecoq* (1875), borrowed Gaboriau's character. In his *Le coup de pouce* of the same year he invented a priest-detective, Père Jean, who anticipated Chesterton's Father Brown, and

Right: *Ponson de Terrail, one of the most prolific of the* feuilleton *writers and inventor of the famous Rocambole, a daring and adventurous rascal, the founder of a family of audacious gentlemen robbers.* Far right: *A cartoon of Rocambole on the cover of* La Lune. *On the seamonster's tail is the* feuilleton's *motto—"To be continued in the next issue."*

Dickens's Dream *(1875)*. *Robert Buss showed Dickens surrounded by all his characters. Elements of criminal fiction exist in all his novels, although, as Poe noted, the whole narrative structure may not be aimed toward the solution of a crime. In this respect it is interesting that Poe predicted the outcome of* Barnaby Rudge *while the first installments were coming out in America, publishing his prediction in* The Saturday Evening Post, *May, 1841. Many critics think this influenced Poe to write detective novels.*

in *Cornaline la Dompteuse* (1887) he created an early example of the journalist-detective Saintonge.

CHARLES DICKENS AND WILKIE COLLINS

In France criminal fiction developed from the romantic novel, the *feuilleton*, and memoirs in the style of Vidocq's. In England it is the direct heir of the Gothic novel and horror story. The "threedecker," a three-volume novel that sold for a guinea and a half, and the "shilling pamphlets" were the English equivalent of the *feuilleton*.

Charles Dickens used crime and detection in the low-life scenes in *Oliver Twist* (1837), particularly in Mr. Brownlow's investigations into Oliver's past. Elements of criminal fiction also appear in his historical novel *Barnaby Rudge* (1839–1841). In the 1850s, however, his interest in crime and detection was reawakened, stimulated by a growing friendship with Sergeant Whicher of Scotland Yard, who was to be the model for Sergeant Witchem in a series of short stories (Wilkie Collins also used him for his more famous Sergeant Cuff), and who helped inspire *Bleak House* (1851–1853) and *The Mystery of Edwin Drood* (1870).

Bleak House illustrates the human damage that

Right: *Wilkie Collins, the father of English detective fiction, caricatured by Adrian Cecioni.* Far right: *Inspector Bucket of Dickens's* Bleak House *(watercolor by Clayton Clark). Bucket was inspired by Sergeant Whicher of Scotland Yard, who was also used by Collins as a model for his Sergeant Cuff. Bucket is helped by his wife in his investigations, the first of many detective couples.*

might be caused by interminably drawn-out judicial proceedings—Dickens had been a lawyer's clerk when young—but the last chapters are a typical piece of detective fiction. A man threatens to reveal to Sir Dedlock a secret concerning his wife, but that very night the man is found murdered. The evidence appears loaded against Lady Dedlock and, when Inspector Bucket arrives from Bow Street to arrest the guilty party, everyone expects her to be charged with the murder. Instead, Bucket arrests Hortense, Lady Dedlock's French maid, whose hatred for both the murdered man and her mistress had led her to kill the first and try to have the blame placed on the second.

Nearly twenty years later, following the example of Wilkie Collins, who published *The Moonstone* in 1868, Dickens began writing *The Mystery of Edwin Drood*. It was published in serial form in the magazine *All the Year Round* but was unfinished at Dickens's death in 1870. Attempts have been made to complete it by using the clues in the first chapters and the notes left by the author. One of the most notable recent contributions to the body of Droodiana is Leon Garfield's *The Mystery of Edwin Drood* (1981).

The true father of English criminal fiction is, however, William Wilkie Collins (1824–1889), a prolific writer who grew up in Dickens's school and began his brilliant career with a long historical novel, *Antonina*, in 1850. In 1856 he wrote a series of short detective stories based largely on a collection of famous trials,

Maurice Mejeau's *Recueil des causes célèbres* (1807–1814), which he had bought in France during one of his numerous continental tours with Dickens. The *Recueil* was also the inspiration for *The Woman in White* (1859–1860), a complex novel that reflects the strong influence of Balzac. The woman is Laura Fairlie, forced to marry Sir Percival Glyde, a bastard with no right to his title, who is interested only in the lady's money and soon gets rid of her by locking her up in a lunatic asylum in the place of an actual madwoman. When the madwoman dies, Glyde buries her under his wife's name. However, with the help of a halfsister and an admirer, Walter Hertright, his wife manages to escape from the asylum and discover the plans of her evil husband, who dies in a fire he himself had started.

The greatest innovation in this novel is the first-person narrative's changing from character to character, a technique Collins was to use in his masterpiece *The Moonstone*. Published in 1868 in *All the Year Round*, the magazine edited by Dickens, *The Moonstone* is considered by many to be the first true English detective novel.

The stone is a precious, sacred diamond stolen by the unscrupulous Colonel John Herncastle from an Indian sect in Seringapatam, where he murdered three Brahmins who were guarding it. But the diamond carries a curse, which is visited upon him and his family. Pursued by avenging Indians, despised and deserted by his friends and relatives, Herncastle dies and leaves the diamond to his niece Rachel Verinder.

Carrying out the terms of Herncastle's will, Franklin Blake, the son of the executor, gives the diamond to Rachel. To make matters a little more complicated and

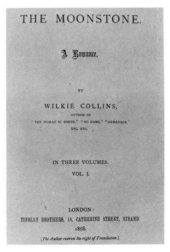

Wilkie Collins, and the title page of the original edition of The Moonstone, *the first work in the English school of detective fiction.*

interesting, Rachel is also Franklin's cousin, and the two young people are in love with each other. Within twelve hours of the diamond's being handed over to Rachel, it disappears. The police are immediately called in and unsuccessfully search the house and its occupants—except for Rachel, who mysteriously refuses to be searched. Faced with the local police force's lack of success, Franklin Blake calls Sergeant Cuff from Scotland Yard. Cuff arrives, arrogantly self-confident, to make blunder after blunder by first suspecting Rachel herself, then the maid Rosanna (an ex-thief who commits suicide), and finally some mysterious Indians who for some days have been seen in the vicinity of the house. Finally, after various false starts, a humbled Cuff solves the mystery by tracing the movements of one of Rachel's rejected suitors, who had stolen the stone and pawned it.

Among his many merits as author, Collins can be credited with establishing the principle of playing fair with the reader. In the first chapters of the book he gives all the clues necessary to the solution of the crime. He conceived of the idea of choosing the culprit from among the least suspect characters and, in his works, portrayed medical, legal, and police procedural details with complete accuracy.

Many critics have judged *The Moonstone* the greatest detective novel ever written. T. S. Eliot said that everything that is good and effective in the modern detective story can be found in *The Moonstone*. Modern writers have added the use of fingerprints and such other technological trifles, but they have not materially improved upon either the personality or the

An illustration from The Woman in White.

methods of Sergeant Cuff. Sergeant Cuff is the perfect detective. Our modern detectives are most often either efficient but featureless machines, forgotten the moment we lay the book down, or they have too many features, like Sherlock Holmes. Sherlock Holmes is so heavily weighted with abilities, accomplishments, and peculiarities that he becomes an almost static figure; he is described to us rather than revealed through his actions. Sergeant Cuff is a real and attractive personality, and he is brilliant without being infallible.

Various writers of Collins's school deserve to be remembered: Arthur Griffiths (*Fast and Loose*, 1884); G. Manville (*The Dark House*, 1885); Mary Elizabeth Braddon, author of more than eighty novels; Charles Gibbon (*A Hart Knot*, 1885); B. L. Fargeon, who created the first detective-journalist in *Great Porter Square* (1884); and even Robert Louis Stevenson, who "crossed" the genre various times. It is enough to note Stevenson's "Suicide Club" from the collection *The New Arabian Nights* (1882) and, above all, *The Strange Case of Dr. Jekyll and Mr. Hyde*. Without the example of *Dr. Jekyll and Mr. Hyde*, Oscar Wilde probably would not have written *The Picture of Dorian Gray*, nor would Conan Doyle have immortalized London's pea-soup fog as the essential backdrop to Sherlock Holmes's adventures. Among Stevenson's works should also be mentioned a novel written with his stepson Lloyd Osborne, *The Wrong Box* (1888), in which an exchange of boxes with totally different contents creates a black-humor story that unfolds along dramatic and criminal lines.

Sheridan Le Fanu also deserves a position among the authors of the Collins school. Author of *Uncle Silas* (1864) and a modest detective novel, *Checkmate* (1870–1871), in which an ex-detective uses the information gathered in his investigations to blackmail people, LeFanu is more famous for his stories of vampires, which were to inspire, among others, Carl Theodor Dreyer's famous film *Vampyr* (1932).

An 1871 poster by Frederick Walker advertising the play based on Collins's book The Woman in White. *The plot for Collins's story came from a collection of famous French criminal cases which Collins found while browsing in a bookshop in Paris with Charles Dickens.*

2 | THE FOUNDING FATHERS

Arthur Conan Doyle in cap and gown when he was at the University of Edinburgh.

L ondon, 1881—The corpse of a well-dressed gentleman has been found in an empty house, No. 3, Lauriston Gardens. Murder? Suicide? Death by natural causes? A total mystery; there is no clue to how the man died. The police grope hopelessly for ideas, and finally the detectives involved, Gregson and Lestrade, turn for help to Sherlock Holmes, a bizarre dilettante who has already advised the police on a number of occasions. He arrives with a certain Dr. John H. Watson, a military doctor recently returned from colonial service in India, with whom Holmes shares rooms in 221B Baker Street.

Holmes begins his investigation at once: he examines the surroundings of the house, questions the police, and then whips "a tape measure and a large, round magnifying glass from his pocket." With these he searches the room intently, occasionally muttering to himself, kneeling or even lying down to take a better look, and every so often breaking out with a satisfied exclamation. He finds and notes marks the previous investigators overlooked and discovers a small pile of gray dust, which he carefully picks up from the floor and puts into an envelope. Finally he turns to the police, who have been following his movements with a certain amount of skepticism as well as curiosity, and says: "They say that genius is an infinite capacity for taking pains. It's a very bad definition, but it does apply to detective work. . . . I'll tell you one thing that may help you in the case. There has been a murder done, and the murderer was a man. He was more than six feet tall, was in the prime of life, had small feet for his height, wore coarse, square-toed boots, and smoked a Trichinopoly cigar. . . . In all probability the murderer had a florid face, and the fingernails of his right hand were remarkably long."

With these startling revelations, the curtain is raised on "A Study in Scarlet" (1887), the first of many fascinating stories starring the greatest fictional detective of all time. Holmes's creator was a young Scottish

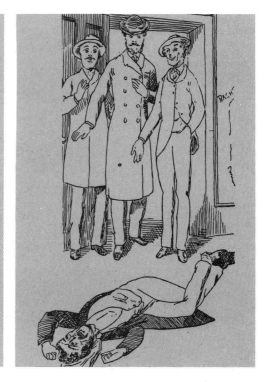

A letter from Arthur Conan Doyle to his mother. The two enjoyed a very close relationship, Arthur keeping her constantly informed about the progress of his work while she often replied with specific criticisms which he valued highly. Right: *The discovery of the body of an unknown man in a house in Lauriston Gardens from "A Study in Scarlet". The drawing is by Charles Doyle, Arthur's father, who shows himself as Holmes between Inspectors Gregson and Lestrade of the Yard. When he made this drawing (published with other drawings and watercolors in 1978), Charles was in a Scottish mental hospital. Perhaps for this reason not much is known of him. Conan Doyle's biographers have always treated the subject as taboo.*

medical student, Arthur Conan Doyle (1859–1930), who had studied at the university in his native Edinburgh. There he was taught by the famous Professor John Bell, the champion of the theory of deductive methodology in the diagnosis of diseases. Bell never tired of telling his students to use their eyes, ears, hands, brain, intuition, and, above all, their deductive faculties. The patient's illness must be deduced from the various symptoms, seen in relation to each other and to their various degrees of importance.

Bell's method made a great impression on Conan Doyle, as his acute biographer John Dickson Carr, himself a detective novelist, points out. The young student was sure that the same principles could be equally well applied in many other fields, even in the complex and incongruous world of criminal fiction, which, with historical novels in the Walter Scott tradition, made up his favorite reading. So while waiting for his first patients in the practice he had set up in Southsea (he wrote to his mother that in twenty-five minutes twenty-eight people had stopped to read his brass plaque and then walked straight past), Conan Doyle decided to write a revolutionary detective story.

First, he had to create a protagonist, a detective

capable of using Bell's modern methods, not a lout like Gaboriau's Lecoq—that "miserable bungler; he had only one thing to recommend him, and that was his energy." No, someone more like Dupin, Edgar Allan Poe's "magisterial" detective, or even, perhaps, someone better, for Dupin was in fact "a very inferior fellow. . . . He had some analytical genius, no doubt; but he was by no means such a phenomenon as Poe appeared to imagine."

This is, of course, Holmes's opinion, perhaps revealing a certain amount of professional jealousy. Conan Doyle himself was far more generous, and in his memoirs he credits Gaboriau with influencing the way in which he constructed his stories, while citing Poe's Dupin as one of his favorite heroes.

Conan Doyle's first problem was choosing a name for his detective. "Ormond Sacker" was rejected as being too snobbish, suggestive of Bond Street and dandies rather than the world in which the readers of popular novels lived. "Sherrinford Holmes" was an improvement, and it was nearly adopted when Conan Doyle came across a rather strange Irish Christian name: Sherlock—Sherlock Holmes! Marvelous. Conan Doyle had already thought up a plot, and in a few months "A Study in Scarlet" was written, with Holmes committed to solving the murder at Lauriston Gardens.

The dead man turns out to be Drebber, an Ameri-

Sherlock Holmes and Dr. Watson in their richly decorated rooms at 221B Baker Street (a reconstruction by the Sherlock Holmes Society). The lodgings, described in "A Study in Scarlet," were made up of two comfortable bedrooms and a large sitting room lit by two big windows.

can who had come to London with his secretary, Stangerson. The police immediately set out to interview the secretary but are beaten to it by the murderer. Stangerson is found stabbed to death. In the meantime Holmes carries on with his own investigations, and when these end he summons the detectives involved in the case to Baker Street. Before giving his explanation, he has the coachman called in on the pretext of having some heavy luggage that needs moving. In this way he stages the denouement, holding the coachman and announcing, "Gentlemen, let me introduce you to Mr. Jefferson Hope, the murderer of Enoch Drebber and of Joseph Stangerson." The coachman turns out to be one of Drebber's old rivals in love, his identity and story having been ascertained by

A CATALOGUE OF THE INGENIOUS MR. HOLMES

1. Knowledge of Literature—Nil.
2. Knowledge of Philosophy—Nil.
3. Knowledge of Astronomy—Nil.
4. Knowledge of Politics—Feeble.
5. Knowledge of Botany—Variable. Well up in belladonna, opium, and poisons in general. Knows nothing of practical gardening.
6. Knowledge of Geology—Practical, but limited. Tells at a glance different soils from each other. After walks has shown me splashes on his trousers, and told me by their color and consistence in what part of London he had received them.

7. Knowledge of Chemistry—Profound.
8. Knowledge of Anatomy—Accurate, but unsystematic.
9. Knowledge of Sensational Literature—Immense. He appears to know every detail of every horror perpetrated in the century.
10. Plays the violin well.
11. Is an expert singlestick player, boxer, and swordsman.
12. Has a good practical knowledge of British law.

"A Study in Scarlet"

Holmes's telegraphing American authorities. Holmes had suspected him from the beginning. From the coach's tracks outside the abandoned house in Lauriston Gardens, it was clear that after the murderer and his victim had alighted, the coach had moved around quite a bit, an indication that no coachman had stayed behind to hold the horse.

Sherlock Holmes's first adventure, which is narrated by his constant companion and biographer Dr. Watson, was published in *Beeton's Christmas Annual* in December 1887. Public response was only lukewarm, and a disillusioned Conan Doyle consoled himself by devoting his professional energies to his first patients and his literary energies to a series of historical novels with which he hoped to become famous.

He did not return to Holmes for almost two years. He might never have done so, might never in fact have

The king of detectives searching for clues with his famous hand lens (a reconstruction by the Sherlock Holmes Society).

Sherlock Holmes in mortal struggle with his sworn enemy Professor Moriarty in an illustration by Sidney Page for "The Final Problem": "An examination by experts leaves little doubt that a personal contest between the two men ended, as it could hardly fail to end in such a situation, in their reeling over, locked in each other's arms. Any attempt at recovering the bodies was absolutely hopeless, and there, deep down in that dreadful cauldron of swirling water and seething foam, will lie for all time the most dangerous criminal and the foremost champion of the law of their generation."

returned to criminal fiction, had it not been for a request from the American *Lippincott's Magazine* for one of Sherlock Holmes's unpublished adventures. Conan Doyle began working immediately and in a few months wrote *The Sign of Four*, in which Holmes investigates the mysterious disappearance, ten years before, of a certain Captain Morstan. The novel was published in *Lippincott's Magazine* in February 1890 and in London later in the same year.

This time Conan Doyle's success was great, both in the United States and in England. Both publishers and readers swamped him with requests for more stories. Within a year, he was more or less forced to publish a series of twelve stories in the *Strand Magazine*, one of the most popular journals of its day. These were later published together under the title *The Adventures of Sherlock Holmes* (1892).

Portraits on glass of Sherlock Holmes and Dr. Watson. In giving Holmes's constant companion an identity Doyle used a real name. John Dickson Carr notes in his biography: "A friend of his at Southsea, also a leading member of the Portsmouth Literary and Scientific Society, was a young doctor named Watson: Dr. James Watson. Surely Watson wouldn't mind the use of his surname if the first name were changed to John? Down it went as John M. Watson. (But can we wonder if, in later years, the author's pen slipped and Watson's wife called him James? . . .)"

At this point Conan Doyle was growing weary of the rather demanding character he had created. He found himself a slave to what was originally designed as a mere pastime. In order to discourage his publishers, he decided to charge inordinate sums for his Sherlock Holmes stories, but when even his most extravagant requests were met—he was paid the enormous sum of £1,000 for twelve stories—he reconciled himself to the worst. As Conan Doyle wrote to his mother at the time, Holmes was taking up far too much of his time, and he saw no solution but to kill Holmes off at the end of the series he was then writing. This in fact happened in the last story of *The Memoirs of Sherlock Holmes* (1894), in which Conan Doyle leaves Holmes plunging into the thunderous falls of Reichenbach in Switzerland in mortal embrace with his sworn enemy, Professor Moriarty.

The public's reaction to Holmes's "murder" was immediate; protests came from every corner of Britain, France, and even America. City businessmen dressed in mourning; workers went out on strike; questions were raised in Parliament. Giving way to pressure from both the public and his publishers, Doyle wrote a third Sherlock Holmes novel, *The Hound of the Baskervilles* (1902). He insisted, however, that Holmes was still dead, and that the adventure in the book had taken place before the mortal struggle at Reichenbach.

The expediency of this solution turned out to be faulty, for the writer was soon forced to "reveal" that Holmes had in fact survived, healthy in mind and body, his terrible ordeal in Switzerland. So his adventures continued with the thirteen stories in *The Return of Sherlock Holmes* (1905).

Between 1905 and 1915, however, Doyle refused to give the public any more of his gentleman's (as he called Holmes) adventures, seeking success instead in the theater. He put on *The House of Temperley*, an evocation of the sporting England of 1812, at his own expense; although it was well received, it made no money. In fact, within a few months Doyle managed to lose a large amount of money. *The House of Temperley* was replaced by *The Speckled Band*, starring Sherlock Holmes and Dr. Watson. It not only recouped all the previous losses but made a substantial profit.

Throughout his life Conan Doyle unsuccessfully pursued a literary success that was not tied to Holmes and Watson. But neither the theater, nor historical novels, nor his writings on the paranormal phenomena that fascinated him, nor his cautious experiment with science fiction (*The Lost World*, 1912) brought him close to achieving his aim. In 1915, encouraged by public enthusiasm for his master creation, he published the last novel in the Holmes cycle, *The Valley of Fear*, followed by his last two collections of stories—*His Last Bow* (1917) and *The Case Book of Sherlock Holmes* (1927). The stream of adventures involving the greatest detective in criminal fiction—four novels and fifty-six short stories in all—had finally dried up.

What is it in these stories that even today captivates millions of readers? Their attraction lies partly in their sense of place and the way in which they reconstruct a bygone age—the atmosphere of Victorian England, somewhat grandiose and high-minded, depicted with a love for tradition and for the calm optimism of a self-satisfied society quite unaware of the storms that were to break over it. Above all, however, their success is dependent on their protagonist: the character created by Conan Doyle is far more convincing than his greatest fictional predecessors, Auguste Dupin and Lecoq.

Sherlock Holmes, a complete character in every sense, developed his own infallible method of investigation, turning criminology into a precise science—the science of deduction. He is not only a detective but also a theorist. At the beginning of "A Study in Scarlet" he reads parts of an article on criminology he has written for a magazine:

Like all other arts, the Science of Deduction and Analysis is one which can only be acquired by long and patient study. . . . Before turning to those moral and mental aspects of the matter which present the greatest difficulties, let the inquirer

begin by mastering more elementary problems. Let him on meeting a fellow mortal, learn at a glance to distinguish the history of the man, and the trade or profession to which he belongs. Puerile as such an exercise may seem, it sharpens the faculties of observation, and teaches one where to look and what to look for. By a man's finger-nails, by his coat-sleeve, by his boot, by his trouser-knees, by the callosities of his forefinger and thumb, by his expression, by his shirt-cuffs—by each of these things a man's calling is plainly revealed. That all united should fail to enlighten the competent inquirer in any case is almost inconceivable.

In this, Holmes is not simply a character created by Conan Doyle but also an example of the effect of late nineteenth-century logical positivism. His scientific methods are no less than the positivist approach based on the systematic collection and identification of all the facts, an approach adopted in all fields of study by the prominent thinkers and scientists of the time—

Auguste Comte, John Stuart Mill, Herbert Spencer, and Charles Darwin. Doyle's works might therefore be seen as an example of this movement in the literature of the time.

Over the years Holmes has become dissociated from Conan Doyle and has taken on an independent existence—people even write to him at his address on Baker Street. Through movies, radio, television, and theater, he has become the symbol of a literary genre, and in this way he has left the confines of criminal fiction to assume a more universal character. Thus, he holds a minor place among the great universal characters of literature, along with Ulysses, Don Quixote, and Faust.

Holmes has been a great influence on subsequent authors, both as a model and even as a character. One of the first writers to use him was Mark Twain, who, in *A Double-Barreled Detective Story* (1902), has Holmes failing to provide a solution. In the 1950s, Conan Doyle's own son Adrian wrote *The Exploits of Sherlock Holmes* with John Dickson Carr, taking as his starting point stories mentioned by Holmes but never actually told by Sir Arthur. Beyond these, Holmes has been used by innumerable writers of works ranging from detective to comic fiction and even science fiction: Schlock Homes was invented by Robert L. Fish, Herlock Sholmes was invented by Maurice Leblanc; and *Hoka Holmes* by Poul Anderson and Gordon R. Dickson, who place their protagonist on a faraway planet. Recently we have had Nicholas Meyer's *Seven Per Cent Solution*, which was filmed with Laurence Olivier and Vanessa Redgrave. Here Holmes is shown as a drug addict who goes to see an up-and-coming doctor in Vienna, one Sigmund Freud. Holmes is not only cured of his addiction to a 7 percent solution of cocaine, but he learns from Freud the reason for his addiction, which is entangled in his subconscious with his father's murder of his mother and her lover.

ANNA K. GREEN AND THE INVENTION OF THE DETECTIVE STORY

Although Sir Arthur Conan Doyle (knighted for his humanitarian work during the Boer War and not, as is still sometimes claimed, for his literary achievements) deserves the credit for having securely established the genre of criminal fiction, some recognition must also be given to the American Anna Katharine Green (1846–1935). She was not only the first woman to write a detective novel, some ten years before Doyle, but she

Anna K. Green, who coined the term "detective story." After taking a degree in English at the Ripley Female College in Poultney, Vermont, she turned first to poetry, winning the praise of R. W. Emerson. However she won fame through her detective novels.

also coined the term "detective story," using it as a subtitle to her most famous book, *The Leavenworth Case* (1878).

Before Green, the word *detective* had been used only after *police*, describing the body of police investigators set up in 1843–44 by Sir James Graham. In *Bleak House* (1852–1853) Dickens created Inspector Bucket of the Detective, meaning the Detective Police Force, although the word was also used to describe his job. French etymological dictionaries trace the word back to 1871 when it was used by Jules Verne, although it had in fact been used in 1869 by Ponson du Terrail in *Rocambole en prison*.

In *The Leavenworth Case* the hero is Ebenezer Gryce, a regular police detective, not a private investigator. Gryce is middle-aged, portly, simple, and amiable, his most striking characteristic being that he never stares at or scrutinizes the people he is questioning. His gaze falls instead on some insignificant object in the room such as a vase, an inkpot, or a book. He solves his cases in the same way one might make a complex mosaic or a finely detailed embroidery—his investigations progress methodically, step by step, as he pieces together small facts, and builds up theories from accumulated minute details.

Daughter of a famous New York criminal lawyer, Anna K. Green knew a great deal about penal law and its practice—knowledge that was very useful in her writing and makes her books technically perfect. The threads of a good plot, she claimed, must always pass from one character to another, so that an atmosphere of suspense is maintained and the ending retains an element of surprise.

Although these ideas may now seem to be rather obvious, it is because they were adopted and added to through the years by other authors that the detective novel developed into an effective literary form, a skillfully created product with a large market.

Anna K. Green published more than forty works, not all detective stories, and in addition to Ebenezer Gryce, she created one of the first women detectives —Violet Strange, whose adventures are now completely forgotten. Green died in Buffalo in 1935, a year after the publication of a special edition of *The Leavenworth Case* with an introduction by S. S. Van Dine, one of the greatest detective novelists between the wars.

NICK CARTER AND THE DIME NOVEL

While Anna K. Green and Arthur Conan Doyle, together with numerous minor authors who are now forgotten, helped establish and develop the detective story and give criminal fiction some literary status, a publishing breakthrough occurred in America equal in its impact to the much later introduction of pocket editions and paperbacks—the dime novel.

Dime novels—they were sold for ten cents—were introduced around 1860. They were cheap books written in the tradition of James Fenimore Cooper's *The Last of the Mohicans*. The American frontier was expanding, and the heroes of these stories were westerners—Buffalo Bill and Kit Carson. Dime novels enjoyed immediate and immense success. In a short time over a hundred million copies were sold.

Another series—whose heroes were James Brady, Iron Burgess, Manfred the Metamorphosist, Lord Lister, Nat Pinkerton, and Nick Carter—enjoyed even greater success. Nick Carter was particularly popular; he had been created by a circle of writers who signed themselves variously as "The Author of Nick Carter," "Sergeant Ryan," or "Nicholas Carter," and among them, it is worth mentioning, was Frederick Van Rensselaer Dey, writer of over a thousand stories!

Today Nick Carter—as always, written by a group of writers—is a sophisticated spy in the style of James Bond. In 1886, however, when his first adventure— "The Old Detective's Pupil," by John Russel Coryell, based on a story by Ormond G. Smith—came out in *The New York Weekly*, Nick Carter was a detective. He was the spiritual heir of Buffalo Bill and his contemporaries, living in a changing world where the "last frontier" had moved to the city and the cowboy had been replaced by the elegant gangster who wears his gun in a shoulder holster instead of on his belt.

Nick Carter would have little place in the history of the detective novel except for the fact that he anticipated a literary "type": the solitary detective struggling against the dangers of the concrete jungle, the lover who became the hero of the "hard-boiled novel." This school of writing, which developed in the 19040s with a lively, violent style, was led by Raymond Chandler, William R. Burnett, and Dashiell Hammett. Nick Carter's many adventures all have the same basic structure—beginning with his search for his father's murderer in his first story—and never rise above the monotonous and sterotyped style of highly commercial fiction.

Nick Carter, 1886 style, and illustration from one of the weekly comic magazines in which his adventures were published. The cover of one of the first Nick Carter dime novels shows a row of portraits illustrating the disguises Carter would adopt during his fantastic adventures.

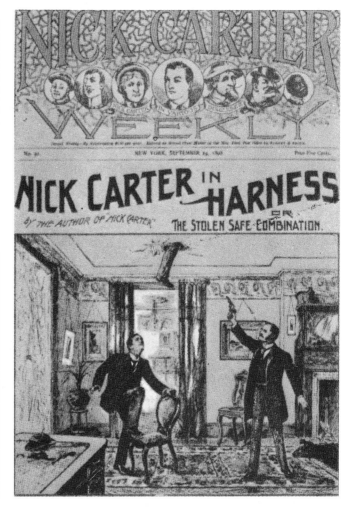

Nick Carter, 1940 style. Florence Rice, Walter Pidgeon (as Nick Carter), and Joseph Schildkraut in Phantom Raiders, *one of the many films of Nick Carter adventures.*

The contemporary Nick Carter. Since World War II Carter has become a sophisticated spy in the style of James Bond.

JACQUES FUTRELLE AND R. AUSTIN FREEMAN—THE BEGINNINGS OF THE SCIENTIFIC DETECTIVE NOVEL

At the turn of the century and during the years before World War I the popularity of detective fiction grew substantially. Its readership increased, spreading among all classes of society, while the number of writers also grew. The most important—Poe, Collins, Doyle, and Green—were joined by hundreds of others perhaps less imaginative but often highly skilled, who helped establish the genre.

In The Problem of Cell 13 *Jacques Futrelle's hero, "The Thinking Machine," accepts the challenge of two scientifically minded friends to escape from an escape-proof cell (illustration by C. Beck).*

Although the detective novel became more refined, it retained its homogeneous character, writers of the American school preferring to follow English models. New themes and motifs came, therefore, from individual writers rather than from general social trends. Apart from the freak example of Nick Carter no challenge to the English genre emerged from the American detective novel for twenty years.

The most significant developments in criminal fiction at this stage came from Jacques Futrelle and, perhaps more importantly, R. Austin Freeman, who together gave it an aura of intellectual and scientific respectability. Jacques Futrelle (1875–1912) was a journalist who lived and worked in Boston. In 1906 and 1907 he published two curious books entitled *The Chase of the Golden Plate* and *The Thinking Machine*. The protagonist in both books is a new type of cultivated detective, Augustus S. F. X. Van Dusen, Ph.D., L.L.D., F.R.S., M.D., a professor at a university never actually named, located on the outskirts of a city that seems remarkably like Boston.

Augustus S. F. X. Van Dusen, significantly enough called "The Thinking Machine," is about five feet seven inches tall, weighs about 160 pounds, and wears a size eight hat. His fair hair is disheveled and falls over his ears; his mouth is usually set in a slight scowl; and he has a large, curving forehead that accentuates the grotesque quality of his looks. His motto and rule is "Logic, logic, logic"; he believes that, given some fact to start from, a logical brain can easily follow an investigation to its natural conclusion.

One of Sherlock Holmes's worthier successors, Van Dusen typifies the scientific approach to investigation—he values very highly the importance of identification through blood groups, as well as of other scientific methods, such as ballistics, which were then being developed by criminologists. He is also creative, however, claiming that imagination is essential to a good scientific brain. Another amusing way in which he differs from his predecessors, most of whom were misogynists, is in his appreciation of women; women surround him and charm him, yet he is never thrown off balance or diverted. The era of the Don Juan detective was yet to arrive.

Before his premature death in the sinking of the *Titanic*, Futrelle had written several other detective novels, including *The Diamond Master, Elusive Isabel*, and *My Lady's Garter*.

Futrelle's scientific style was further developed in 1907 with the appearance of Dr. John Thorndyke, the most important scientific detective in the history of the

THE PUZZLE
LOCK

R. Austin Freeman

BRUCE

Nine Cases of Dr. Thorndyke

The cover of a collection of Dr. Thorndyke's adventures. R. Austin Freeman, who created Thorndyke, was also the author of The Art of the Detective Story *(1924), a study of criminal fiction.*

genre and the protagonist of the novels of Richard Austin Freeman (1862–1943).

Born in London, R. Austin Freeman was the son of a tailor. He studied medicine and graduated from the Middlesex Hospital Medical College as an ear, nose, and throat specialist. Like Doyle, he was deeply influenced by the methods of his tutor, a Dr. Alfred Swayne Taylor, who worked a great deal for the police, and he decided to use Taylor as a model in his books. It is no mere coincidence that Dr. Thorndyke is a police doctor.

In 1907, when he was forty-five years old, Freeman published the first Thorndyke adventure, *The Red Thumb Mark*, which was to be followed by twenty more novels and forty-two short stories. Thorndyke spe-

Dr. Thorndyke, dating from the early years of the century. In The Art of the Detective Story, *Freeman wrote that the characteristic of a detective novel that distinguishes it from all other literary genres is the intellectual satisfaction it offers the reader.*

cialized in those cases that can be clarified only by precise medical or scientific study. In his method of investigation he concentrated far more on facts than on people, and, although he was a perfectly normal man without any superhuman powers, he possessed an encyclopedic knowledge. He was quite at home with subjects as varied as oceanography, astronomy, anthropology, international trade, fingerprinting, zoology, botany, metallurgy, codes, locks of any kind, chemistry, entomology, biology, mineralogy, tattooing, typewriters, medieval history, ballistics, precious stones, and geology. He could identify different types of paper and their sources, as well as different fabrics and tobaccos. Naturally he was also fully acquainted with London's history and knew its streets backward and forward.

R. Austin Freeman's most important contribution to criminal fiction was the way in which he securely established the scientific detective story. It is not for nothing that critics like Howard Haycraft, Boileau, and Narcejac speak of him as the father of this particular strain of detective novel. Previously the sense of suspense had always lain in such questions as "Who is the criminal?" and "Will he be caught?" In Freeman's books, however, the reader witnesses the crime, and the excitement therefore lies in *how* and *why* the criminal is eventually caught.

One of Freeman's greatest admirers was another great detective novelist, Raymond Chandler, who praised him for his ability to combine excitement and suspense with a restrained and low-key style of writing. Another aspect of Freeman's style that particularly appealed to Chandler was the warmth and charm with which he described London and its citizens.

MARY ROBERTS RINEHART, G. K. CHESTERTON, AND THE PSYCHOLOGICAL DETECTIVE NOVEL

In 1908, with the publication of *The Circular Staircase*, another important American writer of criminal fiction, Mary Roberts Rinehart (1876–1958), appeared on the scene. She had already gained some measure of success with short stories published in the more important American magazines.

The novelty of Rinehart's style consisted in her shifting the focus of attention away from the private or police detective, who therefore occupies only a position of secondary importance in her work, to the victim and the criminal, now in the forefront of the action. Her books are filled with heiresses and fortune hunters, chauffeurs and butlers. Luxurious villas set in beautiful parks become buildings to be murdered in, rather than to live peacefully in. The sense of adventure and mystery becomes more important than the role of the detective, and her books were described as mystery stories rather than detective stories.

In constructing her novels, Rinehart always followed a fixed pattern—the first murder of the book is an introduction to a series of violent deaths that will strike down the characters with a fatal regularity throughout the story. In *The Great Mistake* the shadow of death follows pretty Patricia Abbott from the moment she becomes the secretary of the rich Maud Wainwright. The first victim is Donald Morgan, an adventurous figure whose body is found on the banks of the moat dressed only in a pair of pajamas—blue, for those who like precise detail. The next corpse is that of Maud Wainwright herself, who suffered a violent, though elegant death; she is found shot beside the swimming pool (which is, as you might imagine, part of her luxurious country residence). This second murder seems to be completely unconnected to the first and as a result two separate investigations are embarked upon, following two different trails. Matters are made even more complicated when a third body turns up, Maud's daughter-in-law, Bessie Wainwright. Suspicion for this murder falls on Bessie's husband, Tony; he hated his wife and made no secret of it. The third crime also appears to be unconnected to the earlier ones. Only when all three investigations finally converge is the murderer brought forward.

Of Rinehart's other works, which extend over a career of some forty years, *The Door, Miss Pinkerton, The Album, The Wall*, and *The Case of Jenny Brice* are all noteworthy.

By the beginning of the century the scope of criminal fiction had widened so much that it had come to be considered a legitimate and respectable genre that might be used even by writers who had achieved substantial fame in other fields. Gilbert Keith Chesterton (1874–1936)—journalist, poet, critic, and author of various books considered among the world's classics—published a "Defence of the Detective Story" in *The Defendant* in 1901. He also wrote a series of studies on Sherlock Holmes for the *Daily News*. From 1910 on, G. K. C. (as he was popularly known) also wrote a series of detective stories whose protagonist, Father Brown, was an unusual priest.

In his writings on criminal fiction Chesterton maintained that the narrative had to be simple and straightforward although it had to preserve a sense of

Mary Roberts Rinehart began to write because of financial difficulties (photograph from the 1920s).

Above: *G. K. Chesterton building a puppet theater. Chesterton was already famous as a serious writer when he created the character of the detective-priest Father Brown.* Right: *Father Brown, as interpreted by Alec Guinness on the screen and in an illustration from the first edition of* The Incredulity of Father Brown *(1926).*

mystery and a final denouement. To achieve this, he argued, the writer of detective stories should find his model in short stories rather than novels.

Chesterton heeded his own advice and wrote fifty-one stories between 1910 and 1934. These make up the adventures of Father Brown, collected in five volumes—*The Innocence of Father Brown, The Wisdom of Father Brown, The Incredulity of Father Brown, The Secret of Father Brown,* and *The Scandal of Father Brown.* In addition, there are, in the style of Conan Doyle, the stories of *The Club of Queer Trades* (1905), in which Chesterton takes on the role of Watson.

Father Brown made his first appearance in "The Blue Cross," published in *The Storyteller*, September 1910. A small priest with "a face as round and dull as a Norfolk dumpling" and "eyes as empty as the North Sea," he is constantly dropping the large, cumbersome umbrella he carries around with him. Having arrived at a complete understanding of the criminal mind through the sacrament of confession, his detective methods differ significantly from those of Sherlock Holmes. "I try to get inside the murderer. . . . Indeed it's much more than that, don't you see?" Father Brown confides. "I wait till I see the world with his bloodshot and squinting eye, looking between the blinkers of his half-witted concentration; looking up the short and sharp perspective of a straight road to a pool of blood. Till I am really a murderer."

His secret is psychology, or rather a knowledge of men's souls, which he regards as a religious study. External clues, traces, and marks are of little importance compared to the *internal* clues. "When they say criminology is a science," he tells an American who has asked him to explain his method, "they mean getting *outside* a man and studying him as if he were a gigantic insect. . . . They mean getting a long way off from him, as if he were a distant prehistoric monster" (*The Secret of Father Brown*). The most terrifying things about evil, he goes on to explain, are that it is so close to us and exists in all of us.

Chesterton's influence on detective fiction was therefore twofold: he ennobled the genre with his critical writings (he believed it to be the only popular literary medium of the time able to interpret the present with any poetic feeling); and he was largely responsible for establishing the psychological detective novel as an independent type. With him the first period in the history of criminal fiction came to an end, a period in which the foundations—of types, styles, and plots—were laid, ready to be built on by the next generation of writers.

THEIR CONTEMPORARIES

Brander Mathews, Charles Gibbon and Detective Hadden, Catherine Louisa Pirkis, Louis Tracy and Inspector Fourneau, Matthew Phipps Shiel and Prince Zaleski, the Russian exile who lives in complete isolation—who remembers these names today? Yet at the turn of the century some were nearly as famous as the characters created by Doyle, Green, and Rinehart. English, American, and French creators of detective

A caricature of Chesterton.

The old man in the corner, as described by his creator, Baroness Emmuska Orczy. Seated at the corner table of a café, he solves all the crimes that are brought to him without moving from his chair.

novels and stories added hundreds of titles to the increasing amount of criminal fiction. Not always highly skilled, sometimes naive or simplistic, these writers are nevertheless important because they provided the environment out of which the great postwar novelists were to develop.

Some deserve a closer, if necessarily cursory, look because they established specific characters, situations, or plots that were later to be adopted and refined by others.

1887: New Zealander Fergus W. Hume (1859–1932) wrote *The Mystery of a Hansom Cab*, a story set in Melbourne and written in the style of Gaboriau, which enjoyed greater popular success than Conan Doyle's early works. In little more than ten months it sold 340,000 copies, making it the best-selling detective novel of the nineteenth century.

1892: Israel Zangwill (1864–1926) published *The Big Bow Mystery*. Zangwill, an important Jewish writer (*The Children of the Ghetto*, 1892; *The King of Schnorrers*, 1894), is universally recognized as the inventor of the locked-room crime novel, set in a room completely sealed from the inside.

1894: Arthur Morrison (1863–1945) published a se-

Raffles, the gentleman thief created by Ernest William Horning, in action beneath the gaze of his "Watson," Bunny Manders (illustration by Cyrus Cuneo, 1905). Right: The Australian edition of The Mystery of the Hansom Cab *by Fergus W. Hume.*

ries of short stories in *Strand Magazine*—they were brought out in a single volume in the same year—whose protagonist, Martin Hewitt, stands halfway between Sherlock Holmes and Dr. Thorndyke.

1899: Ernest William Horning (1866–1921), Conan Doyle's brother-in-law, created Raffles, a gentleman thief who finally turns detective. A character halfway between Rocambole and Arsène Lupin, Raffles was very popular and provided Agatha Christie with some of her favorite reading.

1901: Baroness Emmuska Orczy (1865–1947), Hungarian-born resident in England, where her Scarlet Pimpernel books enjoyed considerable popularity, wrote some detective stories for *Royal Magazine* in which the mysteries are solved by an old man who never moves from a corner table in a café. These were published together in 1909 under the title *The Old Man in the Corner*.

1906: Godfrey Rathbone Benson (1875–1956) published *Tracks in the Snow* in which a clergyman, James Callaghan, searches for his best friend's murderer. In *The Triumphs of Eugène Valmont* by Robert Barr (1850–1912), a French detective appeared in English criminal fiction for the first time, at the head of a long line of similar characters—Valentin, Popeau, Hanaud, Poirot.

1907: Carolyn Wells (1870–1942) in America published a story in *Lippincott's Magazine* whose protagonist, the detective Fleming Stone, was to have a career of some thirty years. In 1913 she published *The Technique of the Mystery Story*, a study of the genre. She is also remembered as one of the first people to compile an anthology of detective stories.

1910: Alfred Edward Woodley Mason (1865–1948) published *At the Villa Rose*, whose main character was Inspector Gabriel Hanaud of the Sûreté.

1911: Melville Davisson Post (1871–1930), an American lawyer, wrote some short stories whose protagonist, Uncle Abner, was the sole administrator of justice in a small, provincial town in the Deep South. In 1918 the best of these were collected under the title *Uncle Abner: Master of Mysteries*. In addition to Uncle Abner, Post created five other detectives: Randolph Mason (*The Corrector of Destinies*), Sir Henry Marquis (*The Sleuth of St. James, The Bradmoor Murder*), Monsieur Jonquelle (*Monsieur Jonquelle: Prefect of Police of Paris*), Walker (*Walker of the Secret Service*), and Colonel Braxton (*Silent Witness*).

1912: American lawyer and journalist Arthur B. Reeve (1880–1936) published *The Silent Bullet*, which marked the appearance of Craig Kennedy, hailed by

A caricature of Alfred E. W. Mason by Max Beerbohm.

The title page of Trent's Last Case *by Edmund C. Bentley. Bentley was the first writer to include a complete love story in a detective novel; Philip Trent, his detective, falls in love with the beautiful widow of the murder victim shown on the frontispiece.*

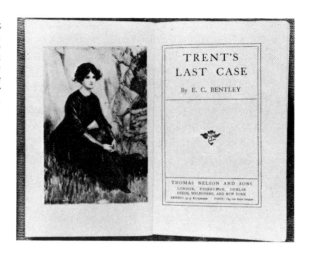

critics of the day as the American Sherlock Holmes. In England Marie A. Belloc Lowndes (1868–1947) published *The Chink in the Armour* in which a French detective, Hercules Popeau, appeared. Some regard his name as the model for Agatha Christie's Hercule Poirot.

1913: Edmund Clerihew Bentley (1875–1956) published *Trent's Last Case*, dedicating it to G. K. Chesterton, who five years before had dedicated *The Man Who Was Thursday* to him. Instead of following the Sherlock Holmes model, Bentley created in Trent a dilettante painter and writer who tried his hand at detection out of a desire for adventure. Most importantly, Trent was not infallible. The solution he proposed, though perfectly rational, was not the right one. E. C. Bentley was one of the first writers to introduce a love affair into a detective story.

3 | LA BELLE EPOQUE OF CRIME

Alas, no more shall I find
the absurd and magnificent lyricism of Fantômas,
the naive enchantment of Arsène Lupin,
the melancholy tenderness of Rouletabille

Jean Cocteau

The similarity between detective fiction and Greek tragedy, which many critics have noted, stems not only from general parallels in structure and setting but more particularly from the construction of an important series of early twentieth-century French novels built around the characters of Arsène Lupin (1905), Rouletabille (1907), and Fantômas (1911).

Like Oedipus, Rouletabille is a young orphan who pursues a difficult investigation into his past, searching for his true identity and a strange "lady in black" whom he remembers only by her perfume (anticipating Proust's Madeleine?). Finally Fate leads him into a fight for his mother against his father, a notorious criminal. Rouletabille defeats and kills him.

There is also an Oedipal element in the fortunes of Arsène Lupin and the man who created him, Maurice Leblanc. The literary offspring soon assumed a fame and importance large enough to eclipse/kill his "father." It is significant that shortly before dying Leblanc asked the Etretat police for protection "against Mr. Lupin." Another element of Greek tragedy is the enmity between Fantômas and his twin, the policeman Juve—an enmity that, in the first series of adventures, ends tragically with the death of both.

With Rouletabille, and above all with Lupin and Fantômas, the quality of criminal fiction increased radically; the detective novel entered the field of the literary epic. The creators of Fantômas and Lupin introduced political and social themes into their works, which were far more mature and less haphazard than those of their predecessors. While Lupin, with his critical, quizzical humor, satirizes the world of the

LE MYSTÈRE
de la chambre jaune

GASTON LEROUX

The title-page of the theatrical program for The Mystery of the Yellow Room *(1912). A number of films have been based on Leroux's books, the most popular of which is* The Phantom of the Opera *(1911). This thriller has had many film versions, the most noted being Brian de Palma's* Phantom of the Paradise *(1974), in which the plot is adapted to a setting in a rock music hall in New York.*

Above: *Joseph Josephin, called Rouletabille, or round head, the youngest of the great investigators of detective fiction.* Right: *Gaston Leroux in an amusing cartoon. When he was writing, Leroux used to lock himself in his study and impose a rule of silence on his family. As soon as he had written the words "The End" he leaned out the window and fired off a whole magazine from a handgun. At this signal, according to Hoveyda, his wife and children threw themselves at the crockery, sending plates flying to a deafening accompaniment of banging pots and pans.*

Belle Époque from the inside, Fantômas represents the more direct and brutal anarchistic destroyer of a corrupt society.

GASTON LEROUX AND THE OEDIPUS MYTH

Although, historically speaking, the adventures of Rouletabille date from a few years after Arsène Lupin's, they are far closer than the famous thief's, in writing style and in spirit, to the great tradition of criminal fiction as represented by Poe, Gaboriau, and Conan Doyle.

A more romantic personality than the characters of his books, Gaston Leroux (1868–1927) was born in Paris into a rich family. Orphaned at twenty, he inherited an immense fortune—a million gold francs—which he squandered in six months of gambling. For a while he practiced law and then went into journalism. He became a crime reporter, establishing his fame with a scoop he managed to get by using a faked pass from the prefecture to interview a marquis in jail for a bloody crime involving one of the oldest families in France. Leroux, tired of journalism, tried the theater without success and finally became a writer of popular criminal fiction.

Ambitious by nature, he set out to achieve something "a little stronger" than either Conan Doyle or Poe. Deciding to meet these great masters on their own ground, Leroux wrote a story based on the classic mystery of criminal fiction, the locked room: *The Mystery of the Yellow Room* (*Le Mystère de la chambre jaune*, 1907–1908).

The apartment in Poe's rue Morgue only seemed to be completely locked (the murdering ape went in and out through the window), and in Conan Doyle's "The Speckled Band" the mystery was explained by a small hatch in the ceiling through which the poisonous snake entered the room. Leroux's sealed room, however, has absolutely no exit that the criminal might escape from. And in fact the explanation Leroux provides at the end of four hundred pages—full of dramatic scenes, twists, and mysterious, well-informed quotations—is both ingenious and simple: The attacker escaped through the fourth dimension, time. The screams that bring Professor Stangerson running to the locked "yellow" room where Mathilde, the professor's daughter, is found gravely wounded, are a sort of replica of the victim's screams at the time of the crime. The attack actually

Two illustrations, dating from the early years of the century, depicting the main scenes from The Mystery of the Yellow Room: *Larsan, the chief of police, leads the investigation into his own crime, one of the first examples of guilty policemen.* Below: *Rouletabille promises to reveal the name of the real criminal to the judges.*

took place many hours before, at which time the assassin had already made good his escape.

The genius who provides the brilliant solution to the mystery of the yellow room is Joseph Josephin, a very young journalist of unknown parentage who is nicknamed Rouletabille because of his small round head. He is certainly the youngest detective in the history of criminal fiction: when he was working on this case, he was only eighteen years old! However, he already has had an eventful past, worthy of a Dickens novel.

Rouletabille was born in 1874 in the United States, of a sad and secret marriage between Mathilde Stangerson and a swindler and murderer named Ballmeyer. Returning to France, Mathilde left her child in the school at Eu (where Leroux himself went) under an assumed name. The boy is therefore completely ignorant of his family, aware only of a mysterious and very beautiful "lady in black" who comes to visit him every so often and whose perfume will stir his feelings for many years.

Entering as a crime reporter for *L'Époque*, Rouletabille follows the investigations on the case of the locked room closely, managing to clear Mathilde's fiancé, the shy Professor Robert Darzac, against whom the head of the police, Frédéric Larsan, had collected a mass of evidence and imputations. Larsan follows Sherlock Holmes's theories on criminal investigation to the letter, but Rouletabille protests that he relies on a preconceived notion of the criminal and that it is very dangerous to search for a culprit who fits one's own preconceptions, an attitude which he says will lead to a grave miscarriage of justice. However, it is just such a miscarriage of justice Larsan is hoping for, because the real culprit is no less than Larsan himself, alias Jean Roussel, alias . . . Ballmeyer, Rouletabille's father!

Unmasked by his son, Larsan escapes by sea, although he quickly returns in *Le parfum de la dame en noir* (1909) to persecute Darzac, Mathilde, and her father. After another five hundred pages of cruel violence Larsan, pursued under various ingenious disguises and finally parading as the poor Darzac, is discovered by his son and—commits suicide. Thus, having won back his mother and killed his father—one might see the suicide here as patricide—Rouletabille fulfills his Oedipus-like destiny and, having freed himself from the nightmares of his youth, can devote himself to another six adventures (from *Rouletabille chez le tsar* to *Le crime de Rouletabille*), each one increasingly melodramatic and farther removed from the world of detective fiction.

In 1914, following the examples of Rocambole and Fantômas, Leroux wrote a cycle of five adventures centered on the warped character of Chéri-Bibi, the most violent force in France. Accustomed to the evil deeds of men and the forces of destiny ("Fatalitas" is his motto), Chéri-Bibi, following a popular French literary tradition, turns into a defender of the innocent.

A last note: Chéri-Bibi's stories contain a great many slang words, anticipating by some fifty years the great boom in the use of slang after World War II in the stories of Simonin (*Le Grisbi*), Le Breton (*Rififi*), and Sanantonio.

ARSÈNE LUPIN, THE GENTLEMAN-THIEF

Arsène Lupin was born in decidedly boring circumstances compared to the brilliant life he was later to lead, first as an author, later in the theater and motion pictures, and finally in that peculiarly modern form of popular storytelling, the television series.

At the request of the publisher Pierre Lafitte, who had recently started the magazine *Je sais tout* and wanted a "typically French" counterpart to Sherlock Holmes, Maurice Leblanc (1864–1941), writer and journalist, wrote a short story about a gentleman-thief, obviously modeled on Holmes's literary rival, Raffles. "I have always enjoyed telling stories," Leblanc said later, "so I took pen in hand, and Arsène Lupin came to me. I changed the name of the old Parisian town councillor, Arsène Lopin, and I wrote, without really know-

Born to compete head-on with Sherlock Holmes, endowed with the characteristics of Robin Hood and the gentleman-thief Raffles, Arsène Lupin (above) enjoyed tremendous success from his first appearance and was translated into thirty-three languages. Far left: *Lupin, in jail, in pleasant conversation with his sworn enemy, Inspector Ganimard, the first of a long line of honest but obtuse policemen who are the constant victims of the amiable criminal's tricks.* Left: *Lupin's creator, Maurice Leblanc.*

One of the famous covers which Léo Fontan designed for the Arsène Lupin stories. The character created by Maurice Leblanc is the most complete and famous of that long stream of criminals, from Rocambole to Diabolik, who fill the pages of popular fiction.

ing where it was leading, *L'Arrestation d'Arsène Lupin.*"

Published in the sixth issue of *Je sais tout* (July 15, 1905), *L'Arrestation d'Arsène Lupin* is the first of more than sixty adventures of the "thief in yellow gloves" which ended in 1939 with *Les milliards d'Arsène Lupin.* The first story was such a success that Lafitte commissioned other stories and eventually whole novels about Lupin. Soon the "son" consumed the father; "It's hard," Leblanc lamented. "Lupin follows me everywhere. He is not my shadow, I am his shadow." To free himself of this too burdensome son, he tried—like Conan Doyle with Sherlock Holmes—to kill Lupin by having him fall off a rock on Capri. However, the public, and the almost independent life which his character had assumed, forced him to arrange one of those convenient resurrections that are so typical in popular fiction.

In the imaginary society of his novels Arsène Raoul Lupin was born in 1874, the son of the aristocratic Madame d'Andresy and of Théophraste Lupin, a boxing and *savate* coach imprisoned for fraud in the United States (where he died).

Through the years and various adventures (*Arsène Lupin, gentleman cambrioleur*, 1907; *Arsène Lupin contre Sherlock Holmes*, 1908; *L'aiguille creuse*, 1909; *813*, 1910; *L'Éclat d'obus*, 1915; *L'Île aux trente cercueils*, 1919; *Les huits coups de l'horloge*, 1923; *La comtesse de Cagliostro*, 1923; *La demoiselle aux yeux verts*, 1926; *Victor de la brigade mondaine*, 1934, to cite only the most important works) the reader realizes that such a birth could in no way produce such a rich and superior character, one who is so nobly French. In a learned study by Valère Catogan, pseudonym for Raymond Lindon (*Le secret des rois de France, ou la véritable identité d'A.L.*), it is shown that the famous thief is actually the heir of the kings of France.

The elusive Lupin makes his debut in a catastrophic manner—through love he ends up in the hands of his lifelong enemy, the policeman Ganimard, in the process losing the precious booty which he had stolen on one of his jobs. This is but one of his many arrests during his long career. These are not just occupational hazards; they are chances to carry out spectacular escapes, a pleasant way in which to publicize himself. Arsène Lupin was in fact among the first to realize the awesome power of the press and to use it to his own ends: in general, his statements are prominently reported in the papers. He influences his adversaries' way of thinking to such an extent that they end up confused and frightened, leaving him to carry out his plots with ease.

Arsène Lupin's character is drawn quite fully from his earliest adventures. A gentleman-thief, protector of orphans, widows, and the ignorant and exploited, Lupin also has an eye for the ladies, which means he often allows himself to fall into a trap and be arrested. Only once, however, does he kill a beautiful traitress, even though he is deeply in love with her. A master of disguise, Lupin adopts a series of costumes and characters—Vicomte d'Andrésy, Horace Valmont, Prince Sernine, Colonel Sparmiento, Jim Barnett (an American detective), Don Louis Perenna, Louis Valmeras, and even Victor Hautin, the head of the vice squad, as well as Lonormand, the head of the Sûreté (like Vidocq!). Lupin could take on, with equal ease, the disguise of a nobleman or of a tramp, of a "chauffeur, tenor, bookmaker, dissolute young spendthrift, aged old man, commercial traveler from Marseilles, Russian doctor, Spanish bullfighter" (*A. L., gentleman cambrioleur*). All these changes are in constant motion, in situations that flare up like fireworks, Lupin con-

A 1978 study devoted to Arsène Lupin. The famous French thief is one of only two characters in criminal fiction—the other is his great rival Sherlock Holmes—to have a foundation and a journal devoted to the study of his career.

trolling them as a puppeteer handles his performers, finding some way of getting the upper hand even in the tightest corners.

Lupin is no vulgar thief. He does not steal for money, but, rather, to turn robbery into an art form. In a detailed study of twenty-seven of Lupin's crimes, Marcel Hovenot concludes that, given the benefit of the doubt, the thief might have just covered his expenses ("Butin de Lupin," in the *Revue d'Études Lupiniennes*, no. 4). Between payments to his workers, the cost of materials, entertainment expenses, the renting or buying of places to work from and cars—he is the first to make full use of this important technical innovation—he spends all the money that he makes from crime; "I've got so many incidental expenses," he confides to Ganimard. "If you could only see my bank balance!"

His only guaranteed return, as Francis Lacassin writes, is psychological satisfaction—the pleasure of defying society, of ridiculing its oldest institutions, and of calling attention to its repressive customs. In Lupin's adventures, as opposed to Fantômas's, there are no bloodthirsty deeds; Fantômas terrifies, Lupin amuses.

Lupin's aim is, in a certain sense, the recovery of ill-gotten gains. His preferred victims are usurers, shady collectors, banks, insurance companies, churches, the Treasury, thieves, murderers, blackmailers, spies, politicians, the excessively wealthy (even including Kaiser Wilhelm II of Prussia). He is clearly the heir—even if more pedantic criticism tends to discount it—of the famous anarchist Alexandre-

Arsène Lupin's screen career began in 1917 with a series of French and American silent movies, followed in 1919 by The Teeth of the Tiger, *in 1932 by* Arsène Lupin, *in 1938 by* Arsène Lupin Returns *and in 1944 by* Enter Arsène Lupin. *However, the most famous Lupin is the television one, Georges Descrières (*right*).*

Marius Jacob (1879–1954), the leader of the organization Travailleurs de la Nuit.

Jacob was brought to court three months before the first Lupin adventure came out, accused, in a spectacular trial, of no less than a hundred and fifty-six crimes, all against banks, the wealthy, and churches (where he left notes: "Omnipotent God, try and catch your thieves"). In his criminal inventiveness Jacob was very close to Arsène Lupin—he was the inventor of the hollow shooting umbrella that was to make Auguste le Breton's *Rififi* famous. Among other examples of Jacob's Lupin-like sensitivity was his decision not to rob the owner of a castle once he discovered that the owner was laboring under the weight of many debts. During one of his other "jobs" he learned that the house he was staying in belonged to Pierre Loti; he departed empty-handed, leaving a respectful note praising the famous writer.

But perhaps Lupin's most important characteristic is that he is a patriotic Frenchman; as Jean-Paul Sartre noted in *Les mots*, Lupin worshiped the siren of evil without knowing that he owed his Herculean strength, his arrogant fearlessness, and his typically French intelligence to the defeat suffered by France in 1870 at the hands of the Prussians, leading to the loss of Alsace-Lorraine. Evading and making fools of his adversaries (he leaves a visiting card at the site of each crime and publishes accounts of the fiascos that befall his enemies), triumphing over them with a style and exhibitionism that are typically French (for instance, his dramatic encounter with Sherlock Holmes, who comes from England to destroy him only to return ridiculed), Arsène Lupin vindicates the honor that was betrayed in 1870. He also did something more for his country: he left France his treasures, fought for the return of Alsace-Lorraine and the advancement of French interests in the colonies, and acquired the secret plans of the *Seven of Hearts*, the submarine that would assure France complete mastery of the seas.

Leblanc himself thought of the Lupin books as adventure stories although, as Jean-Jacques Tourteau has written, they are also, and above all, detective novels. As Tourteau wrote, the mere commission of a crime is not Lupin's starting point; the real problem is the mystery it represents, which Lupin, as a sort of outlaw detective, solves before the police and the rival gangs do, thereby getting away with a large amount of booty.

If Lupin is the French answer to Sherlock Holmes and Raffles, the Lone Wolf, a character invented by Louis-Joseph Vance (1879–1933), is America's answer to Lupin. This can be seen quite clearly from the first of his eight adventures, *The Lone Wolf* (1914), in which one of the characters comments that Arsène Lupin closely resembles a lone wolf. The Wolf is Michael Lanyard, a gentleman-thief trained by the Irishman Bourke, an expert in the criminal arts. The Lone Wolf, like many other Lupin imitations, has already been forgotten.

FANTÔMAS, THE ANGEL OF EVIL

Against Arsène Lupin's exploits can be placed, after 1911, the adventures of Fantômas, created by the team of Marcel Allain (1885–1969) and Pierre Souvestre (1874–1914).

To be truthful, Fantômas hardly belongs to this history. He is mentioned for merits different from those usually directly associated with criminal fiction. His appeal was wide and his influence in doing away with the conventional happy ending was considerable. His stories also featured far more vivid and anarchic violence than that found in Rocambole. Here was a savagery elevated to a philosophical level, with no holds barred. Most important, however, was the influence of the spontaneous literary style of *Fantômas*, which has been commented on by surrealist critics from Apollinaire ("Extraordinary stories full of life and imagination, written it does not matter how, but with an abundance of color") and Blaise Cendrars ("*Fantômas* is the *Aeneid* of modern times") to playwright Antonin Artaud, poets Aragon and Queneau, and Robert Desnos, author of the famous *Complainte de Fantômas*.

Who is Fantômas? Nothing . . . and everything. What is he? Nobody . . . but someone! Well, what does this being do? He terrifies. The genius of evil is intro-

Pierre Souvestre, one of Fantômas's creators.

Born a few years after Arsène Lupin, Fantômas, the genius of evil, enjoyed an even greater success. The publication of his books was advertised by large posters in which the great outlaw's shadow falls menacingly over Paris. The Fantômas comics were also launched with a great publicity campaign, as evidenced by this 1926 photograph.

duced in his first adventure (*Fantômas*, February 10, 1911), describing himself with these terrible words: "I am the master of all, of Time, of the Elements. . . . I am Death!"

The publication of the Fantômas stories, written by Souvestre and his friend and "ghost" Allain for the publisher Arthème Fayard, was preceded by a publicity drive of unprecedented scale—the whole of France was covered with posters showing the sinister criminal's menacing silhouette overshadowing Paris. Fantômas's success was so spectacular that Allain and Souvestre had to write many more than the five stories specified in their contract with Fayard. In three years—until Souvestre's death in 1914 from Spanish flu—the team produced thirty-two Fantômas stories and, as if that were not enough, they wrote another fifty or so as comic magazines.

"We assigned ourselves three days to working out the plot," Allain said later. "Then in three days we dictated the story to a dictaphone. Another ten days were used to read it over, correct the mistakes, check the proofs . . . and the book was finished." After working out the plot, the two authors used to alternate chapters, one writing the even-numbered one and the other the odd-numbered ("though we may perhaps swap over, depending on our particular skills"). To avoid confusion Allain always began with the word *toutefois* ("however") and Souvestre with *néanmoins* ("nevertheless").

In *Le fin de Fantômas* (1913), the last adventure written by the two writers, the fiendish criminal drowns in the sinking of the *Gigantic*, accompanied by his two sworn enemies: the policeman Juve (his good twin) and the journalist Fandor. But a few years later, at his publisher's request, Allain continued the stories on his own, resurrecting all the main characters: Fantômas was saved by the submarine that sank the *Gigantic*, while Juve and Fandor were thrown onto an iceberg where they hibernated. So the series continued with another twelve adventures, from *Fantômas est-il ressucité?* to *Fantômas mène la bal* (1963).

4 | THE GOLDEN AGE

World War I brought irreversible changes to
Europe. The tragic experience of five years
of bloodshed, the social upheavals—
particularly the Russian Revolution of
1917—and the conditions stipulated by the
Treaty of Versailles spelled the end of the Edwardian
Age in England and the Belle Époque in France and
much of the rest of Europe.

As these two periods disappeared, literary and
artistic styles changed. This change did not stop short
of affecting what for many is a minor form of literature:
the detective story. Criminal fiction modified many of
its less essential parts—for instance, the social and
physical settings—in adapting to the new reality.

In its early years criminal fiction had acquired a
definitely conservative character for which it was
eventually to be criticized (the discovery of the culprit
always leads to the reestablishment of the social order
he disturbed). Now it began opening up. Also important were the scientific and technical innovations developed during World War I.

Cars, radio, airplanes, and movies, to mention only
the most "disturbing" inventions, accompanied as they
were by hundreds of other technical innovations,
helped to deepen the rift between prewar and postwar
society.

The new methods of transportation and communi-
cation meant that countries no longer remained isolated. The first signs of this new way of life were already apparent during the war, with soldiers rapidly
moving from one front to another and refugees leaving
their homelands after foreign occupation to seek safety
in more secure countries. Agatha Christie's Hercule
Poirot, a Belgian who found a second home in England,
is one of many examples in criminal fiction that illus-
trate how the detective story mirrors contemporary
society.

A broadcast of a detective play from NBC studios. In order to capture the drama of the script, the actors read their roles as if they were performing before a live audience rather than a microphone. During the 1920s and 1930s radio plays became an established, independent form of literature to which many detective novelists turned.

News, new ideas, and new styles spread with increasing rapidity. In the field of detective fiction, English crime stories reacted to the English public's sudden awareness of American writers, who were to make their influence felt throughout Europe.

All these changes had a profound effect not only on the young writers whose careers began after the war but also on the older ones—Conan Doyle, Freeman, Chesterton, and Edgar Wallace—who continued to write, adapting their work to the times. Thus was born what many critics have described as the golden age of detective writing, marked by the literary birth of Agatha Christie, who dominated criminal fiction for over fifty years.

Those were the years when writers such as S. S. Van Dine and R. A. Knox tried to apply fixed canons and rules to criminal fiction, while writers like Eden Phillpotts and G. D. H. Cole, carried on the tradition, begun by Chesterton, of making the genre respectable. Still others opened completely new fields: A. A. Milne created the humorous detective novel that was, in a few years, to have many followers.

During this period, which lasted until the 1930s, criminal fiction was dominated by the English detective novel, generally accepted as the classic type, not only because of its proliferation but also because its canons were so faithfully followed. However, if such writers as Freeman Wills Crofts, and Philip Mac-Donald remained faithful to the mystery novel, others concentrated far more on description of character and setting (Dorothy L. Sayers) or gave more importance to psychological aspects (H. C. Bailey and A. B. Cox, whose work marked the beginning of the end for the simple, straightforward mystery novel).

Nearly all these writers, however, whether English or American, structured their plots with a minimum of action. But the formal detective sitting at a Chippendale desk with a cup of tea in his hand began to be replaced by a detective who, when necessary, could jump out a window, chase a criminal, and let loose a few punches. This change marked the beginning of the thriller, with its roots in American westerns—remember Nick Carter?—and the *feuilletons* and shilling pamphlets of Europe.

The term *thriller* was coined to describe a narrative work (although it could also be extended to the theater and film) that centers on some criminal plot and is constructed to build up maximum tension. The ingredients were not new. Suspense and intrigue have always been essential parts of criminal fiction. The novelty lay in the combining of suspense and intrigue with action and excitement.

One of the first writers to modify the English detective novel to create a thriller was Earl Derr Biggers, an American. Biggers was one of the "new" writers who, significantly, achieved his greatest fame through motion pictures.

However, the most striking change in the golden age of detective writing was the increased and wide-ranging appeal criminal fiction enjoyed throughout the world. To this period, for example, belongs the most prolific early detective-story writer, Edgar Wallace, even though his first work was published in 1905. Wallace's real achievement in criminal fiction, strictly speaking, came in 1925 with his stories about the detective Mr. Reeder. Edgar Wallace spread the appeal of the detective story among all classes of society and nearly all countries of the world. The fact that his writing style and, at times, the plots of his stories were characterized by a rather slap-dash and hurried attempt to get as much in as possible is not important; his enormous output, his great success, and the fact that he was sought after and read by people who had never bought a detective novel before are enough to entitle him to a prime place in this pantheon of crime writers.

THE MOST PROLIFIC: EDGAR WALLACE

Some idea of the writing speed of Edgar Richard Horatio Wallace (1875–1932) may be gained from a letter he wrote in 1927, in which he advised his publisher that he would be sending in four stories in January—*The Flying Squad, Again the Ringer, Sanders*, and one as yet untitled. To follow in February was *The Orator* and another as yet untitled work; in addition, he promised two serials to be finished by the end of the first half of the year. This all added up to eight books in only a few months. An idle boast by an extravagant personality? Nothing of the sort. Although he did not keep up the demanding rate suggested in the letter, he kept very close to it. In his twenty-seven-year career, in fact, Wallace produced over a hundred and seventy books and an impressive number of short stories, as well as comedies and scripts for the theater and movies (including *King Kong*). He averaged six important works a year, or one every two months.

Even during his lifetime it was suggested that Wallace used ghostwriters, publishing other people's work under his own name. In order to dispel any possible doubt, Wallace offered a reward of £1,000 to anyone

Edgar Wallace, author of the Just Men *series, said the reader must always be satisfied. Accordingly he avoided controversy in his works and steered clear of such taboo subjects as sex. Arnold Bennett accused him of being too complacent and uncritical of contemporary society, never expressing any unorthodox ideas. This is unfair in light of the bitter criticism of justice implied, at times quite explicitly, in his* Just Men *books and other works.*

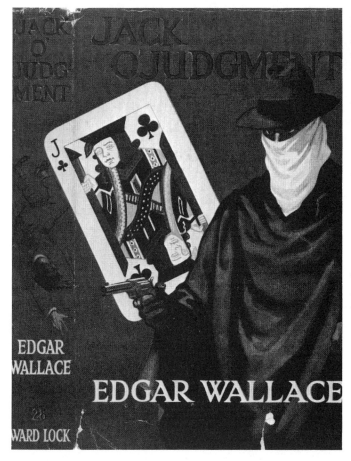

The jackets of first editions of Edgar Wallace's novels, one illustrating the jack of clubs calling card of the Four Just Men.

who could prove his "dishonesty," but nobody came forward to claim the prize.

Once Wallace wrote a book in just one weekend, between Friday night and Monday morning. (Wallace never actually wrote, but dictated to a "very modern" dictaphone, and later had the text copied by two or even three typists, as many as were needed to keep up with him).

His own life was a "Wallace-style" adventure, and it is worth noting its most important phases. He was born in Greenwich in 1875, the son of an actor and a ballerina, to share with nine other children the meager benefits of a poor household, and was denied the chance of a regular education. He was sent out to work selling newspapers when very young—a plaque commemorates him in Fleet Street—and then worked as a cobbler and an office boy. At eighteen he joined the army and was sent to work with the hospital services in South Africa. He was discharged in 1899, before the

fighting against the Boers began, and became the war correspondent for Reuters and then for the *Daily Mail*.

After his return to England at the end of the war, he continued working for the *Daily Mail* but had to leave after some incautious articles by him had brought complaints against the paper.

At the outbreak of World War I he became a correspondent for the *Birmingham Post*. Probably spurred on by an ever-increasing need for money (his daughter-in-law wrote in her biography of him that he earned too much but also spent too much and ran up debts with an extravagant panache), he entered the field of popular writing in 1905 with *The Four Just Men*. It was a success; with his first effort he had found a formula that had instant appeal to the public at large. His characters were drawn with light, masterly strokes and his plot was full of surprises and dramatic scenes.

His novels, like his movie scripts, cover the widest possible range of subjects and have, as protagonists, the unlikeliest possible characters—businessmen, detectives, tearful heroines, gorillas, avengers, scientists, madmen, and ferocious animals.

Wallace rarely became so attached to one character that he made him the protagonist of a series of books. His attention was completely concentrated on the plot, his inexhaustible creativeness enabling him to produce a constant stream of new ones, adjusting the settings and protagonists. From the few characters to whom Wallace dedicated a series of novels there stand out Mr. J. G. Reeder, a detective whose adventures he recounted in a style that gave free reign to his humorous style, and the Just Men of his first novel, daring paladins dispensing inflexible justice to a cross section of

EDGAR WALLACE'S.
AVENGERS

people who become the objects of the author's psychological, and often satirical, observations.

In evaluating Wallace's characters and the right they assume to redress wrongs perpetrated by others, one must bear in mind the times when these characters were created; in Britain as in nearly all countries, the death penalty was habitually applied. If in one of Wallace's books an illegal avenger applies capital punishment to a murderer who has escaped the hangman through some failing in the judicial system or lack of incriminating evidence, one must remember that, by the accepted natural law of man, that murderer *had* to suffer capital punishment.

The Four Just Men made their appearance in 1905. However, from the beginning this quartet was made up of only three people. Once there had been four, but during a previous adventure one was caught and killed by the police. Although lacking one member, the group continued quite appropriately to sign its deeds "The Four Just Men," since an outsider often joined them in the business of executions. In a certain sense the situation is like Dumas's *Three Musketeers* in reverse—the Three Musketeers are in fact four; the Four Just Men are in fact three. However, they are always musketeers, romantic avengers.

The type of the avenging hero—redresser of wrongs standing above the common fray, seeing the failings from which the justice of men suffers, and deciding to provide a remedy—has always fascinated writers and has been widely used. This is particularly true in modern times, when the type has been adopted with increasing realism and less and less romanticism.

A scene from the movie The Mind of Mr. J. G. Reeder *(1939). The detective, acted by Will Fyfe, stands at the center.*

Robin Hood, the Scarlet Pimpernel, the cowboys of the Far West, and many others are heroes of this type. There is no lack of these incorruptible avengers in criminal fiction. The dilettante detective who, for no personal gain, sacrifices his time and even risks his life to bring a criminal to justice or to save an innocent person from condemnation is no less than a Robin Hood of the criminal world. Sherlock Holmes is usually cited as the prototype of this particular kind of detective, the clear line of descent running through Hercule Poirot, Miss Marple, Philo Vance, and Ellery Queen. Today that line continues with the various American private eyes who work for money rather than for glory but who nearly always take to heart the duty they are entrusted with, facing immense personal danger and sometimes forsaking financial reward in order to see justice done.

The three Just Men—Leon Gonzalez, Raymond Poiccart, and George Manfred—are all of unimpeachable character. They intervene "for the love of justice" when they see that an evil, criminal character is able to corrupt his fellows, violate moral code, and escape the arm of temporal law. This, they say, is what distinguishes them from and lifts them above the mass of common hired killers. The fourth protagonist in Wallace's first novel is not a judge but an executioner—Miguel Thery, also known as Saimont, a dangerous but retired criminal. When invited by the Just Men to join them, he at first refuses; he feels outclassed by them, saying that he understands only half of what they have discussed—they talked of governments, kings, constitutions, and causes. According to Thery's view of jus-

The cover of The Council of Justice, *part of the Four Just Men series. This is one of the first Italian editions of Wallace's works.*

tice, if somebody wronged him, he simply caved in his skull and left it at that. What really repelled Thery, however, was that the three cold-bloodedly kill people who have not done them any personal wrong. However, lured by the possibility of personal gain, he did eventually join them.

Wallace wrote a number of books about his Just Men (*The Council of Justice, The Just Men of Cordova,* etc.) and took up the same theme in other books, one of the best among them being *Jack O'Judgement* (1920). In this book, along with the avenging hero there appears a character type that crops up throughout Wallace's books: the arch-criminal, leader of a ring whose activities the police are never able to stamp out. The avenger does, however, succeed where the police have failed. Having discovered the ring's hiding place, he makes lightning raids on it, leaving his calling card—a jack of clubs—and gradually wipes out the criminals one by one. It is immediately obvious that the avenger is someone leading a double life—not a Jekyll/Hyde type of schizophrenic, but somebody who, for personal motives, has made a conscious decision to do what the law cannot. Wallace's protagonists might appear in various guises, but they never hesitate between good and evil. The criminal is a criminal through and through, while the avenger's character is spotless. If he makes mistakes, as must happen to someone who takes the law of God and man into his own hands, he does so in good faith, convinced of his sacred mission and prepared to sacrifice even his own life to it.

John G. Reeder, private investigator, first appeared in 1925 in a series of stories published under the title *The Mind of Mr. J. G. Reeder* and reappeared in two novels and various other stories. Reeder is a man a little over fifty, with a long face, silver-gray hair, and a pair of metal-framed spectacles which nobody ever sees him look through and which he takes off whenever he wants to read. His hat elegantly matches his carefully buttoned frock coat; he wears square-toed shoes and an old-fashioned cravat with folds covering his chest and a false knot attached to his wing collar. His smartest accessory is an umbrella, so tightly furled that it might be mistaken for a walking stick. Rain or shine, Mr. Reeder carries his umbrella everywhere, though nobody can actually recall having seen him open it.

A secretary to the attorney general in London, he is in appearance timid and obsequious. (He says "sorry" to doormen when he rings the bell.) In reality, however, criminals fear him as a mortal enemy. According to them, he is worse than both hell and poison and would be perfectly capable of cutting a man's throat

and then writing a poem over the corpse. He has an excellent memory, allowing him to register a vast range of facts and news that can be recalled whenever needed. Added to this is his "perverse" vision, which finds evil everywhere—in withered roses, horseshoes, even in poetry.

Mr. Reeder never stops repeating (it is as if Father Brown were speaking) that he has the mentality of a criminal and is therefore capable of understanding or divining facts the majority of people—those without such a criminal mentality—would be completely unaware of.

Others of Wallace's works worth remembering are *The Man Who Knew, On the Spot* (a play based on Al Capone's career), *The Case of the Frightened Lady*, and *The Ringer*.

Agatha Christie in a caricature by Nicholas Bentley.

AGATHA CHRISTIE'S IMMORTAL CHARACTERS: HERCULE POIROT AND MISS JANE MARPLE

July 18, 1917. In Styles, Essex, the rich Mrs. Emily Inglethorpe, owner of the old manor house Styles Court, is found dead, poisoned with strychnine. In order to find the murderer, Arthur Hastings, an army captain who is at Styles for a short time convalescing—one must not forget that England is at war with Germany!—asks for help from Hercule Poirot, an old friend whom he had recently come across after many years.

Poirot, a Belgian refugee, has been driven away from his own country by the horrors of war and has found, through Mrs. Inglethorpe's generosity, security with seven other compatriots in Styles. When Hastings first met him, he had been "one of the most celebrated members of the Belgian police. As a detective his *flair* had been extraordinary, and he had achieved triumphs by unraveling some of the most baffling cases of the day."

Tony Randall, one of the first cinematic Hercule Poirots, in a rather curious scene from The Alphabet Murders *(1966), which was based on* The ABC Murders. *For many years Hercule Poirot, unlike Miss Marple, enjoyed little success on the screen. When* After the Funeral, *one of the Poirot books, was made into the motion picture* Murder at the Gallop *(1963), Miss Marple was the detective, instead of Poirot. However, in the past few years the Belgian detective has made a startling comeback in two very successful films,* Murder on the Orient Express, *with Albert Finney as Poirot, and* Death on the Nile, *with Peter Ustinov (below), as the detective.*

Poirot accepts Hastings's suggestion with enthusiasm. A crime? Exactly what he wanted to bring back the good old times. Unleashed on the trail of the criminal, he puts forward his investigating philosophy: "Presently, when we are calmer, we will arrange the facts neatly, each in its proper place. We will examine—and reject. Those of importance we will put on one side; those of no importance, pouf! Blow them away!"

A little later, Poirot clearly explains his method: "*Voyons!* One fact leads to another—so we continue. Does the next fit in with that? *A merveille!* Good! We can proceed. This next little fact—no! Ah, that is curious! There is something missing—a link in the chain that is not there. We examine. We search. And that little curious fact, that possibly paltry little detail that will not tally, we put it here! . . . It is significant! It is tremendous!"

At the scene of the crime the Belgian detective immediately finds five clues: the fragments of a coffee cup; a few threads of green cloth; a stain, still damp, on the carpet; another stain; and wax—enough clues for him to find and unmask the murderer, who is hiding among the residents of Styles Court.

In the eyes of the small Belgian all the residents are suspect, from the servants to the victim's second husband (younger than she), from the daughter-in-law and stepchildren to the dead lady's female companion, from her young protégée to a mysterious foreign doctor who lives in the village. For each Poirot discovers both a motive and an opportunity for the murder of Mrs. Inglethorpe. But only in the last chapter, following the classic structure of the detective story, does he explain the crime and unmask the culprit.

This, in short, is the plot and the crime detection philosophy in *The Mysterious Affair at Styles* (1920), the first novel written by Agatha Mary Clarissa Miller (1891–1976), better known by her first husband's name: Agatha Christie. And so the curtain rose on the career of another great fictional private investigator, a worthy heir to Sherlock Holmes. The curtain was to fall only after fifty-five years in a second affair at Styles, significantly enough called *Curtain*, in which Poirot meets his death. However, in contrast to his great predecessor, Poirot's entrance was not at all theatrical, although his final exit was.

Edgar Wallace had concentrated on the extravagant, the exotic, and the freely fantastic, all interpreted in a style derived from the Gothic novel. In contrast, Agatha Christie, in working out her plots and developing her characters, always tried to remain close to the realities of everyday life. Throughout *The Mysterious Affair at Styles* there are many directly autobiographical details: Mrs. Inglethorpe's young protégée Cynthia Murdoch works, like the author, in a hospital dispensary. In fact, there lived near the Christie house a small colony of Belgians on whom she drew to create the character of Poirot and color his language.

Born in Torquay to an English mother and an American father, Agatha Christie did not have a regular education. Her family was well-off, and she was taught at home by her mother and private tutors. The first love of her life was music. She studied piano and singing in Paris (1906) but stopped short of entering a professional career in music, realizing that she was not made for it. Her first modest literary efforts, mostly short stories and poems, began soon afterward.

Her second love, a few years later, was a colonel in the Flying Corps, Archibald Christie. She married him in 1914 and later gave birth to a daughter, Rosalind. However, in 1926 Archibald asked for a divorce, having fallen in love with another woman, Teresa Neele. Agatha, upset by her mother's recent death, disappeared from home for three weeks. Her concerned husband and family called in the police. Soon all England became involved in "the Christie case" (the writer had been famous since the publication of *The Mysterious Affair at Styles*).

At the end of three weeks she was found in a small provincial hotel. She told the police that she had lost her memory; the police doctor confirmed the story and no further light was ever shed on this disappearance—it is not even mentioned in her autobiography.

The idea of writing a novel came to her during the war, in 1917–1918, while her husband was fighting and she was working as a volunteer nurse in a hospital dispensary. She became fascinated by the crystal vials that contained the most dangerous and deadly poisons. As she wrote in *An Autobiography* (1977): "It was while I was working in the dispensary that I first conceived the idea of writing a detective story. . . . Since I was surrounded by poisons, perhaps it was natural that death by poisoning should be the method I selected."

An avid reader of detective stories, before working out a plot she decided to create a completely new type of investigator. She considered and rejected all those she had come across in her reading. "There was Sherlock Holmes, the one and only—I should never be able to emulate *him*." Arsène Lupin—"was he a criminal or a detective?" Rouletabille, hero of Leroux's *The Mystery of the Yellow Room*, was interesting, as was Raffles the gentleman-thief, one of her favorite characters—

The Daily News *offered a reward for information about Agatha Christie after she disappeared in December 1926. The event was reconstructed by the novelist Kathleen Tynan in her book* Agatha—The Agatha Christie Mystery, *which was turned into a motion picture starring Vanessa Redgrave and Dustin Hoffman.*

and yet also a criminal. A student? A scientist? It was her everyday life that came to her rescue: "Then I remembered our Belgian refugees. . . . Why not make my detective a Belgian? I thought. There were all types of refugees. How about a refugee police officer? A retired police officer. Not too young a one." He had to be quite brilliant—"he should have little gray cells of the mind—that was a good phrase. I must remember that. . . ."—and he had to have a name. "How about calling my little man Hercules? He would be a small man—Hercules: a good name. His last name was more difficult. I don't know why I settled on the name Poirot, whether it just came into my head or whether I saw it in some newspaper or written on something. . . ." Anyway, putting the two together she found that they did not fit exactly. "It [Poirot] went well not with Hercules but Hercule—Hercule Poirot. That was all right—settled, thank goodness."

Looking over the thirty-three novels that Agatha Christie wrote about Poirot—among which the best known are *The Murder of Roger Ackroyd* (1926), *Murder on the Orient Express* (1934), *The ABC Murders* (1936), *Death on the Nile* (1937), *Sad Cypress* (1940), and *After the Funeral* (1953)—one cannot help asking why this amusing, small, and quaintly old-fashioned character is so different from his colleagues and is able to inspire so much more sympathy from his readers than they. Detective novelists who have sought to create a strong character have invariably tended to create a hero to be taken very seriously. Poirot, instead, provides a slightly comic note in Christie's novels. He inspires admiration for his ability to unravel even the most tangled knots, but he also makes the reader smile because of his character, his behavior, and his attitudes; yet he never sinks to the level of caricature.

A small man in a world that admires those who "walk tall," he sports a moustache, which in England makes him look almost as alien as a Martian. His hair is cropped so close that he is practically bald. He is a meticulously fussy dresser, to the point even of being ridiculous—down to his patent-leather shoes. His language, even taking into account the fact that he is a foreigner, is full of rather odd turns of phrase and excessively excited exclamations.

His immense self-esteem, even if justified by his successes in thwarting criminals, is irresistibly comic. In short, Poirot is entertaining; the reader is in no way forced to feel belittled by him.

An eccentric, colorful character such as Poirot might have soon tired the public, but Christie prevented this by always slightly distancing her Belgian detective from the plot. In all her novels, in fact, she created a microcosm of English society, with its own typical characters and events, into which Poirot entered almost as a stranger. In some novels, notably *Cat Among the Pigeons* (1959), he does not appear until the last quarter of the book.

While not a superman, Poirot and his approach to crime detection have become something of an institution. Through hard work and the use of his highly active "little gray cells," Poirot scrutinizes all the possible culprits, brings all the suspects out into the open, and by doing so invites the reader to try with him, or in competition with him, to unravel the complex mystery before reaching the last page. He is a difficult rival!

The debut of Agatha Christie's other great character, Miss Jane Marple, was to be even more low-key than Poirot's. As Agatha Christie wrote in her autobiography, "Miss Marple insinuated herself so quietly into my life that I hardly noticed her arrival." Assigned to write a series of stories for a magazine, Christie decided to link them in a narrative centered on the village of St. Mary Mead, where every week six people meet to discuss mysterious and unsolved criminal cases. Among the six friends is an elderly spinster, Miss Jane Marple, a keen gardener and passionate bird watcher. She was clearly modeled on the writer's grandmother, who led a quiet, typically Victorian life

Miss Marple's popularity is partly due to Margaret Rutherford's exceptional portrayal of her, here with Robert Morley in Murder at the Gallop, *directed by George Pollock.*

but was also quite aware of the depths of human degradation.

Agatha Christie later wrote that Jane Marple's character had appealed to her instantly, and her hope that the public at large would feel the same way was not disappointed. At that stage, however, she felt that Miss Marple could be used only in short stories, not whole novels. She was wrong. As often happens, authors can lose the initiative to their characters; Christie was forced by Miss Marple's success to try her out in a full-length novel, *Murder at the Vicarage* (1930), in which the old lady succeeds in discovering the murderer of Colonel Protheroe, a distinguished figure whose death had brought the most important police inspectors and private detectives in England to the little village. Eleven more novels followed; the last was *Sleeping Murder* (1976).

Miss Marple is a quiet woman who solves even the most complex mysteries from her armchair, finding in her knitting the necessary calm for concentration. She came to criminology through chance: since her youth she had been very successful at a game, fashionable in those days, in which one had to find the culprit in a criminal case chosen by one of the players. It is not therefore surprising that, with the passing of years, her acuity and intuition became increasingly refined.

In practice, Miss Marple's technique was unique and, at the same time, very simple. Taking as a premise the idea that human nature is always and everywhere the same—from film stars to night watchmen, from the inhabitants of St. Mary Mead to New York City or the remotest Pacific island—and ever mindful of the axiom that even the least suspicious is suspect, Miss Marple registers in her extensive memory all the different types that one might come up against. At a certain point she realizes that there are no more new character types, that everyone resembles at least one other person she has already come across, and that, given a particular situation, people tend to behave in a particular, predictable way. To reach this conclusion, it was enough for her to look at the new part of her village: houses, street names, and manner of dress may have been different, but actual human nature and behavior were the same.

Miss Marple is part of an exclusive circle of companions, all spinsters like herself, all enduring the ravages of time, and quietly buried in their respective, neatly pretty houses. Usually they are stuck to the window, curiously staring out and noting everything and then exchanging views in long phone calls or visits over scones. "Did you see what a hurry George's wife was in? She seemed nervous," "Annette wasn't wearing makeup today, it's very strange," "By the way, Old Hopkins didn't have his pipe."

The tool of their trade is not Sherlock Holmes's traditional hand lens, but gossip. However, placed side by side in a wider context, the observations of Miss Marple and her friends can become the basis for an intricate and complex mystery—a mystery that, naturally enough, will be solved by Miss Marple.

The other tools of her trade? Sight and hearing, as well as an imaginative brain combined with strict logic. Miss Marple looks, listens, and puts two and two together. Naturally it is not as easy as that, and at times she risks making big mistakes, although she rarely comes to the wrong conclusion. With her old-fashioned clothes and her knitting needles, she rather resembles the famous Madame de Farge, who sat peacefully knitting beneath the guillotine during the French Revolution. Miss Marple does not, however, limit herself to being an onlooker at the moment of execution; she practically takes part in it, inasmuch as it is she who prepares the way for it. However, one must remember that it would be difficult to show pity for the criminals whom the old lady sends to the gallows or life imprisonment.

Miss Marple has survived for well over a generation and has a skeptical view of changing customs. She remains convinced that anything might change—except human nature. She has a nephew, a young and rising writer, who gets the idea of keeping her up with the times. He sends her strange books, novels written in some incomprehensible idiom, full of unpleasant characters who do the most senseless things and never enjoy themselves, not even the ones who are continually talking about *sex*. Miss Marple scratches her head—and not because the word *sex* did not exist in her day. Rather, one had the good sense to use it sparingly then.

The young *think* the old are foolish, but the old *know* the young are foolish, Miss Marple muses. Anyway, the young are not even fully aware of their surroundings; her nephew thinks of St. Mary Mead as no more than a stagnant backwater, even when his aunt shows him that he has only to look at that backwater to find its vital and interesting human problems opening up a large and fertile field of conjecture.

Miss Marple is part of the England of lace curtains and Sherlock Holmes, representing the triumph of the old technique of detection through logical analysis over a more modern investigative technique based on brute force and trained on protein-balanced diets.

Agatha Christie's detective comedy, The Mousetrap, *has been running for more than twenty-five years. The stage set for the first scene (above, right) was designed by Robert Furse. Peter Saunders, who produced the play, once noted that if all the programs for the play were collected they would weigh one hundred and fifteen tons.*

Apart from her short stories, Agatha Christie's vast oeuvre in detective fiction comes to sixty-six novels. Among those not devoted to Poirot or Miss Marple are spy stories—for instance *Passenger to Frankfurt* (1970)—while four feature Tommy and Tuppence Beresford, a couple, first engaged and then married, who never caught the public imagination (nor Agatha Christie's, judging from the long gaps between the books—1922, 1941, 1968, and 1973). The sixteen remaining books do not feature any common characters. One of these, *Ten Little Indians* (1939), has been judged by many as her greatest work. It tells the story of ten people stuck on an island, all destined to die because one of their number is an implacable murderer. Three films of this novel have been made, directed by René Clair, George Pollock, and Peter Collinson.

Some of Agatha Christie's short stories feature Mr. Quin, a protagonist completely different from all her other characters. As she noted in her autobiography, "Mr. Quin was a figure who just entered into a story—a catalyst, no more—his mere presence affected human beings. There would be some little fact, some apparently irrelevant phrase, to point him out for what he was: a man shown in a harlequin-colored light that fell on him through a glass window; a sudden appearance or disappearance. Always he stood for the same things: he was a friend of lovers and connected with death."

Agatha Christie's literary work was not limited to detective fiction. The "queen of the detective story," as she has been described, also wrote romantic love stories under the pseudonym Mary Westmacott. An autobiographical novel, which evokes the most beautiful moments of her second marriage, to the archaeologist Max Mallowan whom she wed in 1930, is

Agatha Christie with her second husband, the archaeologist Max Mallowan. The famous writer's second marriage was very happy. She often joked about the fact that her husband was much younger than she, once telling a journalist that because he was an archaeologist, the older she got, the more he loved her.

signed Agatha Christie Mallowan to prevent its being confused with any of her other books. She also worked for the theater, writing various comedies, one of which, *The Mousetrap*, has been running in London for more than a quarter of a century. At seventy-five she wrote *An Autobiography*, a 550-page book that runs through

A scene from the first film version of Ten Little Indians, *directed by René Clair (1945).*

The Russian edition of The ABC Murders. *Agatha Christie's works have been translated into many languages, even Esperanto. Some unscrupulous publishers have even used her name on books she did not write.*

her life lightly and yet with profound insight. At her request, it was published posthumously. Agatha Christie finished this work ten years before her death, years in which she was able to rest comfortably on her laurels—the sales of her books throughout the world increased greatly, making her the most widely read English author after William Shakespeare. She was granted the title of Dame of the British Empire.

All this might well have induced her to change the last sentence of her autobiography. She could have ended it on a high, triumphant note, with a smug piece of self-acclaim. Instead, Agatha Christie preferred to change nothing and ended with these simple words: "Thank God for my good life, and for all the love that has been given to me."

THE MOST CULTIVATED: DOROTHY L. SAYERS

Oxford, 1915. In one of the oldest and most famous universities in the world, Dorothy L. Sayers (1893–1957) was granted a degree in medieval literature. It was a momentous event in that it was one of the first degrees given to a woman. Considering the difficulties she overcame in earning it, it is not surprising that in her work as a writer she also showed herself to be exceptional.

In the year following her graduation she published a book of poetry, *Opus I*; two years later came *Catholic Tales and Christian Songs*, another collection of poems. Between 1917 and 1919 she edited the magazine *Oxford Poetry*. Twenty years later she published *The Devil to Pay*, a comedy set against a religious, Faustian background. Her intellectual masterpiece, however, was an English translation of Dante's *Divine Comedy*, which she took more than ten years to complete.

Dorothy Leigh Sayers at nine years old.

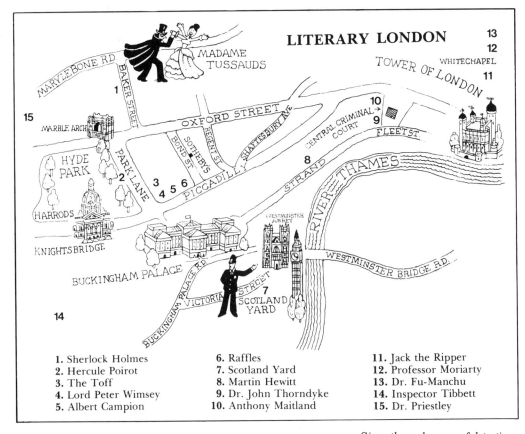

LITERARY LONDON

MADAME TUSSAUDS

MARYLEBONE RD

BAKER STREET

OXFORD STREET

REGENT ST

SHAFTESBURY AVE.

BOND ST

SOTHEBY'S

PICCADILLY

PARK LANE

MARBLE ARCH

HYDE PARK

HARRODS

KNIGHTSBRIDGE

BUCKINGHAM PALACE

BUCKINGHAM PALACE RD.

VICTORIA STREET

SCOTLAND YARD

WESTMINSTER ABBEY

WESTMINSTER BRIDGE RD.

STRAND

CENTRAL CRIMINAL COURT

FLEET ST

TOWER OF LONDON

WHITECHAPEL

RIVER THAMES

15 13 12 11 10 9 8 7 1 2 3 4 5 6 14

1. Sherlock Holmes
2. Hercule Poirot
3. The Toff
4. Lord Peter Wimsey
5. Albert Campion
6. Raffles
7. Scotland Yard
8. Martin Hewitt
9. Dr. John Thorndyke
10. Anthony Maitland
11. Jack the Ripper
12. Professor Moriarty
13. Dr. Fu-Manchu
14. Inspector Tibbett
15. Dr. Priestley

Since the early years of detective fiction London—its fogs, the Thames, and Scotland Yard—has been the ideal setting for criminals and adventure. London is, however, also the home of many crime fighters, from Sherlock Holmes to the lawyer Anthony Maitland, created by Sara Woods.

Aside from this impressive body of scholarship, Sayers also actively devoted herself to criminal fiction. Like Edgar Wallace and many other great authors, she began writing detective stories for quick and easy money. Her first novel, *Whose Body?* (1923), marked the debut of Lord Peter Wimsey, destined to become one of the most refined and original dilettante investigators in the history of criminal fiction.

Peter Death Bredon Wimsey, born in 1890, is the second son of Mortimer Gerald Bredon Wimsey, fifteenth Duke of Denver. Beneficiary of a very good background and education, Lord Peter goes to Oxford, where he very soon becomes totally intolerable, adopting affectations and exaggerated airs—such as wearing a monocle—typical of the university town.

In 1921 he solves his first case and so finds a way of filling his rather meaningless, vacuous life. A while later he opens an office at 97 St. George's Square and gains, through his successes, the reputation of being the Sherlock Holmes of the upper-class districts. He has two all-consuming passions—criminal cases and

Lord Peter Wimsey's motto and coat of arms.

rare books, as reflected in the two works he himself wrote: *The Murderer's Vade-Mecum* and *The Collecting of Incunabula*. He admires Dante. He enjoys music and every so often sits down at the piano and throws himself into some Bach or Scarlatti (his predecessor Sherlock Holmes was even more famous for his music; he played the violin).

Naturally enough, Lord Peter Wimsey also has his own method for solving the cases he becomes involved in. Above all, he works with his good friend Inspector Parker of Scotland Yard. In fact, it is Parker who does all the legwork, while Wimsey puts forward all sorts of supposedly farfetched theories the Inspector has laboriously to refute until, by a process of elimination, they reach the real explanation, for which the young aristocrat gets all the credit.

During Lord Peter Wimsey's long career there is also room for a love affair. It all begins in *Strong Poison* (1930), when he meets Harriet D. Vane, a detective-story writer (*Murder by Degrees* and *The Fountain Pen Mystery*) who ends up in the dock under a charge of murder. Harriet, young and intelligent, brought up with solid Christian principles, had fallen in love with a writer, Philip Boyes. As he did not want to marry her, Harriet finally yielded to his wishes and went to live with him. Some time later Boyes died, poisoned with arsenic, and Harriet was accused of his murder.

Lord Peter Wimsey took on the job of investigating this complex mystery. One look at Harriet was enough to convince him of her innocence, and, of course, at the end he succeeds in getting a complete acquittal for her. In addition, he also proposes marriage. Harriet refuses because she thinks their marriage would be overshadowed by the debt she owes Peter for his having saved her life.

Seven years later (although only five fictional years have passed) in *Busman's Honeymoon* (1937) Sayers brings the love affair to a happy ending in marriage, sealed by the birth of three children, Bredon, Paul, and Roger.

Sayers also created another detective, Montague Egg, who appears only in some short stories and never really threatens Lord Peter Wimsey's supremacy. With Robert Eustace (Eustace Robert Barton's pseudonym) she also wrote another detective novel, *The Documents in the Case* (1930), in which Wimsey does not figure.

Dorothy L. Sayers's greatest achievement lay in her ability to combine detective writing with expert novelistic writing, concentrating particularly on a psychological approach and the creation of credible characters. At times she ignored the classical canons of detective fiction: In *Gaudy Night* (1935) the mystery story is essentially psychological, lacking even the customary murder. *Busman's Honeymoon* is, in fact, subtitled "A Love Story with Detective Interruptions." Critics have indeed credited Sayers with succeeding in creating a new type of detective novel.

Despite Sayers's important place in the history of criminal fiction, her books have not all enjoyed an international following. Only a few have been widely translated into other languages: *The Unpleasantness at the Bellona Club* (1928), *Clouds of Witness* (1926), *Unnatural Death* (1927), and *Murder Must Advertise* (1933). However, through televised serials of her novels she has recently gained a new readership.

THE MOST EXOTIC: CHARLIE CHAN

The view of the Dutch novelist Robert Van Gulik that the detective story came to Europe at the end of the nineteenth century with other chinoiserie from the Far East is not strictly true. It is true, however, that many early writers of criminal fiction gave in to the temptation of introducing a touch of the mysterious Orient into their novels, from Wilkie Collins with *The Moonstone*, to Sax Rohmer, whose stories revolve around the evil and mysterious figure of Dr. Fu-Manchu. In 1928 the writers of the Detection Club in London called for an end to these hordes of sinister Chinamen.

No one, at that stage, had ever thought of creating a character who could apply the sharpness and wisdom of his Oriental brain to the fight against crime. Despite the edicts of the Detection Club, Earl Derr Biggers filled the gap with Charlie Chan, a Chinese detective from Honolulu. Acutely intelligent, Chan is graced with the manners and cultivation that belong to the Chinese of the ancient régime, always ready to quote Confucius—not haphazardly or for easy laughs, as does Peter Cheyney's Lemmy Caution, but in order to cite the verities that lie at the root of ancient Chinese civilization. Very soon Chan took his place among the most famous fictional detectives (thanks largely to movies), even though he appeared with his inscrutable detective techniques in only six of Earl Derr Biggers's novels.

Born in Warren, Ohio, Biggers (1884–1933) graduated from Harvard in 1907. He then began to work for the *Boston Traveller* as its humor writer. Every so often he also wrote theater reviews, which led him to catch the theatrical bug and write his first com-

Earl Derr Biggers, the creator of Charlie Chan, the amiable Chinese detective from the Honolulu police department.

edy, *If You're Only Human*, which opened in 1912. It was an unmitigated flop.

Biggers did not give up, but changed genre. In 1913 he published a detective novel, *Seven Keys to Baldpate*, which enjoyed a great deal of success and was later adapted for theater and film (one of the well-known film versions starred Richard Dix). *Love Insurance* (1914) and *The Agony Column* (1916) followed. After this, Biggers stopped writing fiction for nearly ten years. In the middle of the 1920s he returned to detective writing with a novel, *The House Without a Key* (1925), published serially in *The Saturday Evening Post*. Here Charlie Chan appeared for the first time, the reverse of the "sinister Oriental" type so popular in the early twentieth century. That character type had in fact been completely used up by popular novelists but, as Biggers himself noted, there had never been a proper Chinese character on the side of law and order.

The success of Charlie Chan's first meeting with the public was not comparable to the enthusiasm engendered by his contemporary, Philo Vance, although this imbalance was soon to be redressed. *The Chinese Parrot* (1926) had a very enthusiastic reception and was immediately bought by a major film company. Warner Oland, who certainly had the looks for the part although he was not of Oriental origin, played Charlie Chan. It was a role he was to keep for a long time, even after Biggers's death, for Hollywood continued to produce Charlie Chan films, commissioning stories from various scriptwriters (there are more than forty-five Charlie Chan films).

Warner Oland, the most popular of the various screen Charlie Chans, in Charlie Chan in Egypt. *After Oland's death the part was taken by Sidney Toler, who acted in twenty-two Chan films; after Toler, six more adventures were acted by Roland Winters, and a 1981 film starred Peter Ustinov in the role.*

After these first two novels, Biggers published another four Chan adventures: *Behind that Curtain* (1928), *The Black Camel* (1929), *Charlie Chan Carries On* (1930), and *Keeper of the Keys* (1932). His early death from heart disease brought an end to the successful series.

As the story goes, Charlie Chan, Chinese by birth, moved to Honolulu in 1900, when he was about fifteen. There he joins the police. He immediately distinguishes himself for his detective abilities and, in 1925–26, at the time of the first novel, is already a sergeant in the crime-detection squad. In this capacity, in *The Chinese Parrot*, he has to leave Honolulu for California; at first it seems he has only to deliver a precious necklace belonging to an impoverished lady who wants to sell it to an American millionaire. Chan therefore has to take his priceless charge to New York to deliver it to its buyer personally. However, the millionaire behaves capriciously, insisting that the delivery be made to his ranch in the middle of the desert, which is called, symbolically enough, Eldorado.

Charlie Chan, the most human detective in the history of criminal fiction, in a 1930s drawing. Charlie Chan's qualities are courtesy, a sense of humor, patience, thoroughness, resignation, humility, and prudence.

Chan cannot refuse the request, although he realizes, with his infallible intuition, that "there's something rotten in the state of California," and so decides to go in disguise, dressed as a Chinese cook. While it is true that the disguise loses him the immunity policemen expect (so much so that at one moment he is charged with murder), in the end the plan works very well. He unmasks a sophisticated criminal who had almost accomplished a master stroke that would have gone down in the pages of crime history. Thanks to his success, Chan is promoted to the rank of inspector.

Charlie Chan is very polite (he always says "please" and "thank you," and when he bows, he folds in half "like a penknife"); he has a very large family (nine children, who are joined by two more born during the course of his adventures), and naturally his speech is colored with proverbs, aphorisms, and epigrams—an inexhaustible mine of Chinese wisdom: "A man without enemies is like a dog without fleas"; "Fresh weeds are better than withered roses"; "Hurry only when you have to pull your hand from the tiger's jaw"; "A weak alibi is like a fish: neither can stand the test of time."

THE MOST REFINED: PHILO VANCE

In 1926, at the time of the publication of *The Benson Murder Case*, whose hero, Philo Vance, was one of the first American detectives in criminal fiction (Poe's

Dupin was French), everybody thought that its author, who signed himself S. S. Van Dine, was a promising new writer. Doubts began to appear after only a few months, however, when the book was enjoying a phenomenal success with both the critics and the public. The first to air these suspicions was Harry Hansen, literary critic of the *The New York World*, in an article arguing that the book was too perfect to be the work of a new writer and that, therefore, S. S. Van Dine must surely be a pseudonym; he had to be a brilliant, expert author or at least a very good professional writer.

The hunt was on, to end only when Bruce Gould of the *New York Post* announced that S. S. Van Dine was no other than the well-known journalist and art critic Willard Huntington Wright. Bruce Gould brought curious and amusing proof in support of his case: Wright had invited him to dinner at the Pierre, and, Gould wrote, he was sure that no journalist writing for an arts page in America would ever earn enough money to invite his friends to dinner at the Pierre. Therefore, he went on to assume, Mr. W. H. Wright must have enriched himself at the expense of his intimate friend S. S. Van Dine.

So Willard Huntington Wright (1888–1939) rose to the greatest heights of criminal fiction after having been for many years one of the brightest lights of the New York intelligentsia. Born in Charlottesville, Virginia, Wright had a very good education, completing his literary studies at Harvard. He soon made a name for himself as a journalist and art critic. He wrote a series of monographs on modern artists, an essay on Nietzsche for the *Encyclopaedia Britannica*, and *The Man of Promise* (1916), an experimental novel that was praised by the critics but sold very few copies.

In 1923 Wright fell dangerously ill with tuberculosis and was forced to stop all his work. The doctors allowed him only light reading, so the noted critic began reading detective novels. In a short time he developed such an interest in the genre that the pastime became an object of study. Painstaking and fastidious as he was, Wright acquired all the detective novels ever published, including rare and first editions—over two thousand books in all, which he catalogued according to author and chronology. (The number of titles Wright was able to buy reflects the large-scale development of criminal fiction in its first fifty years.)

Wright studied the technique of detective writing closely, with the idea of writing a history of the detective novel, although he soon decided to enter the ring

S. S. Van Dine, alias Willard Huntington Wright, in a sketch by Jon Taska.

TWENTY RULES FOR DETECTIVE STORIES

From an article published in the September 1928 issue of *The American Magazine*.

1. The reader must have equal opportunity as the detective for solving the mystery. All clues must be plainly stated and described.

2. No wilful tricks or deceptions must be placed on the reader other than those played legitimately by the criminal on the detective himself.

3. There must be no love interest. The business at hand is to bring a criminal to justice, not to bring a love-torn couple to the hymeneal altar.

4. The detective himself, or one of the official investigators, should never turn out to be the culprit. This is bald trickery, on a par with offering someone a bright penny for a five-dollar gold piece. It's false pretenses.

5. The culprit must be determined by logical deductions—not by accident or coincidence or unmotivated confession. To solve a criminal problem in this latter fashion is like sending the reader on a deliberate wild-goose chase, and then telling him, after he has failed, that you had the object of his search up your sleeve all the time. Such an author is no better than a practical joker.

6. The detective novel must have a detective in it; and a detective is not a detective unless he detects. His function is to gather clues which will eventually lead to the person who did the dirty work in the first chapter; and if the detective does not reach his conclusion through an analysis of those clues, he has no more solved his problem than the schoolboy who gets his answer out of the back of the arithmetic book.

7. There simply must be a corpse in a detective novel, and the deader the corpse the better. No lesser crime than murder will suffice. Three hundred pages is far too much bother for a crime other than murder. After all, the reader's trouble and expenditure of energy must be rewarded.

8. The problem of the crime must be solved by strictly naturalistic means. Such methods for learning the truth as slate-writing, ouija-boards, mind-reading, spiritualistic seances, crystal-gazing, and the like, are taboo. A reader has a chance when matching his wits with a rational objective, but if he must compete with the world of spirits and go chasing about the fourth dimension, he is defeated *ab initio*.

9. There must be but one detective—that is, but one protagonist of deduction—one *deus ex machina*. To bring the minds of three or four, or sometimes a gang of detectives to bear on a problem, is not only to disperse the interest and break the direct thread of logic, but to take an unfair advantage of the reader. If there is more than one detective, the reader does not know who his co-deductor is. It's like making the reader run a race with a relay team.

10. The culprit must turn out to be a person who has played a more or less prominent part in the story—that is, a person with whom the reader is familiar and in whom he takes an interest.

11. Servants must not be chosen by the author as the culprits. This is begging a noble question. It is a too-easy solution. The culprit must be a decidedly worth-while person—one who wouldn't ordinarily come under suspicion.

12. There must be only one culprit, no matter how many murders are committed. The culprit may, of course, have a minor helper or co-plotter; but the entire onus must rest on one pair of shoulders: the entire indignation of the reader must be permitted to concentrate on a single black nature.

13. Secret societies, camorras, mafias, *et al.*, have no place in a detective story. A fascinating and truly beautiful murder is irremediably spoiled by any such whole-sale culpability. To be sure, the murderer in a detective novel should be given a sporting chance; but it is going too far to grant him a secret society to fall back on. No high class, self-respecting murderer would want such odds.

14. The method of murder and the means of detecting it must be rational and scientific. That is to say, pseudo-science and purely imaginative and speculative devices are not to be tolerated in the *roman policies*. Once an author soars into the realm of fantasy, in the Jules Verne manner he is outside the bounds of detective fiction, cavorting in the uncharted reaches of adventure.

15. The truth of the problem must at all times be apparent—provided the reader is shrewd enough to see it. By this I mean that if the reader, after learning the explanation for the crime, should re-read the book, he would see that the solution had, in a sense, been staring

him in the face—that all the clues really pointed to the culprit—and that, if he had been as clever as the detective, he could have solved the mystery himself without going on to the final chapter. That the clever reader does often thus solve the problem goes without saying.

16. A detective novel should contain no long descriptive passages, no literary dallying with side issues, no subtly worked out character analyses, no "atmospheric" preoccupations. Such matters have no place in the record of crime and deduction. They hold up the action and introduce issues irrelevant to the main purpose, which is to state a problem, analyze it, and bring it to a successful conclusion. To be sure, there must be sufficient descriptions and character delineation to give the novel verisimilitude.

17. A professional criminal must never be shouldered with the guilt of a crime in a detective story. Crimes by housebreakers and bandits are the province of the police departments—not of authors and brilliant amateur detectives. A really fascinating crime is one committed by a pillar of the church or a spinster noted for her charities.

18. A crime in a detective story must never turn out to be an accident or a suicide. To end an odyssey of sleuthing with such an anticlimax is to hoodwink the trusting and kindhearted reader.

19. The motives for all crimes in detective stories should be personal. International plottings and war politics belong in a different category of fiction—in secret-service tales, for instance. But a murder story must be kept *gemütlich* so to speak. It must reflect the reader's everyday experiences and give him a certain outlet for his own repressed desires and emotions.

20. And (to give my Credo an even score of items) I herewith list a few of the devices which no self-respecting detective story writer will now avail himself of. They have been employed too often and are familiar to all true lovers of literary crime. To use them is a confession of the author's ineptitude and lack of originality.

a. Determining the identity of the culprit by comparing the butt of a cigarette left at the scene of the crime with the brand smoked by the suspect.

b. The bogus spiritualistic seance to frighten the culprit into giving himself away.

c. Forged fingerprints.

d. The dummy-figure alibi.

e. The dog that does not bark and thereby reveals the fact that the intruder is familiar.

f. The final pinning of the crime on a twin or a relative who looks exactly like the suspected, but innocent, person.

g. The hypodermic syringe and the knockout drops.

h. The commission of the murder in a locked room after the police have actually broken in.

i. The word-association test for guilt.

j. The cipher or code letter which is eventually unraveled by the sleuth.

—*The American Magazine*
(September 1928)

"Vance was sitting in a large armchair, attired in a surrah silk dressing gown and gray suede slippers, with Vollard's book on Cézanne open across his knees."
Inspired by this description of Vance from The Benson Murder Case, *E. M. Jackson produced this illustration. He also showed Philo Vance in his study (right).*

himself and write the ultimate detective novel. So was born *The Benson Murder Case*. The Benson in question is a noted Wall Street stockbroker who is found dead, shot from the front by a pistol. The corpse is discovered in an armchair, sitting normally but without dentures or toupee. John F. X. Markham, the New York district attorney, finds the case complex and baffling and asks his good friend Philo Vance to help. There are many clues, but there are also many possible suspects. Philo Vance pursues his inquiries in a rather unusual way: He establishes the alibis of all the suspects, then pulls them apart one by one, destroying them completely, and finally, with a certain panache, announces that they are in fact true. At last he arrives at the alibi of the least suspect character, who was included in the list almost as a formality. This man, seemingly above suspicion, turns out to be the criminal (as usual in detective novels, the culprit often turns out to be the least suspect person). Vance in fact recognized him from the beginning, but had he leveled an accusation against him at that stage, as he later explained to Markham, he would probably have been charged with calumny; it was only by waiting and hiding the culprit's identity that he could eventually persuade others of his guilt.

Once he had finished writing his first detective novel, the famous critic suffered an intellectual reaction and decided not to publish it under his own name, because, after all, it was an escapist novel, in complete contrast with his work as a scholar. So he invented the pseudonym S. S. Van Dine.

Curiously enough, this pseudonym has captivated the attention of many students and inspired the most absurd and complex explanations; some argue that the initials S. S. represent "sob story" or "steam ship." Some considered Van Dine to be a combination of his mother's surname (*Van* Vranken) and letters from "*di*me *no*vel." Wright's own explanation, that Van Dine was an old family name while S. S. simply did not signify anything, has never succeeded in supplanting these other theories.

In response to the great acclaim that greeted *The Benson Murder Case*, Van Dine wrote another eleven novels, all of which feature the refined Philo Vance (the author's alter ego). Among these are *The "Canary" Murder Case* (1927), his greatest success; *The Greene Murder Case* (1928); *The Kidnap Murder Case* (1936); and *The Winter Murder Case* (1939).

Philo Vance is the most refined, cultivated, and aristocratic detective in American criminal fiction, and in this series of novels, Van Dine recounts his complete life history. Extremely intelligent, Vance found the normal course of study limiting and therefore privately dedicated himself to theology, Greek and Persian classics, Sanskrit, Egyptology, ethnology, and ancient and modern languages (particularly Egyptian, Hebrew, and Arabic). The list does not end here, as Vance also has a passion for medicine, surgery, and psychology (particularly practical psychology, an indispensable tool in his criminal work).

Naturally, given his "father's" area of study, he could not leave the history of art and literature out of his curriculum. After Vance's graduation from Harvard (of course) he finished his education with two

One of the first Philo Vances on screen: Warren William (center) in The Dragon Murder Case (1934). Later William was to make a career in crime movies, acting in the "Lone Wolf" and "Perry Mason" series.

"In his dress [Philo Vance] was always fashionable— scrupulously correct to the smallest detail—yet unobtrusive. He spent considerable time at his clubs: his favorite was the Stuyvesant because, as he explained to me, its membership was drawn largely from the political and commercial ranks and he was never drawn into a discussion which required any mental effort" (The Benson Murder Case). The elegant and refined Philo Vance in a drawing by Clark Agnew.

years at Oxford, as might also have been expected. Finally, he traveled for three years through Egypt, Belgium, Spain, the south of France, the Netherlands, Italy, Switzerland, Monte Carlo, Greece, China, Japan (where he learned the martial art of jujitsu), India, and Arabia.

At the death of an aunt, he inherited a substantial fortune, which allowed him to follow a leisurely lifestyle and dedicate himself to his hobbies and his priceless collection of paintings (Cézanne, Matisse), drawings (Michelangelo, Picasso), Chinese prints, and so on.

Vance lives in the top two floors of a house on East Thirty-eighth Street in New York City. Aristocratic by birth and instinct, he stands aloof from the world of common men, regarding the insignificant with a certain indefinable disdain.

At the basis of his success as a detective lie all these qualities, which at first might appear to be slightly negative. Fascinated by art, music, and literature, Philo Vance is an esthete, who therefore approaches a crime in exactly the same way that he would examine a work of art. He tries to understand its character, to place it in a particular school. Material details, such as physical clues, interest him only afterward, as a proof and confirmation of what he has already intuitively deduced.

Enrico Piceni, an art critic as well as a translator and follower of the detective novel, has commented on how Philo Vance does not search for the artist's signature, which might easily be false (all fakes are signed), as do inexperienced amateurs; instead, his expert's eye concentrates on brushstroke, tone, and composition. Discovering the artist is no more than a process of elimination. Piceni notes how, for instance, in *The Casino Murder Case* (1934), Vance reaches his solution through visual sensation: In the "Picasso style" abstract "landscape" of the inside of a small medicine cabinet a certain detail is missing. The presence of that detail would have been just as important to the whole as is the small dot of color on a Cézanne watercolor hanging in Vance's study.

Like many other dilettante investigators, Philo Vance needs a contact to introduce him to criminal cases, and this is provided by New York District Attorney John F. X. Markham. The official policeman who calls to his aid a dilettante or private detective is a figure used quite often in criminal fiction. For instance, the Paris prefect of police resorts to asking for Dupin's help in the case of the stolen letter; Sherlock Holmes is asked by Gregson and Lestrade to solve the case of Lauriston Gardens; and, three years after

Vance's first appearance, Ellery Queen works with his father, a New York police inspector.

The first-person narrator in all Vance's adventures is the author, S. S. Van Dine. Given his cultured background and his pedantic tendency toward classification, Van Dine, drawing on his wide reading and personal experience of novel writing, decided to draw up a sort of Magna Carta for criminal fiction, a set of

"Simple case of strangulation from behind. Digital bruises about the front of the throat; thumb bruises in the suboccipital region. Attack must have been unexpected. A quick, competent job, though deceased evidently battled a little." So runs the diagnosis of the police doctor on the body of the ballerina Margherita Odell, the "canary" in S. S. Van Dine's The Canary Murder Case. *Louise Brooks played the canary in the first film based on the book. Italian actor Giorgio Albertazzi played Vance in an adaptation of the book for Italian television.*

twenty unquestionable rules that should govern detective writing. However, even he contradicts himself when he says that the criminal's actions and the methods of investigation must be strictly logical and rational (Rule 14), and, on the other hand, that the detective story must reflect the everyday life of the reader, acting as a safety valve through which he might vicariously work off his energies and emotions (Rule 19). In fact, as one of the most perceptive students of criminal fiction, Thomas Narcejac, has noted, this illustrates a fundamental contradiction in the character of detective stories in general. One would like to make intellectual games out of them, formulating precise, rigid rules. And yet one is forced to recognize that, because of its character, the detective story will tend to break those rules. For there is within this genre an impure and rebellious element that Van Dine could never bring himself to name: emotion.

A detective novel built on pure mystery, a sort of intellectual game of chess as is suggested by Van Dine's rules, would invariably end up being extremely boring. Had this been the case, the genre might not have preserved its vitality but suffered the same fate as the Gothic novel of the eighteenth and nineteenth centuries. Luckily, human errors and human emotions, in short the lifegiving vitality that has always been captured by the greatest writers, have stimulated the genre's development, which has been so impressive that even writers outside the field of detective fiction—Greene, Faulkner, Borges, Dürrenmatt—have been influenced by its techniques in describing the warped contradictions of our times.

CONTEMPORARIES

Besides the birth of such new talent as Agatha Christie, Dorothy L. Sayers, Earl Derr Biggers, and S. S. Van Dine, and at the end of the 1920s Ellery Queen, Stuart Palmer, and Dashiell Hammett, the golden age of detective fiction still included the work of the great writers from before the war: Doyle, Chesterton, Wallace, and R. A. Freeman. The readership was so vast that many countries saw the publication of special crime and detection or "crime club" series—for instance Le Masque, begun in France in 1927, and the Gialli series published by Mondadori in Italy.

At the base of this large structure of major writers there flourished an active mass of minor followers. These writers occupy many well-earned lines in that bible of criminal fiction, *Who Done It?* by Ordean A.

Hagen (1969), and in Allen J. Hubin's *The Bibliography of Crime Fiction, 1749–1975*. Writers in this group who made a particularly important contribution to the genre were Freeman Wills Crofts, H. C. Bailey, Eden Phillpotts, Howard Cole, A. B. Cox, Philip MacDonald, A. A. Milne, and R. A. Knox, to mention only a few.

Freeman Wills Crofts, whose first detective novel, *The Cask*, came out in 1920, is famous for a rather unique detail: All his plots are built up on apparently foolproof alibis that break down at the last moment. In 1925 Crofts, who until 1929 held the position of chief engineer on the railways, published *Inspector French's Greatest Case*, in which Joseph French makes his first appearance. The public's reaction was so favorable that Crofts decided to continue the inspector's adventures with a long series of novels—*Inspector French and the Cheyne Mystery* (1926), *Inspector French and the Starvel Hollow Tragedy* (1927), and so on. For Crofts the detective novel was a game, a crossword puzzle to be solved.

The Irish writer Freeman Wills Crofts. A railway engineer, Crofts took up writing during a long illness. His novels are often built up around unquestionable alibis; for him the detective novel was an intellectual game, a crossword puzzle.

Another contributor was Henry Christopher Bailey (1878–1961), an Englishman who wrote a historical novel before graduating from college—*My Lady of Orange* (1901)—and only much later published his first detective work, *Call Mr. Fortune* (1920), a collection of short stories featuring Reggie Fortune, a doctor by profession and detective by chance. Fortune is the direct successor to Father Brown and, like him, relies more on psychology and intuition than on material evidence. Another recurring protagonist in some of Bailey's novels is the lawyer Joshua Clunk—*Garstons* (1930), *Shrouded Death* (1950)—an old hypocrite who never really won the public's sympathy.

Among these writers of the golden age of criminal fiction an important place belongs to Eden Phillpotts (1862–1960), judged by Jorge Luis Borges to be one of the ablest formulators of criminal intrigues. Born in India of English parents, Phillpotts was sent home to England as soon as he reached school age. After finishing his regular studies he spent a short time in acting school but soon gave up the idea of going into the theater, preferring to work in an insurance company. He began writing in 1890, and during his long life completed over 150 works of poetry, prose, essays, and plays.

His first detective novel, *The Grey Room* (1921), was an immediate success for the originality of its plot and principal theme. The story takes place in a country house where some people die in a mysterious and unnerving manner: all the bodies are found in a fine old bed in the macabre gray room of the title. Finally it is discovered that the murders were carried out by means of a very unusual weapon—the mattress. The weight of the person sleeping on the bed caused a deadly poison to seep out of the mattress.

The next year Phillpotts published a second detective novel, *The Red Redmaynes*, which featured Peter Gams, an American detective who was called upon to investigate the mysterious deaths of a whole family.

Under the pseudonym Harrington Hext, Phillpotts also wrote *The Thing at Their Heels* (1923), in which the culprit is a priest. With the writer Arnold Bennett (1867–1937), who had published the detective novel *The Grand Babylon Hotel* in 1902, he wrote *The Sinews of War*.

The creator of the two characters Inspector Ringrose (who appears in the books published under Phillpotts's own name) and Inspector Midwinter (who appears in those published under his pseudonym), Eden Phillpotts enjoys even greater honor in the world of criminal fiction for having encouraged Agatha Christie in her first efforts, for which she gives him due credit in her autobiography.

The ennoblement of the genre, begun by Chesterton and carried on by Phillpotts and Arnold Bennett, con-

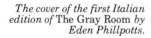
The cover of the first Italian edition of The Gray Room *by Eden Phillpotts.*

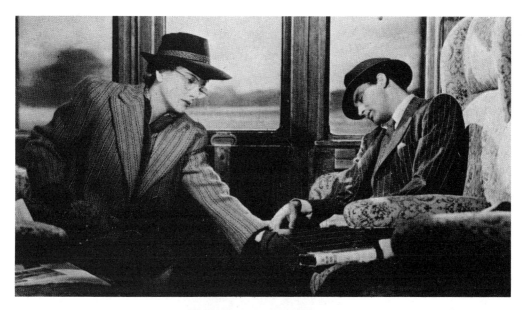

Cary Grant and Joan Fontaine,
in two scenes from the film
Suspicion, *directed by Alfred*
Hitchcock. Suspicion, *was based*
on the novel Before the Fact *by*
Francis Iles, the pseudonym of
A. B. Cox.

tinued with George Douglas Howard Cole (1889–
1959), a noted economist, lecturer at Oxford, founder
and president of the Fabian Society, writer of historical
and politicoeconomic studies (among which is the very
long *A Short History of the British Working-Class
Movement, 1789–1947*). Cole's first detective novel was
The Brooklyn Murders (the Brooklyn of the title has
nothing to do with New York but is the name of an
English family), in which appears for the first time
Superintendent Henry Wilson, an incorruptible

policeman who has had to leave Scotland Yard for daring to accuse a senior official in the Home Office of committing a crime.

After this work G. D. H. Cole wrote another thirty-two books with his wife, Margaret Isabel Postgate (born 1893), in which Superintendent Henry Wilson often reappears and is restored after a few years to his old position at the Yard. The Cole couple are among the first examples in criminal fiction of a prize-winning company, a fashion which was soon to produce a top couple of cousins, Manfred B. Lee and Frederic Dannay, alias Ellery Queen.

While many journalists and writers began their careers as detective novelists because they were drawn by the possibility of the easy money, Anthony Berkeley Cox (1893–1970) took it all up for amusement. In 1925 he published *The Layton Court Mystery* anonymously. At that time Cox was enjoying a very good career as a journalist and a humorous novelist (*Brenda Entertains* and *The Family Witch*), and he was later to distinguish himself by his social and political essays (*O England!*, 1934).

In *The Layton Court Mystery* Cox created Roger Sheringham, a detective who intelligently solves a murder disguised as suicide—a typical locked-room crime—but also shows himself to be rather unusual in that he is both violent and unpleasant.

Seeing the great success that his first book enjoyed, Cox decided to continue writing detective novels. He chose the pseudonym Anthony Berkeley and published a large number of novels, all successful, among which *The Poisoned Chocolates Case* (1929), with its various solutions, is considered a textbook for mystery writing.

In his Preface to *The Second Shot* (1930) Cox made the prophetic assertion that the old-fashioned crime mystery was dead and that detective fiction was developing novels centered on the character of a detective or a criminal, concentrating the reader's attention on the psychological workings of the plot rather than the rational or mathematical ones.

Anthony Berkeley Cox was also responsible for the founding of the Detection Club (1928), whose members are English detective-story writers. Self-effacing as he was, Cox accepted only the post of honorary secretary, G. K. Chesterton being unanimously elected the first president.

Cox (arguably with a collaborator) also wrote three novels under the name Francis Iles. The first is *Malice Aforethought* (1931), the story of a mean, twisted doctor who murders his equally miserable wife. (This novel, based on a real story, the Armstrong case, was recently serialized for television by the BBC.) The second book, *Before the Fact* (1932), is a psychological study of a would-be murderer through the eyes of his intended victim. Alfred Hitchcock based one of his most famous crime movies, *Suspicion* (1941) with Cary Grant and Joan Fontaine, on this book.

Philip MacDonald followed in the footsteps of Edgar Wallace, settling in Hollywood in 1931, where he wrote scripts for some of the Charlie Chan and Mr. Moto crime movies. For MacDonald the ideal was "a sort of competition" between writer and reader, and from his first novel, *The Rasp* (1924), in which the detective Anthony Gethryn appears, he achieved this ideal. He also published various novels under the pseudonyms Martin Porlock—*Mystery at Friar's Pardon* (1931) and *X v. Rex* (1933)—Oliver Fleming (the trademark of Philip and his father Ronald)—*Ambrotox and the Limping Dick* (1920)—and Anthony Lawless— *Harbour* (1931).

A caricature of Anthony Berkeley Cox by G. Morrow (1925).

Alan Alexander Milne's (1882–1956) importance lies in having introduced a definitely humorous vein into criminal fiction with his dilettante detective Anthony Gillingham, called Madman, and his Watson-style companion-narrator Bill Beverly—a pair of amusing bunglers. They appear in *The Red House Mystery* (1922), which records their attempts to solve a complex mystery that begins with the murder of Robert Ablett, a rich emigrant who has just returned to England from Australia after an absence of fifteen years. The chief suspect is Mark Ablett, Robert's brother (the two did not get on well), but to complicate the plot, Mark disappears from the Red House in which he lives. Naturally Gillingham and Beverly manage to solve the case, which had left the police completely in the dark.

If Father Brown was the first detective-priest, Ronald Arbuthnot Knox (1888–1957) was certainly the first priest to write detective stories. Monsignor Knox, an Anglican who converted to Roman Catholicism in 1917, graduated from Oxford, where he was to remain for many years as a lecturer and chaplain.

Rising through the years in the ecclesiastical heirarchy, he devoted many years to a new translation of the New Testament (1944) and the Old Testament (1949–1950). A member of the Detection Club and writer of critical essays on Sherlock Holmes (1930), the monsignor published *The Viaduct Murder*, his first detective novel, in 1925. The narrative starts off in a light, seemingly satirical tone; a party of golfers comes across the body of an unknown person. As the plot thickens, however, the tone becomes more dramatic, with an increasing number of corpses and other *coups de scène*.

Others of Knox's detective novels worth noting are *The Three Taps* (1927), *Still Dead* (1934), and *Double-Cross Purposes* (1937). In the Preface to *The Best English Detective Stories of 1928*, edited by H. Harrington, Knox handed down to detective writers his "Ten Commandments," ten rules on how to write a crime novel. After 1937 he stopped writing because of pressure from his superiors. But by that time detective fiction had seen it all: a detective-priest from Chesterton, a murdering priest from Phillpotts, and in Knox's work, a priest who alternated theological studies with criminal fantasies.

MONSIGNOR RONALD KNOX'S TEN COMMANDMENTS FOR DETECTIVE NOVELISTS.

I The criminal must appear at the beginning of the book and not at the last moment.

II The solution of the crime must be logical without involving the supernatural.

III It is only permitted to use one secret room or passageway.

IV It is prohibited to use poisons which are new, unknown, or which leave no trace.

V No sinister or evil-looking foreigners (particularly of the oriental type).

VI The solution to the crime must never be brought about by a fortunate coincidence.

VII The detective must never be the culprit as well.

VIII The detective should never hide clues or the reasoning behind his deductions from the reader.

IX If a "Watson" figure becomes involved, he should not hide his opinions.

X One should never resort to identical or similar twins.

5 | AMERICAN DETECTIVE FICTION COMES OF AGE

The last act is bloody,
however fine the rest of the play.
They throw earth over your head,
and it is finished forever.

Blaise Pascal (*Pensées*)

ELLERY QUEEN

The classic detective story was at the peak of its development when there appeared in America a detective writing "concern" destined to become famous all over the world. It went by the name Ellery Queen, the pseudonym of two young American cousins, Manfred B. Lee (1905–1971) and Frederic Dannay (b. 1905).

Their first novel, *The Roman Hat Mystery* (1929), featured a unique amateur detective who shared the name Ellery Queen with the presumed author of the book. The "Roman" of the title refers to the Roman Theater, where Monte Field, an infamous character who was probably the head of a vast criminal organization—is found murdered. He is discovered in seat number 30 in the last row at the back left of the theater where a very topical and successful play called *The Gangster* was showing. Field's death was caused by poisoning (it would certainly be quite a task to draw up a list of all the deaths through poisoning in detective novels), but this time the rather banal sort of death is given a rather more modern touch: the poison used is tetraethyl lead, an additive normally found in gasoline and easily extracted from it. In a sense, this is a tribute on the part of criminal fiction to the new scientific and mechanical age. The plot is a sordid history of blackmail, which Ellery Queen explains with great pleasure to his father, Inspector Richard Queen.

This novel marked the beginning of a very fruitful collaboration between Inspector Richard Queen, one of the most highly decorated members of the New York Police Department, and his son Ellery, a young, athletic intellectual and writer of detective novels. Since

(Top) *In 1935 Frank Goodwin drew America's most famous fictional detective by faithfully basing his work on the description of Ellery Queen provided by his two creators. Far more easygoing and undistinguished is the bottom portrait drawn by an artist for production of Ellery Queen's adventures on radio (1940).*

Before trying out the field of criminal fiction, the Ellery Queen team tried the baseball field; right—the cousins Manfred B. Lee (left) and Frederic Dannay, both seven years old.

the death of his wife, Richard Queen (lots of gray hair, a mustache which he chews on when absorbed in concentration, a teetotaler in a society of heavy whiskey drinkers) has dedicated his life to his son and to the fight against crime, in that order. As a policeman, he is unequaled in his ability to collect clues, but it is his son Ellery (the intellectual partner) who connects them and uses them to solve the various mysteries his father must deal with. Richard and Ellery represent the two sides of investigation: the collection of evidence and its theoretical elaboration through a logical or psychological process. In practice, the Queens work as one person, one detective who, divided in this fictional situation into two individuals, becomes more human and real. They are not conceited, abstract supermen like Sherlock Holmes, Philo Vance, or the other characters who had dominated detective writing, even if they are equally infallible.

In 1930 the two authors published a second Ellery Queen adventure, *The French Powder Mystery*, destined to enjoy an even greater success than the first book. There followed, with continued success, *The Egyptian Cross Mystery* (1932), *The Siamese Twin Mystery* (1933), *The Chinese Orange Mystery* (1934), *The Devil to Pay* (1938), *The Dragon's Teeth* (1939), *Calamity Town* (1942), *There Was an Old Woman* (1943), *The Murderer Is a Fox* (1945), *Ten Days' Wonder* (1948), *Cat of Many Tails* (1949), *The Origin of Evil* (1951), *Inspector Queen's Own Case* (1956), *And on the Eighth Day* (1964), and *A Study in Terror* (1966). In all, the team wrote thirty-three novels and numerous short stories about Ellery.

The puzzles produced for the pleasure of their 120 million readers in the 42 years of the Ellery Queen company's activity all share a similar basic characteristic: they are perfect Chinese boxes. Before arriving at the final solution, the reader is forced to devote his complete attention to opening carefully a succession of boxes in order to clarify a myriad of minor or major mysteries. These side issues, although not generally essential to the final solution, serve two important purposes: they distract the reader's attention from the real explanation without actually cheating him, and they build up a psychological atmosphere in which the plot can develop and the conclusion can seem plausible.

The Chinese box technique is reflected in the way the cousins went about writing their detective novels. The first box surrounds their trademark in mystery: Ellery Queen is the pseudonym for the two cousins, Manfred B. Lee and Frederic Dannay. But those names are also boxes, legally assumed names taken by two sons of poor Jewish immigrants, Manford Lepofsky and Daniel Nathan, in an effort to ease their acceptance by American readers.

The discovery of the real name of Ellery Queen's creators sheds light on some of the famous investigator's psychological characteristics and explains, in part, the reasons for his massive success in America. The detective Ellery Queen provides an example of the American dream, a success story to which all aspire. His father, Richard Queen, is a self-made, middle-class citizen who has fought to improve his social status throughout his life. He has succeeded, but only by killing himself with work and sacrificing any other aspiration on the altar of fundamental needs: a house, a secure job, his family's needs, a little money in the bank. In short, Richard Queen is a first-generation American struggling for dignity and a sense of well-being. Ellery Queen, on the other hand, is of the second generation, completely Americanized in character and

DETECTIVE
DIVISION
INSPECTOR
COMMANDING
OFFICE SQUADS

Tall, athletic, cultivated, an infallible investigator, Ellery Queen was the complete opposite of the violent, rough detective of American popular fiction. The star of a very successful radio series, Ellery Queen began a brilliant film career in 1935. In this photograph, Ralph Bellamy, as Ellery Queen, is shown with Margaret Lindsay; she played Nikki Porter, Queen's secretary, a role with hardly any basis in the novels, that was created for radio and screen.

at ease in the American metropolis. His father has handed down all his own intellectual aspirations: a cultivated upbringing, a university education, a good social position, a comfortable life, personal elegance, refinement, and distinguished manners. Ellery Queen seems, in European eyes, rather affected, clumsy and ridiculous rather than elegant, refined, or distinguished. However, to the middle-class American he is the ideal refined man, and as such is the personification of middle-class aspirations.

Another well-kept secret of this "company of crime" is its technique for formulating and writing mystery novels. It was not until Lee's death in 1971 that any light was shed on their cunning alchemy; at that time Dannay confessed to a journalist that the collaboration had not always run smoothly. Their lives, he revealed, were spent arguing, so much so that they were sometimes competitors rather than collaborators. Once, in a movie studio where an orchestra was playing, recording had to be stopped because the two writers were arguing so loudly that the noise could be heard over the music, even though they were on another floor of the building. In order not to argue too often they ended up living apart, Dannay in Larchmont, New York, and Lee in Connecticut, with more than an hour and a half between them. They preferred to communicate by telephone or mail rather than risk the consequences of working in each other's physical presence.

The ideas for their detective puzzles generally came from actual incidents, some event reported in the newspapers, or from simply chatting with people. One woman's spoonerisms inspired a story in which the solution to the mystery lay in reversing the sense of a series of words.

Dannay went on to say that the Ellery Queen empire expanded rapidly to include novels, short stories, motion pictures, radio plays, a television series, and *Ellery Queen's Mystery Magazine*. They soon found themselves involved in a massive undertaking, without having had time to realize what they were getting into. For them, Dannay said, Ellery was a sort of Frankenstein, a thinking machine that had taken over their whole lives, depriving them of any breathing space. No, Dannay concluded, Ellery was not their slave —they had been his slaves for nearly half a century.

To be truthful, the real slaves were the millions of readers who fed on the fine webs of mystery wrought by Ellery Queen and the famous challenge that he would hurl at the reader near the end of the early novels: "It is a point of honor with me to adhere to the Code. The Code of play-fair-with-the-reader-give-him-all-the-

Calamity Town, *one of Ellery Queen's best-known works.*

Frederic Dannay (left) and Manfred B. Lee, the most highly acclaimed detective story writers in the world, holding two of the many Edgars that have been awarded to them.

clues-and-withhold-nothing. I say all the clues are now in your possession. I repeat that they make an inescapable pattern of guilt. Can you put the pieces of the pattern together and interpret what you see?" (*The American Gun Mystery*, 1933).

The two authors were already feeling constricted by their rather cumbersome character as far back as 1932, so much so that they decided to escape from him by creating a new character—Drury Lane. He was presented under yet another pseudonym: Barnaby Ross. Drury Lane, formerly a Shakespearean actor, now retired from the stage and living in a castle overlooking the Hudson, made his first appearance in *The Tragedy of X*. In this novel, District Attorney Bruno and Inspector Thumm asked Drury Lane to help them solve the murder of an unscrupulous stockbroker.

In his mansion, named, naturally enough, The Hamlet, Lane founded an Elizabethan commune made up of theatrical friends who go about dressed as Shakespearean characters. Lane's career unfolds in a cycle of four novels: *The Tragedy of X, The Tragedy of Y* (1932), *The Tragedy of Z* (1933), and *Drury Lane's Last Case* (1933), in which the plot revolves around the robbery of a Shakespearean manuscript from a New York museum.

Ellery Queen, the writer, is now judged among the greatest writers of the century, even outside the boundaries of criminal fiction. He has received more awards than any other criminal fiction writer, including five Edgars, the "Oscar" of the detective novel. The first was for the radio program of Ellery Queen's adventures, the second for his contribution to the spreading of criminal fiction, the third for *Ellery Queen's Mystery Magazine* which was begun in 1941 and in the forty years of its life has published all the best detective stories of the time, and the fourth for critical writing in the field of criminal fiction. The fifth was the Grand Master, the highest prize awarded. He has been given the Silver Gertrude, a prize for authors who sell over a million copies of a book, and the Golden Gertrude, for having sold over five million copies of his works as a whole. Among the latest prizes have been the Columbia Mystery Prize from Iona College (New Rochelle, New York) and an award from the Mystery Writers of Japan.

THE SAVAGE OF SAN FRANCISCO

Ellery Queen's worldwide success is only one small part of the American reply to the great development of the detective novel in England. In fact, despite its obvious American setting, Ellery Queen's writing always remains faithful to the classic tradition of the English detective novel. However, during the 1930s a distinctly American style emerged, one completely different from the cold, reserved English style. To find an example, it is enough to look at American popular comics and magazines of the 1920s and 1930s and, above all, at *Black Mask*.

Captain Joseph Shaw became the editor of *Black Mask* in the mid-1920s. Shaw wrote that he and his colleagues set out to create a new type of detective novel, breaking with the tradition of Gaboriau, Poe, Doyle, and the others. He regarded this tradition as primarily deductive, with stories built like crossword puzzles, deliberately avoiding any other human emotional values. Shaw wanted a criminal fiction that was closer to the realities of American society and took account of gangsters, political corruption, economic cannibalism, and financial piracy. Above all, it should involve that spirit of individualism and adventure that typify the American frontier tradition.

Searching for somebody capable of turning this new concept of criminal fiction into writing, Shaw discovered a brilliant and original writer in the magazine pages of the day: Dashiell Hammett (1894–1961). As he wrote later, Shaw was deeply impressed by the obvious promise in Hammett's work. It was not that Hammett wrote outside the style that had ruled until that moment, but rather that his stories conveyed an unusual authenticity and immediacy. Thus Hammett, with William R. Burnett and Damon Runyon, the author of *Guys and Dolls* (1931) and many other low-life stories, founded the realistic school of criminal fiction,

Dashiell Hammett, the "savage of San Francisco," who invented the hard-boiled novel. "Hammett gave murder back to the kind of people that commit it for reasons, not just to provide a corpse; and with the means at hand, not with hand-wrought duelling pistols, curare, and tropical fish. He put these people down on paper as they are, and he made them think and talk in the language they customarily used for these purposes" (Raymond Chandler: The Simple Art of Murder, 1950). Before becoming a writer Hammett worked for the Pinkerton Agency—"We never sleep"—as a private detective.

American detective magazines
of the twenties and thirties
described by Raymond
Chandler in a Prefatory Note to
The Simple Art of Murder (1950):

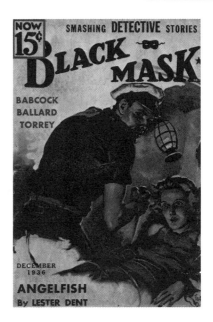

Some literary antiquarian of a rather special type may one day think it worth while to run through the files of the pulp detective magazines which flourished during the late twenties and early thirties and determine just how and when and by what steps the popular mystery story shed its refined good manners and went native. He will need sharp eyes and an open mind. Pulp paper never dreamed of posterity and most of it must be a dirty brown colour by now. And it takes a very open mind indeed to look beyond the unnecessarily gaudy covers, trashy titles, and the barely acceptable advertisements and recognise the authentic power of a kind of writing that even at its most mannered and artificial made most of the fiction of the time taste like a cup of lukewarm consommé at a spinsterish tearoom.

I don't think this power was entirely a matter of violence, although far too many people got killed in these stories and their passing was celebrated with a rather too loving attention to detail. It certainly was not a matter of fine writing, since any attempt at that would have been ruthlessly blue penciled by the editorial staff. Nor was it because of any great originality of plot or character. Most of the plots were rather ordinary and most of the characters rather primitive types of people. Possibly it was the smell of fear which the stories managed to generate. Their characters lived in a world gone wrong, a world in which, long before the atom bomb, civilisation had created the machinery for its own destruction and was learning to use

it with all the moronic delight of a gangster trying out his first machine gun. The law was something to be manipulated for profit and power. The streets were dark with something more than night. The mystery story grew hard and cynical about motive and character, but it was not cynical about the effects it tried to produce nor about its technique for producing them. A few unusual critics recognised this at the time, which was all one had any right to expect. The average critic never recognises an achievement when it happens. He explains it after it has become respectable.

which produced what came to be called the hard-boiled novel. The American hard-boiled novel is filled with violence and action and numbered among its practitioners Raymond Chandler, Thomas Dewey, Day Keene, Ross Macdonald, David Goodis, Brett Halliday, and many others.

Dashiell Hammett's secret lay in his characters and their language rather than in the plot. His characters are flesh-and-blood human beings who think, behave, and express themselves as people do in the real world. Their language is dry and harsh, and their desires, weaknesses, and moods are delineated with an unremitting clarity. As Ellery Queen himself wrote, Hammett broke decisively with the influence of English writers to produce, for the first time, a completely American detective novel. He did not invent a new type of detective story, but he invented a new way of telling it.

Born in St. Mary's County, Maryland, Samuel Dashiell Hammett tried his hand at various trades before joining Pinkerton's Detective Agency as a private detective. During World War I he fell ill with tuberculosis and, returning to the States, soon had to give up his position at Pinkerton's for reasons of health. Using his experiences as a private detective at the agency's offices in Baltimore and San Francisco, he began writing for popular magazines.

Hammett's first novels, *Red Harvest* and *The Dain Curse*, were published in 1929, with *The Maltese Falcon* following in 1930. In the latter, which enjoyed immediate success, Sam Spade, an unusual detective who sees everything through the eyes of the man in the street, appeared for the first time. Spade is not a superman, and he does not perform miracles; he is just a man like so many others, doing a job to make ends meet. His job happens to be that of a detective.

Even though Spade appeared in only one novel and three short stories, he is one of the best-known and enduring fictional detectives of all time. Three film versions have been made of *The Maltese Falcon*; the most famous, made in 1941, starred Humphrey Bogart as Sam Spade.

Samuel Spade's description is very precise: "His jaw was long and bony, his chin jutting V under the more flexible V of his mouth. His nostrils curved back to make another smaller V. His yellow-gray eyes were horizontal. The V *motif* was picked up again by thickish brows rising outward from twin creases above a hooked nose and his pale brown hair grew down from

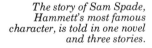

The story of Sam Spade, Hammett's most famous character, is told in one novel and three stories.

In 1931, the year in which Al Capone was jailed for income tax evasion, the artist and writer Chester Gould decided to lead an anticriminal crusade through his work, creating Dick Tracy (below), the first comic-strip detective. Many heroes of criminal fiction soon found themselves in the comic strips —Charlie Chan (drawn by Al Andriola), Perry Mason (Vernon Van Atta Green), and Nero Wolfe (Mike Roy). One of the best-known artists, Alex Raymond, the father of the criminologist Rip Kirby, drew the comic strip adventures of Secret Agent X-9, using a text written by Dashiell Hammett. Above: The last scene from X-9's first story.

high, flat temples—in a point on his forehead. He looked rather pleasantly like a blond Satan" (*The Maltese Falcon*).

In *The Maltese Falcon*, Spade's partner, Miles Archer, is killed. Spade throws himself wholeheartedly into the investigation, even though he despised Archer. His reasons are twofold. First, it reflects badly on a detective's competence if someone can kill his partner and get away with it. Second, Spade was having an affair with Archer's wife, and has no desire to become a prime suspect. Spade becomes involved in a sordid story involving various shady characters united only

The Thin Man, *with Nick (William Powell) and Nora Charles (Myrna Loy). Hammett based only one book on these characters, although Hollywood spun out their adventures into six very successful films.*

by a common, greedy desire to possess a precious gem-studded golden statue of a falcon. Naturally enough, Spade unravels the complex mystery, but he does it his own way—not with a magnifying glass in one hand and the investigator's handbook in the other, but with punch-ups, shoot-outs, and midnight chases down seedy alleyways.

Sam Spade is neither a bully nor an avenger (he does not carry a gun, as he does not like firearms); he is a professional. He fights corruption with obstinacy and courage, even though he is incurably skeptical. He is violent, unpredictable, and disconcerting. He is a fighter who hates to take a punch without returning it and a detective who will find the criminal even though he despises his client. He is, as Queen writes, the savage of San Francisco, a man who never hesitates to call a spade a spade.

Following the success of *The Maltese Falcon*, Hammett went to work as a scriptwriter in Hollywood, where he met playwright and novelist Lillian Hellman, with whom he spent much of the rest of his life.

Hammett sympathized with left-wing movements and was one of the principal victims of the violent witch hunt unleashed in 1950 by Senator Joseph McCarthy against communists and left-wingers suspected of infiltrating the film world and the cultural organizations of the United States. In 1951 he was sent to prison because he would not give the names of the contributors to the bail bond fund of the Civil Rights Congress, of which he was one of the trustees.

It is interesting to note that Hammett, who introduced a social background into his stories, retained a certain fondness for the classic detective story. One of his best-known novels, *The Thin Man* (1934), which was the basis for the successful film series, has as its protagonist Nick Charles, who, quite unlike Sam Spade, is a typical amateur detective in the style of S. S. Van Dine's Philo Vance.

Some measure of the enormous fortune and great fame which Hammett enjoyed can be gained from André Gide's entry in his *Diary* on March 16, 1943:

Read with very keen interest (and why not dare to say with admiration) *The Maltese Falcon* by Dashiell Hammett, by whom I already read last summer, but in translation, the amazing *Red Harvest*, far superior to the *Falcon*, to *The Thin Man*, and to a fourth novel, obviously written on order, the title of which escapes me. In English, or at least in American, many subtleties of the dialogue escape me, but in *Red Harvest* the dialogues, written in a masterful way, are such as to give pointers to Hemingway or even to Faulkner, and the entire narrative is ordered with skill and an implacable cynicism. . . . In that very special type of thing it is, I really believe it is the most remarkable I have read. (*The Journals of André Gide*, Vol. IV, 1951.)

THE METROPOLIS AND THE ASPHALT JUNGLE

During the mid-1930s a young unknown clerk in the office of industrial statistics in Ohio spent his days filling page after page with figures, rates, and percentages. During the evening, at home, he kept on working, though the "job" was completely different from the one that occupied him during the day: he read, one after another, all the important nineteenth- and twentieth-century authors. He also wrote with admirable tenacity, filling one writing pad after another. Nobody encouraged him in his passion for literature except his wife, Marjorie Louise Bartow, who believed in him and shared passionately in his ambitions.

In the traditional American rag-to-riches myth, in a few years William Riley Burnett—this was the young clerk's name—would have reached the apex of popularity, become famous, and be fought over by publishers and Hollywood moguls. Or he would have abandoned his dreams of writing to dedicate himself to a business career. Neither was to be the case. Instead, he remained tied to his work as a compiler of statistics, which allowed him to live through the difficult years of the Depression. He filled several trunks with his manuscripts: nine novels, various theatrical works, and

Edward G. Robinson (far left) in a scene from Little Caesar *(1930), which was based on W. R. Burnett's novel and was directed by Mervyn Le Roy.*

Sterling Hayden (center) in a scene from The Asphalt Jungle *(1950), based on Burnett's book, and directed by John Huston.*

hundreds of stories. In fact, as Burnett was to say himself, he had tried all the literary forms except poetry but had not succeeded in publishing a single line.

Burnett was faced with a drastic decision: to abandon his dreams and literary ambitions or to change his life and seek inspiration in direct experience, not in other people's books. Obstinate, headstrong, unable to renounce his passion for writing, Burnett chose the second alternative. He moved to Chicago, a city which provided writers with an abundance of human subjects, situations, and themes and which in those very years was inspiring the great figures of American literature: John Dos Passos, Ernest Hemingway, William Faulkner, and John Steinbeck.

The impact of the city was enormous. The first result was *Little Caesar* (1929), the violent and realistic story of the rise and fall of a Chicago gangster, Cesare "Rico" Bandello, clearly based on Al Capone. It quickly became a best-seller and was only a year later made into a movie starring Edward G. Robinson, in his most memorable role as Rico. W. R. Burnett finally emerged from anonymity and began to reap the fruits of his persistence.

Burnett continued to write stories inspired by the violence characteristic of the years between the wars. He hit the jackpot a second time, nearly twenty years later, with *The Asphalt Jungle* (1949), an international best-seller which was also made into a very successful film. *The Asphalt Jungle* is the story of criminals who live in the maze of the big American cities, the "asphalt jungles" where the only principle governing human actions is the law of survival.

Burnett's style is economical, his writing terse and pungent, well adapted to realistic image. A conscientious observer of reality, Burnett is, in a sense, a chronicler, as were many other of the literary figures of the day. The plots in his works were never completely invented, even when they were the fruit of his imagination. Burnett described the gangsters' world, with its internal struggles, as a place stained by blood and intimidation, in contrast with the legal world represented by the police. He recounts the eternal fight between good and evil, heightened during the 1930s by the violence and unrest Americans were experiencing firsthand.

ENGLISH FAIR PLAY AND AMERICAN HUMOR

A third American development in the field of detective fiction is the humorous detective novel. Although this particular style had famous precursors—A. A. Milne and, some argue, that extraordinarily provocative book by Thomas de Quincey, *Murder as One of the Fine Arts* (1827)—it was in the United States that it came to be widely adopted, especially after the success of Stuart Palmer, who led a school which included Craig Rice and Rex Stout. This school, keeping its vitality through the years, has enjoyed a renewed success during the 1970s with the novels of Donald E. Westlake.

Before turning to detective fiction, Stuart Palmer practiced various trades: ice-cream vendor, sailor, sandwich man, apple picker, journalist, taxi driver, copy writer, poet, and horror-story writer. He also tried a career as a clown and found work with the Ringling Brothers and the Barnum and Bailey Circus. His first detective novel, *The Penguin Pool Murder*, was published in 1931, when he was just twenty-six. *The Penguin Pool Murder* marked the first appearance of Inspector Oscar Piper of the New York Homicide Squad and a funny old amateur detective, a spinster schoolteacher called Hildegarde Withers.

What does this strange detective look like? According to Piper, one would only have to put on a red wig and wear glass horse-shaped earrings to be the perfect image of Miss Withers. Piper, a small Irishman with grizzled hair, has the good fortune to be one of the most highly regarded members of the homicide squad and the bad fortune to be a friend of Hildegarde Withers. They met over a corpse which had just been fished out of the penguin pool in the New York Aquarium. An unexpected friendship sprang up between the eccentric

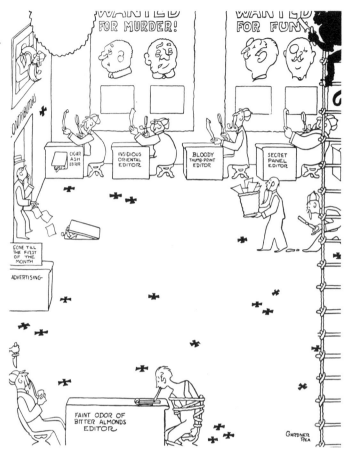

and irrepressible teacher and the stubborn policeman. The bond was strengthened through a series of meetings, or rather confrontations, which at times went as far as blows and vilification. Naturally enough, the relationship soon developed into something sweet and romantic. Oscar, in fact, proposes to Hildegarde, but she has grown used to living alone and turns him down. After his first bout of enthusiasm, Piper is careful not to repeat the offer. Above all, he is convinced that she will gradually get worse, while Hildegarde, apart from the affection that a woman would feel for the only man to propose to her, considers the inspector a symbol of the male-dominated world. A love-hate relationship develops between the two. However, there is always one thing that holds them together: their love of investigation.

Being a busybody is Hildegarde's passion. She describes herself as a dilettante with a fanatic love for puzzles, although in reality she behaves like a sharp professional. If need be, she is quite capable of opening a difficult lock with a hairpin and can quite easily hold a dangerous assassin at bay with her umbrella. Simple intuition is enough to spur her to the attack. An awaited greeting card that fails to arrive could be a sign that the person who should have sent it has died or is in some trouble. For Hildegarde, this presents a complex problem on which to test her wits. It also tests Inspector Piper's patience—he already has quite enough work of his own without Hildegarde's finding any more for him.

Piper is a man who knows his job and carries it out with inventiveness and efficiency. He never overlooks the smallest clue and never accepts evidence without verification. He doesn't have much faith in machines, especially lie detectors. He claims they can be easily fooled if someone knows how they work and has good, steady nerves.

Stuart Palmer, the greatest of the humorous detective story writers.

Piper is a policeman of the old school who refuses to adjust to changing times, trusting more to his instincts than to modern techniques. In this he feels doubly bound to Hildegarde Withers, even if, in the time that he has known her, the eccentric spinster has provided him only with worries. The two form an indivisible pair; they are disciples of the old tradition of logic and deduction, the patient reconstruction of a mosaic whose pieces must sometimes be found in the darkest corners of the city.

Their adventures cover almost twenty novels, including *Murder on the Blackboard* (1932), *Miss Withers Regrets* (1947), *Nipped in the Bud* (1951), and *Cold Poison* (1954). Many films have been made from the books, centered on the character of Miss Withers.

Stuart Palmer's most famous detective is an amusing spinster, Hildegarde Withers, who plagues Inspector Piper. Here she is played by Edna May Oliver to James Gleason's Piper in the film Murder on the Blackboard *(1932).*

John Dickson Carr, American by birth but English by choice. Conan Doyle's biographer, Carr was one of the most prominent specialists in locked-room crimes and the author of some very highly praised historical detective novels.

AMERICAN WRITERS IN THE ENGLISH TRADITION

Despite the emergence of the hard-boiled novel, many American writers remained faithful to the classic formulas of English detective fiction. Among the most famous of these "English Americans" were John Dickson Carr, Mignon G. Eberhart, Rufus King, and Helen Reilly.

Born in Uniontown, Pennsylvania, the son of a noted criminal lawyer, John Dickson Carr (1906–1977) was invariably expelled from the many schools to which he was sent. His scant enthusiasm for study might be ascribed to his parents' determination that he

THE CRIME IN THE LOCKED ROOM

The crime committed in a room hermetically sealed from the inside or in a space which is surrounded or under constant surveillance (for instance, a house or a ship) has always fascinated detective novelists, from Israel Zangwill (the first) to Edgar Wallace (one of the greatest), from S. S. Van Dine to Ellery Queen, from Pierre Boileau to Clayton Rawson, to mention only the most famous. The most active in this field was John Dickson Carr who, through Dr. Gideon Fell, drew up an accurate theoretical catalogue of all the possible ways of committing the apparently impossible crime.

In discussing ways of escaping when both door and window are sealed, I shall not mention the low (and nowadays very rare) trick of having a secret passage to a locked room. . . . We don't need to discuss minor variations of this outrage. . . . The crime committed in a hermetically sealed room which really is hermetically sealed, and from which no murderer has escaped because no murderer was actually in the room. Explanations:

1 It is not murder but a series of coincidences ending in an accident which looks like murder. . . . In this case the means of death is usually a crack on the head—presumably by a bludgeon, but really from some piece of furniture. . . . The most thoroughly satisfying solution of this type of plot, which includes a murderer, is in Gaston Leroux's *The Mystery of the Yellow Room*—the best detective tale ever written.

2 It is murder, but the victim is compelled to kill himself or crash into an accidental death. . . .

3 It is murder, by a mechanical device already planted in the room, and hidden undetectably in some innocent-looking piece of furniture. . . .

4 It is suicide, which is intended to look like murder. A man stabs himself with an icicle; the icicle melts; and, no weapon being found in the locked room, murder is presumed. . . .

5 It is a murder which derives its problem from illusion and impersonation. Thus: the victim, still thought to be alive, is already lying murdered inside a room, of which the door is under observation. The murderer, either dressed as his victim or mistaken from behind for the victim, hurries in at the door. He whirls round, gets rid of his disguise, and instantly comes out of the room *as himself*. The illusion is that he has merely passed the other man in coming out. . . .

6 It is a murder which, although committed by somebody outside the room at the time, nevertheless seems to have been committed by somebody who must have been inside. . . .

7 . . . The victim lies asleep (drugged but unharmed) in a locked room. Knockings on the door fail to rouse him. The murderer starts a foul-play become a lawyer and carry on the family tradition. They insisted that he give up literature and history to concentrate on legal studies.

Since his early youth, Carr was an avid reader of novels. He discovered criminal fiction through the works of Doyle, Futrelle, and Leroux and decided to venture into detective writing himself. During a year's visit to Paris he wrote a cloak-and-dagger novel but soon became ashamed of it and destroyed it. On his return to America he made his debut in criminal fiction with *It Walks by Night* (1930).

The stay in Paris left a deep impression on Carr, so much so that it provided the setting for this, his first novel. His investigator, Henry Bencolin, an examining

---

scare; forces the door; gets in ahead and kills by stabbing or throat cutting, while suggesting to other watchers that they have seen something they have not seen. The honor of inventing this device belongs to Israel Zangwill, and it has since been used in many forms. It has been done (usually by stabbing) on a ship, in a ruined house, in a conservatory, in an attic, and even in the open air—where the victim has first stumbled and stunned himself before the assassin bends over him. . . .

. . . We may list thus a few means of tampering with it (the door) so that it seems to be locked on the inside:

1 Tampering with the key which is still in the lock. . . .
2 Simply removing the hinges of the door without disturbing lock or bolt. . . .
3 Tampering with a bolt. . . .
4 Tampering with a falling bar or latch. . . .
5 The murderer, who is the first to raise a scare and find the body, smashes the upper glass panel of the door, puts his hand through with the key concealed in it, and finds the key in the lock inside, by which he opens the door. This device has also been used with the breaking of a panel out of an ordinary door.

There are miscellaneous methods, such as locking a door from the outside and returning the key to the room by means of string. . . .

And as for windows: I can tell you several brands of funny business with windows if they're only locked. It can be traced down from the earliest dummy nail-heads to the latest hocus-pocus with steel shutters. You can smash a window, carefully turn its catch to lock it, and then when you leave, simply replace the whole pane with a new pane of glass and putty it round; so that the new pane looks like the original and the window is locked inside. (*The Hollow Man*, U.S. title: *The Three Coffins*, 1935)

IT
WALKS
BY NIGHT

BY
JOHN
DICKSON
CARR

HARPER & BROTHERS
NEW YORK
AND LONDON
1930

---

magistrate and the head of the Paris police, continued the long tradition of French detectives in English fiction. In *It Walks by Night*, Carr had not yet developed the half-magical, half-fantastic and supernatural atmosphere that was to make his later works famous. He did, however, employ another of his characteristic themes: the locked-room mystery. The victim in *It Walks by Night* is found decapitated—absolutely excluding any possibility of suicide—in a locked room which is definitely without any secret passages. Furthermore, it is immediately ascertained that the murderer did not hide himself in the room and could not have escaped through a window or the door, which had been watched.

Bencolin's character is developed in the four books that followed: *Castle Skull* (1931), *The Lost Gallows* (1931), *The Corpse in the Waxworks* (1932), and *The Four False Weapons* (1937). The talented judge with sharp tufts of hair and a pointed little beard has eyes that are constantly frowning and a smile described as "ambiguous." His eccentricity is known everywhere but is partly explained by the fact that, from Vidocq on, Parisians have liked colorful guardians. To enhance the legendary aura which surrounds him, Bencolin often encourages his friend and narrator, Jeff Marle (one of Watson's many literary descendants), to divulge the importance of his manner of dress. When he dresses simply, it means that he is seeking no more than simple amusement; when he dons his smoking jacket, it means that he is fully absorbed in the case at hand. When he at last puts on a stylish suit and picks up his silver-headed walking stick, that is a sign that he is ready to spring into action, and that his prey will soon fall into the hands of justice.

In 1932, after marrying Englishwoman Clarice Cleaves in New York, Carr decided to move to England. As he later wrote, he was a great admirer of Conan Doyle and G. K. Chesterton, and he felt that London provided the best possible background for detective stories. The homeland of detective writing proved to be so generous in suggestions and atmosphere that Carr began to write more than one book a year. Since his publisher, then Harper and Brothers, did not see fit to publish all these novels, Carr decided to adopt a pseudonym and find a second publisher. He took the pen name Nicholas Wood, but his new publisher rather unscrupulously decided to change this to Carr Dickson for his first novel. This soon became Carter Dickson after Harper complained that their rights had been infringed.

In 1933 Carr came out with a new character, Dr.

Gideon Fell (*Hag's Nook*). Gideon Fell is a criminologist with free access to Scotland Yard, although he himself is not a policeman. He is always ready to help, particularly in cases involving his great friend Superintendent Hadley. His methods of investigation are not unique, but they acquire an originality through Fell's idiosyncratic behavior. The famous detective paces slowly up and down a locked room or sits heavily in a chair which groans beneath the weight of his portly frame. He poses a constant stream of questions which he then repeats at the risk of appearing simple. After long thought he strikes his forehead, cursing, and reveals the solution. He appears to pull it out from beneath the cloak he always wears, just as a second-class magician might pull out a dove, leaving a speechless audience to scratch their heads and wonder how it was done.

It is in the Gideon Fell novels that Carr builds up the surreal and supernatural atmosphere which at the end dissolves into a straightforward solution.

The technical position of Mr. Carr Dickson in the British detective story is very similar to that of the Messrs. Ellery Queen in the native American product. Both are avowedly "entertainment" writers, presenting sound puzzles in the guise of swift-moving fiction, with characters by no means profoundly drawn but, nevertheless, colorful and adequate to the day. Carr has one important additional asset (present also, it should be said, but to a lesser extent in the Queen novels). His forte has been and remains the rational crime problem, costumed as an eerie tale of the seemingly supernatural. Were not his explanations so meticulously complete and realistic, this would be chargeable error under the canon. As it is, his method represents perhaps the most consistently satisfactory combination to date of the "shudder tale" with bona fide sleuthing. (Howard Haycraft, *Murder for Pleasure*)

Among the many Fell novels (for example, *The Eight of Swords*, 1934; *Death Watch*, 1935; *The Three Coffins*, 1935; *The Problem of the Green Capsule*, 1939; *Below Suspicion*, 1949; *The House at Satan's Elbow*, 1965), perhaps the best is *The Crooked Hinge* (1938), a complex story involving an exchange of characters which only Fell can explain in logical and concrete terms.

During his prolific career Carr created two other characters: Sir Henry Merrivale and Colonel March of Scotland Yard. The former, modeled on Winston Churchill, enjoyed a "prerogative" over locked room murders and made his appearance in *The Plague Court Murders* (1934). The later appeared only in nine short stories. He is the head of the Department of Queer Complaints at Scotland Yard, a position he earns because of his reputation for never being surprised by anything.

The work sometimes considered to be Carr's greatest is *The Emperor's Snuff-box* (1942), which does not feature any of his usual characters. All the facts in the story seem to accuse Eva Neill, the beautiful daughter of an important industrialist, of the inexplicable murder of an old English judge turned antiques collector in the famous French health resort of La Bandelette. Even the police are convinced of the girl's guilt, though Dermont Kinross, a peculiar figure who is both scientist and detective, does not agree. He not only gets to the truth of the facts, clarifying the curious detail of the emperor's snuffbox (made of transparent pink agate mounted in gold and set with diamonds, once the property of Napoleon), but he also reveals the other characters' deception and hypocrisy.

Mignon G. Eberhart (G for Good, her maiden name) shared Carr's appreciation for the classic English detective novel but never felt the need to move to England. Born in Lincoln, Nebraska, in 1899, Eberhart published her first detective novel in 1929, *The Patient in Room 18*, in which she presents Sarah Keate, a nurse at St. Anne Hospital in an unnamed city. Faced with a murdered patient and the robbery of a store of radium, Sarah finds herself acting as an assistant to Lance O'Leary, a young private detective, and helps him to solve the complicated case. It is Sarah who narrates the story, while Lance, the real detective, is reduced to an almost passive participant.

Sarah Keate and Lance O'Leary did not have a long literary life. They appeared in only five more novels: *While the Patient Slept*, 1930; *From This Dark Stairway*, 1931; *Murder by an Aristocrat*, 1932; *Wolf in Man's Clothing*, 1942; and *Man Missing*, 1954. This short career was, however, augmented by a notable list of films—six between 1930 and 1940.

Another heroine created by Mignon G. Eberhart is Susan Dare, who appears only in short stories. Susan

Mignon Good Eberhart, one of the best-known American detective writers. She once said that in order to write a convincing detective story, a writer needed a particular talent and discipline. Bottom: *The jacket of the first edition of* Wolf in Man's Clothing, *one of the six novels featuring the nurse Sarah Keate.*

earns her living by writing detective novels, and lends her services as an adviser to the Chicago police. Among the fifty or more novels by Eberhart that do not feature one of her fixed protagonists, these are worth remembering: *The White Cockatoo*, 1933; *The Dark Garden*, 1933; *The Pattern*, 1937; *Brief Return*, 1939; *Speak No Evil*, 1941; *The Man Next Door*, 1943; *Five Passengers from Lisbon*, 1946; *Hunt with the Hounds*, 1950; *Dead Men's Plans*, 1952; *The Unknown Quantity*, 1953; *Postmark Murder*, 1956; *Message from Hong Kong*, 1968; *Murder in Waiting*, 1973; and *Danger Money*, 1974.

In an interview a few years ago, Eberhart gave her particular recipe for writing. She would sit patiently at her typewriter; as soon as an idea appeared, she would grab it and hold on to it until she had worked it out completely. Ideally, she would start from the wrong end, writing the last chapter first. Then she would try to put in some violence and a crime as a catalyst. She disliked stories in which the author forced the culprit to confess. She liked to develop a good plot to grip the reader's imagination, just as a good juggler might hypnotize his audience, leaving them powerless. She always tried to establish and collect clues, one of her main principles being that the solution must be based on undisputed proof that is strong enough to bring a public accusation.

Another important "English American" was Rufus King (1893–1966). King takes the credit for having created the richest detective in the history of criminal fiction, Reginald de Puyster, who inherited 20 million dollars from his father. However, de Puyster appears in only a few of his books and is in no way equal to King's other major protagonist, the French Canadian Lieutenant Valcour.

Rufus King, the literary father of the French Canadian Lieutenant Valcour, was a writer who cared particularly for character and setting.

Valcour made his appearance in *Murder by the Clock* (1929), but his real impact came in the following year with *Murder by Latitude*. In this case the locked-room crime has a new dimension: it takes place not in a locked room but in a locked setting, aboard a ship.

Valcour was featured in eleven novels, among them *Valcour Meets Murder* (1932), and *The Lesser Antilles Case* (1934). King also created a New York detective, Cotton Moon, who appeared in only one novel, *Holiday Homicide* (1940). In 1941 King wrote a series of stories, *Diagnosis: Murder*, whose protagonist, Colin Starr, is a doctor-detective. Finally, at age seventy-one, he published a series of stories in *Ellery Queen's Mystery Magazine* all of which were set in Florida and featured the young detective Stuff Driscoll. The stories were later collected in three volumes: *Malice in Wonderland*

(1958), *The Steps to Murder* (1960), and *The Faces of Danger* (1964).

The last of this line of British-influenced writers was another Helen Reilly (1891–1962). Reilly not only wrote a number of very good books, but also raised four children, two of whom became, in their turn, detective story writers: Ursula Curtiss, the better and better known of the two, and Mary McMullen.

Helen Reilly's books feature Inspector Christopher McKee of the New York police, a man so dedicated to his work that he does not take off Christmas Day. Surly and bad-mannered (in reality this is due to the little time he can afford to devote to social life outside his work), McKee appeared for the first time in *The Diamond Feather* (1930). Among his exploits are the usual rescue missions to save damsels in distress; these came in the 1940s and 1950s (*The Opening Door*, 1944; *The Farmhouse*, 1947; *The Canvas Dagger*, 1956; *Follow Me*, 1960), when suspense was more fashionable than intellectual mystery and hearts bled easily for a beauty in danger. Among Reilly's books which have had international success are *Dead Man Control* (1936), *Murder in Shinbone Alley* (1940), *Murder at Arroways* (1950), *Lament for the Bride* (1951), *The Double Man* (1952), *The Velvet Hand* (1953), and *Compartment K* (1955).

A GREAT CONTEMPORARY: ENGLAND

In the face of the massive American advances in criminal fiction, Britain provided a contrasting picture of diligent and accomplished artisanship. For years, English writers had dominated the genre. If they did not actually invent it, they ennobled it, spread it throughout the world, and enriched it with works that are still unsurpassed. During the 1930s, however, detective fiction was dominated by American writers. But the United States provided not only the best novels, but also the worst—unreadable books saturated with blood and violence for their own sake, full of impossible, morbidly contrived scenes, and without the slightest literary pretension. In England, on the other hand, there was a steady stream of books that maintained solid if not brilliant quality.

Among the many "honest artisans" (although at times they amounted to something a little greater), Margery Allingham (1904–1966) stands out. She created Albert Campion, a pale, thin, amateur detective with sleek, fair hair who made his first appearance in *The Crime at Black Dudley* (1929), following the same year with *Mystery Mile*. The novels featuring Campion can be divided into two groups: those written before 1934, full of action and even a bit of violence (not, however, of the American style), and the strictly classical ones, with less movement and a great deal of space devoted to psychological characterization. This second strain began in *Death of a Ghost* and carried on with *Flowers for the Judge* (1936), *Dancers in Mourning* (1937), *The Fashion in Shrouds* (1938), and others.

In English criminal fiction there are several serious writers who also devoted themselves to detective stories. One such writer is Cecil Day-Lewis (1904–1972). Well known as a novelist, poet laureate, and critic, he also wrote, under the pseudonym Nicholas Blake, seventeen detective novels based on the character of Nigel Strangeways. Strangeways appeared for the first time in 1935 in *A Question of Proof*. He is well-educated (Oxford, naturally), and he relies on his wide knowledge to help solve his cases. As with all dilettante detectives, Strangeways's greatest problem is his lack of legal justification to allow him to intervene at the scene of the crime; this is provided by his uncle, Sir John Strangeways, Deputy High Commissioner at Scotland Yard.

Writing detective stories was always an amusement for Lewis, an innocent unleashing of the violent tendencies present in all of us. His best works, apart from those already mentioned, are *The Beast Must Die* (1938), *Minute for Murder* (1947), *Head of a Traveller* (1949), *The Widow's Cruise* (1959), and *A Penknife in My Heart* (1958).

Among the many detective writers of the period there was also an immigrant, Ngaio Marsh, born in

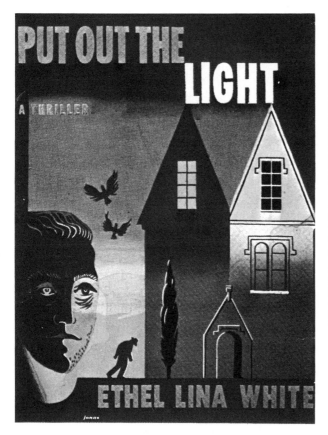

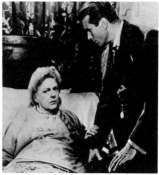

Above: *Ethel Barrymore and George Brent in* The Spiral Staircase, *directed by Robert Siodmak and based on* Some Must Watch *by Ethel Lina White, the story of a homicidal maniac whose ambition is to wipe everyone with any physical defect off the face of the earth.* Left: *The jacket of the first edition of one of White's best-known books.*

1899 in New Zealand to a family of English extraction. She divided her life between her home country and England where, during long visits, she had both studied and worked. Her first novel, *A Man Lay Dead*, came out in 1934, and marked the first appearance of Inspector Roderick Alleyn, who appears in another thirty or so novels among which are *Enter a Murderer* (1935), *Vintage Murder* (1937), *Artists in Crime* (1938), *Colour Scheme* (1943), *Final Curtain* (1947), *Spinsters in Jeopardy* (1953), *Dead Water* (1963), *When in Rome* (1971), and *Black as He's Painted* (1974). Alleyn is very similar to Lord Peter Wimsey, not only sharing the latter's love for investigation but also his aristocratic background. He differs from his great predecessor in that he belongs to the official police force and is far more active, a feature he shares with his contemporary Albert Campion.

Another important English detective novelist was Ethel Lina White (1884–1944). Her career spans barely a dozen novels (notably *Put Out the Light* and *First Time He Died*, both 1935), though her books were to inspire two very successful films: *The Lady Vanishes* (1938), directed by Alfred Hitchcock and taken from *The Wheel Spins* (1936), and *The Spiral Staircase* (1946), taken from *Some Must Watch* (1934).

The vast number of English detective works published in this period was written by a large number of other authors; unfortunately in a broad study it is necessary to make an inevitably subjective choice, albeit one governed as far as possible by popularity and success. However, other writers of the period worth noting are Leonard Gribble, Michael Innes, Raymond Postgate, Basil Thomson, Christopher Bush, Miles Burton, Elspeth Huxley, Leo Bruce, Sidney Horler, and R. A. J. Walling.

6 | MODERN WRITERS

... For my part, I have always been very much in favor of detective stories.

Bertolt Brecht

THE DEVIL'S ADVOCATE

Perry Mason, lawyer; remember that name. You'll be hearing it again. It's going to be famous. . . ." So read the prophetic slogan on the jacket of the young lawyer's first adventure, *The Case of the Velvet Claws*, published in 1933. Since then, Mason has been featured in hundreds of novels, many films, and countless television programs and has become one of the greatest figures in detective fiction.

Perry Mason's literary creator, Erle Stanley Gardner (1889–1970), was born in Malden, Massachusetts, the son of a poor miner. He had a haphazard education, following which he was sent to learn law in a deputy district attorney's office, although he also dedicated himself, with a certain success, to boxing. Gardner was a highly accomplished all-around dilettante. When only twenty, he passed the California Bar, and for twenty-two years he was a respectable criminal lawyer. He then decided to throw himself into criminal fiction. He had already written some short stories and had contributed to *Black Mask*, creating a character who was to a large degree his double—a criminal lawyer who was a defender of the weak, the oppressed, and the persecuted: Perry Mason. Mason owes his surname to a curious ancestor in criminal fiction, Randolph Mason, the protagonist of three novels written by Melville Davisson Post between 1896 and 1908. However, while Randolph was a totally unscrupulous lawyer, Perry is completely honest, a spotless and fearless champion of good.

The feature distinguishing him from other criminal-fiction heroes is that he is neither an official nor a private detective, but a lawyer. He solves his cases through his skills as a lawyer working in court. When he needs to carry out some detective work, he is

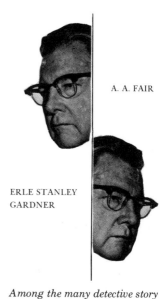

A. A. FAIR

ERLE STANLEY GARDNER

Among the many detective story writers who have published popular series of books under different names, the example of Erle Stanley Gardner/A. A. Fair is one of the most famous. For years nobody, not even his foreign editors, ever imagined that the two writers were, in fact, one. Perry Mason's creator also used other pseudonyms— Charles M. Green, Kyle Corning, Grant Holiday, Robert Parr, and Charles M. Stanton.

forced to rely on the detective agency run by his friend Peter Drake, based in the same building where Mason has his office, on the corner of Broadway and Seventh Street in Los Angeles.

By a strange stroke of fate, every case which Perry Mason accepts involves him in some highly publicized story, his name being dragged into all the newspapers. Mason is forced to deal with all sorts of people, from lying, timid, or untrustworthy clients to policemen and district attorneys who are biased against him. In his first adventure, he is accused of murdering a client who had come to him for help in an embarrassing situation. In at least a dozen other cases, he is forced to break the law (always prudently!) in order to discover the truth. In *The Case of the Drowsy Mosquito* (1943), he even comes near to dying after taking arsenic.

His closest collaborator, apart from Paul Drake, is Della Street. Della is Mason's secretary and personal assistant; beautiful, intelligent, very quick, she complements the "master" ideally. With time, the working relationship between the two transforms itself into an affectionate brother-sister friendship. Della refuses Perry's five proposals of marriage, saying that he needs a secretary, not a wife.

The California lawyer's two most noted adversaries are District Attorney Hamilton Burger, with whom Mason frequently crosses swords in court, and Lieutenant Arthur Tragg. Tragg is the keenest bloodhound in the whole Los Angeles Police Department, although he certainly is not a shrewd intellect; he is generally the one who arrests Perry Mason's clients, and who must listen as Mason, calling on all the skills

The Case of the Turning Tide, an adventure not *involving Perry Mason, Gardner's most famous character. An impressive CBS television series starring Raymond Burr firmly established Mason on film. Below, center and right, Mason on television and in a comic strip.*

Erle Stanley Gardner once appeared in the Perry Mason *television series playing the part of the Judge (here seen with the District Attorney, Hamilton Burger, played by William Talman). Speaking of his work as a detective novelist, Gardner has said that the appeal of a mystery story is that it can fix the reader's attention and involve him in the process of finding the solution. Generally speaking, Gardner maintained, readers are plagued with problems they are unable to solve that follow them even when they want to relax. To escape them, they pick up a mystery story, become completely absorbed, help bring the investigation to a sucessful solution, switch off the light, and go to sleep.*

of his trade as well as some personal detective work, brings to light the immense errors made by the police.

All of Gardner's Perry Mason novels are worth reading, although particularly worthwhile, apart from the titles already mentioned, are *The Case of the Howling Dog* (1934); *The Case of the Stuttering Bishop* (1936); *The Case of the Lame Canary* (1937); *The Case of the Shoplifter's Shoe* (1938); *The Case of the Careless Kitten* (1942); *The Case of the Crooked Candle* (1944); *The Case of the Hesitant Hostess* (1953); *The Case of the Screaming Woman* (1957); *The Case of the Long-Legged Models* (1958); *The Case of the Ice-Cold Hands* (1962) and *The Case of the Postponed Murder* (1973).

While continuing to write detective novels, Gardner never forgot his legal background. He was one of the founders of the Court of Last Resort, an association of jurists and criminologists who, working without pay, sought to provide a solution to unsolved court cases and took up the cause of the innocent and unjustly condemned. He also deserves the credit for an important ruling by the California Supreme Court which plugged a legal loophole by which a murderer might get away unpunished. Gardner had raised this question in 1939, in *The Bigger They Come*, a novel which featured a new protagonist—Donald Lam, a former lawyer who has become a private detective after being disbarred. His expulsion came after he had discovered the loophole in the law and, unknowingly, had "taught" a client how to commit the perfect murder.

After establishing himself as the creator of Perry Mason, Erle Stanley Gardner tried unsuccessfully to base novels on other protagonists. Readers would open the book, see that Mason was not there, and be too disappointed to appreciate the story, even though it had been constructed with great ability. For this reason Gardner decided to sign his Donald Lam adventures with the pseudonym A. A. Fair. He jealously guarded this secret for a long time, so much so that his editors abroad published A. A. Fair novels for years without the slightest idea that they had, in fact, been written by Gardner. Donald Lam, a detective who worked first in the service of and later in partnership with Bertha Cool (a Nero Wolfe in stockings) and her agency, appeared in twenty-nine novels, among which it is worth noting: *Gold Comes in Bricks* (1940); *Top of the Heap* (1952); *Some Women Won't Wait* (1953); *Beware the Curves* (1956); *You Can Die Laughing* (1957); *Try Anything Once* (1962); and *All Grass Isn't Green* (1970).

REX STOUT, OR THE SMILING DETECTIVE STORY

Cigar salesman in Cleveland, dealer in Indian baskets in Albuquerque, guide to the peublos in Santa Fe, courier to holiday-makers in Colorado Springs, librarian in Chicago, Indianapolis, Milwaukee, New York. Before going into the field of criminal fiction, Rex Stout (1886–1975), born in Noblesville, Indiana, tried at least twenty different trades, including writing an experimental novel called *How Like a God*; it was not at all successful.

Stout realized that he had it in him to be a storyteller, but not a great novelist, as he himself was to admit. He therefore set out to produce works of polished craftsmanship better suited to his talents— detective novels. In 1934 there appeared *Fer-de-Lance*, Nero Wolfe's first adventure, in which the large, moody detective finds himself involved in an intricate plot, originating in age-old rivalries and ending in a bloody vendetta. In order to rid himself of the very annoying bother of being investigated, the guilty party puts a snake in a box and leaves it in Wolfe's writing desk, but, by a hair's breadth, the detective saves himself.

Although his date of birth is uncertain (1892 or 1893), Nero Wolfe does know that he was born in Trenton, New Jersey. Around the turn of the century, mother and son moved to Europe. Years of travel followed: Budapest, Zagreb, Albania, Catalonia, Algeria, Egypt, Arabia. During World War I Wolfe returned to the Balkans and was imprisoned in Bulgaria, where he swore obedience to Montenegro and joined its army. When the Serbo-Montenegran army was annihilated in 1916 he came close to dying of starvation. During

For years Rex Stout alternated between novels and collections made up of three long stories, all featuring the famous Nero Wolfe, one of the most eccentric detectives in the history of criminal fiction. Shown is the original cover of one of the first anthologies.

the next two years he walked more than five hundred miles to join the American troops. From 1918 until 1920 he traveled through Europe before finally returning to the Balkans. There followed some "dark" years until 1927, when he went back to the United States, where he established himself permanently except for one trip to Zagreb in 1928 which ended with a stay in jail and forced a sudden return to the United States.

Nero Wolfe lives at the west end of Thirty-fifth Street in New York, one block from the Hudson River. His house, which he owns, has four floors, including the greenhouse on the roof where he grows his famous orchids, for which he has a rather morbid passion. With him live Archie Goodwin—his lieutenant, right-hand man, messenger, and biographer; Fritz Brenner—his butler, cook, and handyman; and Theodore Horstman—his "orchid-nanny." There are no women in the house, apart from the female clients who pass through; Nero Wolfe is a decided, obstinate misogynist.

But what exactly is Nero Wolfe? He himself says that his methods are not those of a policeman, but rather those of a private detective. He marks the criminals and then looks for the evidence with which to nail them. But he also claims to be a philosopher, an artist, and a born actor. And he doesn't hesitate to claim on more than one occasion, "I'm a genius." A rather eccentric genius, he enjoys sitting at home tasting the refined delights of Fritz Brenner's cooking and cultivat-

Rex Stout, the creator of Nero Wolfe.

ing his orchids. He solves his cases while rarely moving from his home. Whenever Archie Goodwin dares to voice the slightest objection to this, Wolfe asks why a man should work so hard to achieve a certain fame, if he must then toil like a normal human being.

To those who ask if he does detective work for the love of it, he replies that this is not exactly the reason. He needs so many pennies, and usually he satisfies his customers and earns them. But the money just seems to disappear, so it's on to more cases.

It has been written that Nero Wolfe is a unique character because his creator was. He is unpredictable, capricious, and a little grotesque, and he manifests many of the same eccentricities as Rex Stout, who has stamped him with the various experiences of his life. There is a distinct resemblance between the two on an intellectual level: They are both committed polemicists, dedicated to verbal battles, not at all disdaining sophistry, quibbling over trifles, and posing paradoxes in order to have the final say. There are, however, many differences: Wolfe is sedentary and irritable; Stout, dynamic and affable. Wolfe is a declared misogynist; Stout loves his wife and is far from indifferent to pretty girls. Wolfe is an inveterate home-dweller; Stout a keen angler and passionate walker, whether in the city or the country. Physically, the two are diametrically opposed—the lazy Wolfe is enormous, the energetic Stout is skinny. Wolfe is clean-shaven while Stout has a beard which, according to the *The New York Times*, was borrowed either from a goat or from George Bernard Shaw.

If Nero Wolfe is the mind, then Archie Goodwin is

the body; Goodwin is the person who physically conducts the investigations, often using the services of Saul Panzer and other private detectives, as the case may need. A young, handsome man, his good looks can create complications during the course of his investigations when he comes across a woman whose beauty is a little too bewitching and who finds that he resembles Humphrey Bogart (though he would prefer to look like Gary Cooper). He has few hobbies, largely because the free time left to him by that taskmaster Wolfe is very limited. A card game every so often, poker or whist, or perhaps billiards, though he is no great fan of the billiard table. He is more or less engaged to the multi-millionairess Lily Rowan whom he would probably marry were she not so rich. Goodwin never hides what he thinks, especially when his lord and master, as he sometimes calls Wolfe, might prefer not to hear it. On these occasions Wolfe teases him by saying that one day he will no longer tolerate him and will have to find a wife to listen to his inanities. Wolfe can hurl no greater insult than this, because for Wolfe, marriage stands first among the great disasters, surpassing flood, famine, and war.

When a journalist asked him how he came to create a couple so different from any other in criminal fiction, Stout replied that as a novelist he might easily invent a number of answers, but to tell the truth he didn't know himself. Stout carefully distinguished between created and constructed characters: created characters are real and three-dimensional, while constructed ones merely fill a slot in the story. In very prolific writers such as Balzac or Dickens, Stout maintained, it was very easy to distinguish one from the other. Wolfe and Goodwin are, like Hamlet, created characters.

Whether functional or created, Goodwin and Nero

Despite Nero Wolfe's great popularity, it has always been difficult to find an actor who can play him convincingly on the screen because of his size. Among the few actors who have established themselves in the role are Edward Arnold (center).

Wolfe have shown themselves, from 1934 on, to be highly successful characters in detective stories combining elements of the classic detective novel with the action-packed novel, fusing them with humor in the style of P. G. Wodehouse.

Among the many Nero Wolfe novels, the best are probably *The League of Frightened Men* (1935), *Too Many Cooks* (1938), *The Golden Spiders* (1953), *Might as Well Be Dead* (1956), *Champagne for One* (1958), *The Final Deduction* (1961), *Gambit* (1962), *Death of a Dude* (1969), and *A Family Affair* (1975).

Like a good father who loves all his children equally, Rex Stout has never disowned the detective novels in which his two famous protagonists do not appear. Critics and readers have judged them as minor works, but he has always rejected that verdict. This does not change the fact that, after trying to give Nero Wolfe two brothers (Tecumseh Fox and Alphabet Hicks) and a sister (Dol Bonner), Stout dedicated all his efforts to Wolfe's orchids and Archie Goodwin's women—apart from their criminal cases, of course.

The marriage of the detective novel to the comic novel was tried again, chiefly by Craig Rice, the pseudonym of Georgiana Ann Randolph (1908–1957). She created the figure of John J. Malone, a lawyer who all too often prefers the bottle to the law. Malone appeared for the first time in *Eight Faces at Three* (1939) and continued his career through about a dozen very original novels. During the 1950s, Craig Rice joined with Stuart Palmer, and the two wrote some stories in which their two most famous protagonists, John J. Malone and Hildegarde Withers, worked together. These were published under the title *The People vs. Withers and Malone* (1963). Two of the stories, "Once Upon a Train" and "Cherchez La Frame," won the *Ellery Queen's Mystery Magazine*'s second prize. Randolph, using the same pseudonym Craig Rice, also created two other interesting characters, Bingo Riggs and Handsome Kusak, both photographers. She also wrote other novels using different pseudonyms, including Daphne Sanders and Michael Venning.

THE LEMMY CAUTION BOMB

Peter Cheyney (1896–1951)—full name Reginald Evelyn Peter Southouse Cheyney—had a very normal education without distinguishing himself at anything, except mathematics, yet succeeded in getting a degree in law and achieving fame as a writer. He began work in 1914 as a barrister's apprentice, but he enlisted in the

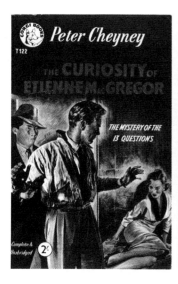

service at the outbreak of war. He stayed at the front until 1916, when, poisoned by German gas, he returned home to stay.

During the months of his convalescence he discovered his vocation as a writer and by 1917 had published a collection of stories of love and war which clearly reflected Kipling's influence. He made little out of it: a certain moral satisfaction but hardly any money. After trying various jobs Cheyney opened a private detective agency in the heart of London. At the same time he also started contributing to the *Evening Standard* and other newspapers. But the "Lemmy Caution Bomb" was still far away. It did not explode until 1936 with *This Man Is Dangerous*, written—at least so the story goes—on a bet between Cheyney and his publisher. Its success was immediate; before the second book of the series was published, the first had been translated into many languages and had achieved massive sales.

Following this success, Cheyney had to create other characters, such as Slim Callaghan and the heroes of his various novels (*The Stars Are Dark*, 1943; *Dark Hero*, 1946; etc.), which were the precursors of the spy narratives that are so popular today. However, none of his other characters ever equaled Lemmy Caution in popularity. In Lemmy, Cheyney had not just created a character, but had inaugurated a completely new genre and style which does not relate to any past model and was destined to create a new school of detective writing.

Lemmy Caution is a daring FBI agent, half hero and half antihero, who succeeds in performing extraordinary tasks. He tells the story of his own adventures

The stylized design for The Saint, which appears on all Leslie Charteris's novels.

in the first person and the present tense; he embraces the readers, calling them "my dears" or "clever people," involving them in the plot as witnesses and judges. He quotes Confucius, mixing more or less apocryphal maxims with the altogether wiser ones he learned from Mamma Caution. His humor is almost black, although rarely totally macabre. His methods are unorthodox, but they are excused on the grounds that the end justifies the means. One of the keys to Peter Cheyney's success is certainly his loose, aggressive, and colorful language which, as the famous *Encyclopédie de la Pleiade* puts it, brought a wind of change to criminal fiction.

Apart from those already cited the best-known Lemmy Caution books are *Dames Don't Care* (1937); *You'd Be Surprised* (1940); *You Can Always Duck* (1943); and *Uneasy Terms* (1946).

Among the many reckless and unconventional heroes of criminal fiction, *The Saint*, created by Leslie Charteris (b. 1907), is particularly worth mentioning, though as a character he is inferior to Cheyney's Lemmy Caution and, especially, to his spiritual forebears, Raffles and Arsène Lupin. Nonetheless the Saint's popularity has been great and survives in part up to this day, thanks largely to a number of television series (the best of which star Roger Moore) which are periodically screened.

The Saint's real name is Simon Templar. His nickname derives from the fact that whatever he does,

The Saint in action—here seen bursting out of the front door onto the scene of a crime.

whether good or bad, he always has the noblest possible motives. Leslie Charteris—born in Singapore of an English mother and a father descended from the Chang dynasty of emperors—moved to the United States in 1932 and became a citizen in 1946. The first Saint novel, *Meet the Tiger*, was published in 1928, but it was not until the middle of the 1930s that the gentleman-thief caught on, with the books *The Misfortunes of Mr. Teal* (1934), *The Saint Goes On* (1934), *Saint Overboard* (1936), *The Saint on the Spanish Main* (1955), and *Thanks to the Saint* (1957).

WOOLRICH-IRISH: A BLACK FANTASY

According to legend, Cornell Woolrich (1903–1968) began his career as a novelist while he was a student at Columbia University. Forced into a long period of immobility by a foot infection, Woolrich killed time by sketching out the plot of his first novel, *Cover Charge* (1926). Anyone acquainted with his work can see that Woolrich would surely have become a writer anyway and would have succeeded in creating something completely new and personal in whatever genre he chose. He is considered the inventor of the suspense novel, one of the most important types of modern detective story.

In fact, Woolrich did not set out to be a mystery story writer; *Cover Charge* was a novel having nothing to do with criminal fiction. It was only in 1934 that he began to dedicate himself to detective stories, publishing the story "Death Sits in a Dentist's Chair" in the magazine *Detective Fiction Weekly*. Within the few pages of this first mystery story—written in Woolrich's evocative, poetic style, based in a kind of stream-of-consciousness writing—one finds the Gothic, ghostly tone that would dominate his works, including *The Bride Wore Black* (1940), *The Black Curtain* (1941), *Black Alibi* (1942), *The Black Angel* (1943), *The Black Path of Fear* (1944), and *Rendezvous in Black* (1948).

Cornell Woolrich was not only the creator and the greatest exponent of the suspense story, he was also a novelist whom many consider the equal of Edgar Allan Poe. As in Poe's works, the dominant theme in Woolrich's work is death—a feared and loved enemy. For him, death will hide its face behind an angelic young girl, or in a majestic old house eaten by fear and decay—themes which are very close to Poe's *The Fall of the House of Usher*.

The distinction between the classic detective novel and a Woolrich suspense story is very clear-cut. At the

Cornell Woolrich led a life which might have come out of one of his novels. Extremely introverted, he lived with his mother, Claire, in a hotel, never going out unless it was absolutely necessary. His exterior life was dominated by Claire Attalie Woolrich's effusive character, while his work provided a tormented reflection of the frustrations and repressions that weighed down on him.

Catherine Deneuve and Jean-Paul Belmondo in Mississippi Mermaid (La sirene du Mississippi, *1969) directed by François Truffaut. Woolrich is one of the most filmed authors. More than twenty-five films of his work have been made. Some of these have had famous directors —Robert Siodmak (1944), Hitchcock, and Truffaut—and have starred well-known actors. Convicted (1938), for example, is distinguished by the acting of Rita Hayworth.* Rear Window *(1954), which critics judged as one of Hitchcock's best films, had an exceptional cast: James Stewart, Grace Kelly, and Raymond Burr. Edward G. Robinson appeared in* Nightmare *(1956) and* The Night Has a Thousand Eyes *(1948).*

end of a traditional detective story in the style of Conan Doyle, Christie, and others, all the questions that the reader asks himself as the story advances are answered in the text. Every piece of the plot is there for a reason, and by studying the novel objectively the reader can discern the way the mosaic is fitted together. At the end of this orthodox type of story, the fear and suspense built up by the author is dissolved: the "devils" are banished, everything returns to normal, and the world is once again free from horrors. Woolrich turned this system on its head: his crime stories, while ending with the logical discovery of the criminal, do not dispel the bogeymen. The suspense does not end when the nightmare is over, since for Woolrich the whole world is a nightmare, dominated by forces committed to human destruction. We are powerless to fight these forces and can only use up all that is good in human nature in the struggle.

Woolrich used two pseudonyms to publish other series of novels. The first, George Hopley, is derived from his real name, Cornell George Hopley Woolrich. The second, and certainly the most famous, is William Irish, with which he signed one of his most tormented and characteristic works, *Phantom Lady* (1942). After a violent row with his wife, Henderson, the protagonist of the story, storms out of the house and asks the first woman he meets in a bar to spend the evening with him. He does not even ask her name. He takes her out to dinner, to the theater, and then back to the bar where they separate, deciding not to see each other again. On returning home, Henderson finds his wife murdered. Naturally, the police accuse him of the crime. To clear himself, it would be enough to show that he spent the night with a woman. But nobody remembers her; nobody saw her. She seems to have vanished without a trace. Henderson's only hope to avoid the electric chair is to find the phantom, to give a face and a name to a woman even he is beginning to think was part of his imagination.

A LEGENDARY HERO: PHILIP MARLOWE

"It was about eleven o'clock in the morning, mid-October, with the sun not shining and a look of hard wet rain in the clearness of the foothills. I was wearing my powder-blue suit with dark blue shirt, tie and display handkerchief, black brogues, black wool socks with dark blue clocks on them. I was neat, clean, shaved and sober, and I didn't care who knew it. I was everything the well-dressed private detective ought to be. I was calling on four million dollars." (Raymond Chandler, *The Big Sleep*, 1939).

This is our first glimpse of Philip Marlowe in the opening lines of his first adventure, *The Big Sleep*, one of the greatest books in the history of criminal fiction. Summoned by the very rich General Guy de Brisay Sternwood to investigate a story of blackmail and gambling debts involving Sternwood's daughter, Carmen, Philip Marlowe is drawn into the affairs of the well-to-do of Los Angeles, for whom wealth is synonymous with corruption. The story is told in the first person by Marlowe, putting the reader in the same position as the detective and allowing him to follow the investigation step by step.

The novels that followed *The Big Sleep* added only a few touches to the description of Marlowe, perhaps because from the start he closely resembled his creator,

Raymond Chandler and the first British edition of The High Window.

Raymond Chandler (1888–1959). Chandler had had a troubled and turbulent life before taking up writing in 1939 at the age of forty-five. His parents' divorce when he was seven left a deep psychological wound. Very closely attached to his mother, he married only after her death in 1924 and then it was to a woman seventeen years older than he was. Born in the United States and educated in England, he fought during World War I with a Canadian regiment on the French front. Re-

"What did it matter where you lay once you were dead? In a dirty sump or in a marble tower on top of a high hill? You were dead, you were sleeping the big sleep, you were not bothered by things like that. . . . You just slept the big sleep, not caring about the nastiness of how you died or where you fell." So says Philip Marlowe in The Big Sleep, *immortalized by Humphrey Bogart and Lauren Bacall on the screen.* Below: *Robert Montgomery, another screen Marlowe, in* The Lady in the Lake.

turning to the United States, he worked picking apricots, stringing tennis rackets, and doing administrative work for small oil companies before turning to criminal fiction, attracted by *Black Mask* and the work of Dashiell Hammett and Erle Stanley Gardner.

Philip Marlowe, however, was born complete because he was the result of seven years of effort and experiment, as Chandler himself made clear in 1949 when he said that he had developed Marlowe's character in stories written for popular magazines. A character much like Marlowe first appeared in 1933 in the story "Blackmailers Don't Shoot," published in *Black Mask*. In the following years, in the process of molding his character and establishing his physiognomy, his psychological traits, his behavior, his way of dress, and his manner of movement, Chandler was to call him first Mallory, then Malvern, Carmady, and Dalmas. Finally Philip Marlowe emerged, incorporating all the most realistic traits of the previous characters. Marlowe immediately won a prominent place in the vast gallery of detective story personalities, a character to be used by subsequent writers—both inside and outside the field of criminal fiction—and on the stage and screen. There have been many successful Marlowe films, and the role has been played by Dick Powell, Humphrey Bogart (called by some the greatest screen Marlowe), Robert Montgomery, George Montgomery, James Garner, Elliott Gould, and Robert Mitchum.

Marlowe is one of the disillusioned, cynical, worried detectives so common to American detective fiction. Unlike many others, however, he is generous, human and sympathetic, gifted with a Don Quixote-like attitude which leads him to take the part of the weak against the strong. His hard-won victories bring him, at best, a quiet sense of moral satisfaction; more often, though, his adventures leave him bitter, feeling that his efforts have been futile. He usually knows this from the outset, although it does not matter to him, and he does not expect any better.

Marlowe embodies the "quality of redemption," as Chandler has written. "Down these mean streets a man must go who is not himself mean, who is neither tarnished nor afraid. The detective in this kind of story must be such a man. He is the hero, he is everything. He must be a complete man and a common man and yet an unusual man. He must be, to use a rather weathered phrase, a man of honor, by instinct, by inevitability, without thought of it, and certainly without saying it" (*The Simple Art of Murder*, 1944).

Marlowe's success with the public was such that Chandler was forced to draw up an authentic biog-

RAYMOND CHANDLER'S TEN COMMANDMENTS FOR THE DETECTIVE NOVEL

1 It must be credibly motivated, both as to the original situation and the denouement.

2 It must be technically sound as to the methods of murder and detection.

3 It must be realistic in character, setting, and atmosphere. It must be about real people in a real world.

4 It must have a sound story value apart from the mystery element; i.e., the investigation itself must be an adventure worth reading.

5 It must have enough essential simplicity to be explained easily when the time comes.

6 It must baffle a reasonably intelligent reader.

7 The solution must seem inevitable once revealed.

8 It must not try to do everything at once. If it is a puzzle story operating in a rather cool, reasonable atmosphere, it cannot also be a violent adventure or a passionate romance.

9 It must punish the criminal in one way or another, not necessarily by operation of the law. . . . If the detective fails to resolve the consequences of the crime, the story is an unresolved chord and leaves irritation behind it.

10 It must be honest with the reader.

—Based on "Twelve Notes on the Mystery Story," *The Notebooks of Raymond Chandler*, 1977.

raphy of the hero for readers' use, which was largely done in two long letters (1951). Marlowe was said to have been born in Santa Rosa, California, some day in an unspecified year. He studied for two years at Oregon State University; his education is reflected every so often in quotations from T. S. Eliot and Flaubert. Moving to Los Angeles, he trained as a private detective with an insurance company and then worked for the city's district attorney. The circumstances in which he lost this last job are not clear, although it is certain that "he got a little too efficient at a time and in a place where efficiency was the last thing desired by the person in charge" (*Raymond Chandler Speaking*, 1962).

Slightly over six feet tall, Marlowe has dark brown hair and brown eyes. He never has a lot of money because he charges very little: usually just twenty-five dollars a day plus expenses, though at times, depending on the case, he will go as low as ten dollars, or perhaps nothing at all.

He is a modest chess player, but "I would not say his chess comes up to tournament standard." His attitude toward women is "that of any reasonably vigorous and healthy man who does not happen to be married and probably should have been long since": he never ignores a good opportunity although he never looks for them. He prefers innocent blonds and does not feel he has to chase every woman he comes across.

His office is made up of two small rooms: a waiting room and a private office, nearly always empty and smelling of dust. Marlowe has no secretary. As for the guns he carries, he started with a Luger but then went on to automatics, Colts of various calibers but never bigger than a .38. He also has a Smith & Wesson .38 Special, although he uses it as little as possible.

Philip Marlowe became a detective just as another man might become a priest. "If being in revolt against a corrupt society constitutes being immature, then Philip Marlowe is extremely immature," Raymond Chandler has written. "If seeing dirt where there is dirt constitutes an inadequate social adjustment, then Philip Marlowe has inadequate social adjustment. Of course Marlowe is a failure and he knows it. He is a failure because he hasn't any money. A man who, without physical handicaps, cannot make a decent living is always a failure and usually a moral failure. But a lot of very good men have been failures because their particular talents did not suit their time and place. In the long run I guess we are all failures or we wouldn't have the kind of world we have" (*Raymond Chandler Speaking*, 1962).

In contrast to many of his colleagues Marlowe is not a sponge. He drinks, certainly, but in moderation, and almost never when on a case. The myth that he is always full of whiskey originates, perhaps, in Chandler's comment that when he wants to drink, he drinks and does not hesitate to admit it.

His career unfolds in seven novels: *The Big Sleep*

Elliott Gould, the penultimate screen Marlowe, in The Long Goodbye *(1973), directed by Robert Altman.*

(1939), *Farewell My Lovely* (1940), *The High Window* (1942), *The Lady in the Lake* (1943), *The Little Sister* (1949), *The Long Goodbye* (1953), which won an Edgar, *Playback* (1958), *The Pencil*, a story posthumously published in 1960, and an unfinished novel, *Poodle Springs Story*, in which Marlowe marries.

Not just a novelist, Chandler was also one of the great theorists of the modern detective story and wrote an important study entitled *The Simple Art of Murder* (1944) and his *Casual Notes*, which contain observations on criminal fiction; these came out during 1949 and 1950, and feature his "Ten Commandments." In these writings Chandler attacks the classic detective novel as reserved for "flustered old ladies" and incapable of creating solid, realistic characters. "The fellow who can write you vivid and colorful prose simply won't be bothered with the coolie labor of breaking down unbreakable alibis." Chandler attacks overrefined settings and artificial crimes, committed "with handwrought duelling pistols, curare, and tropical fish." His world is the real one, the American society of the time, which was dominated by financial sharks and corrupt police, "men who made their money out of brothels, in which a screen star can be the finger man for a mob . . . a world . . . where no man can walk down a dark street in safety because law and order are things we talk about but refrain from practicing" (*The Simple Art of Murder*, 1944). The language of a realistic depiction of such a society must be appropriate to the contents of the novels: no more futile, mundane conversation in the style of Philo Vance, but direct, realistic dialogue, such as one might normally hear in the street, even including slang phrases and, where necessary, vulgar ones.

TWO HEADS ARE BETTER THAN ONE

Names hiding a pair of writers are frequent in criminal fiction. Some are total inventions, like Ellery Queen; others are regularly entered at the register office and the authors' two names appear combined, as in the case of the Gordons (Mildred and Gordon), the Cranes (Frances and Richard), and the Hitchens (Bert and Dolores). This type of collaboration is also found in French detective writing—Allain and Souvestre, the creators of Fantômas, and Boileau-Narcejac. Also in Italy—Fruttero and Lucentini, Feligatti and Pittorru and in Sweden—Sjöwall-Wahlöö.

The case of Patrick Quentin (alias Q. Patrick, alias Jonathan Stagge) is, however, the most unusual. The founder of this "company" was Richard Wilson Webb (1902–1965), a writer who, evidently, needed a shoulder to lean on to be able to write his novels. Webb wrote his first detective novels, which were very good, with the help of Martha Mott Kelley (*Cottage Sinister*, 1931; *Murder at the Women's City Club*, 1932). As always happens in these cases, it is not clear what the cowriter's role was, although it seems quite clear that of the two the real creative force was Webb. After Kelley left, he continued writing and joined up with a young graduate from the University of London, Hugh Cullingham Wheeler (b. 1912), who had left England to live in the United States. It was with Wheeler that Webb wrote the famous series of novels which feature the pleasant couple Peter and Iris Duluth. Peter Duluth is a theater producer and sometime detective; Iris is a movie star. The novels featuring the Duluths are classic detective stories in which "Patrick Quentin" introduced a technique which he was to repeat later in his other novels. For nearly the entire story there seems to be no doubt as to the culprit, but at the end an unexpected fact is revealed which changes everything; the real criminal is usually someone thought to be above suspicion. The series included *Puzzle for Puppets* (1944), *Puzzle for Pilgrims* (1947), and *My Son, the Murderer* (1954).

Another couple created by the Webb and Wheeler duo, this time using the pseudonym Jonathan Stagge, was the young Dr. Westlake and a very unusual assistant: his little daughter Dawn who, with her childish logic, plays an important role in her father's brilliant investigations.

Robert Wade (left) *and Bill Miller used a combination of their names to sign their books—as seen on* Nightmare Cruise.

In 1950 Webb, tired and ill, retired, but Wheeler, whose role had become increasingly important in later years, carried on alone (*Family Skeletons*, 1965) without the readers ever suspecting what had been going on behind the scenes.

A similar story to that of the Quentin duo, if a little less complex, took place a few years later with the couple Robert Wade (b. 1920) and Bill Miller (1920–1961), both Americans, who signed many good novels with a combination of their two names: Wade Miller. Their first novel, *Deadly Weapon* (1946), was written during World War II while one was in Europe and the other in the Pacific, collaborating by mail. The end of the war marked the beginning of a very fertile collaboration which was to create the character Max Thursday. Thursday, a character in the mold of Sam Spade and Philip Marlowe, is a private detective in San Diego, California, who does not like firearms. He is humane and sensitive and follows his own code of honor in the corrupt and brutal world in which he moves.

In 1955 Wade and Miller adopted a new pseudonym, Whit Masterson, in order to write detective stories of a more violent kind, in which the detective work is often done by a gangster who must unmask the spy or policeman who has infiltrated the gang. After the death of his colleague, Wade continued to use the pseudonym Whit Masterson and published books on his own.

THE PESSIMISM AND VIOLENCE OF JAMES HADLEY CHASE

Many readers believe James Hadley Chase to be an American writer, one of the great in the hard-boiled school, a direct descendant of Hammett and Chandler. But they are in error: Chase, born in London in 1906, is completely English and, despite appearances, has never set foot in America. He is more the successor to Peter Cheyney, but while Cheyney was influenced by the American action novel, Chase embraced the violence and cynicism of the hard-boiled school, creating what Boileau and Narcejac have termed the formula of the cruel novel.

A door-to-door encyclopedia salesman, Chase took up criminal fiction in 1939 with the declared intention of making money. In six weeks he wrote *No Orchids for Miss Blandish*, the violent and bitter story of the kidnapping of a young millionairess by a group led by a mad criminal and his mother. The novel, which many critics have said was modeled on William Faulkner's

Sanctuary, had a tremendous success—thirteen million copies have been sold to date, and two films have been made of it—in 1951, directed by St. John L. Clowes, and *The Grissom Gang* in 1971, directed by Robert Aldrich.

James Hadley Chase has never let himself be tempted by the classic formula of a fixed character featured in a series of adventures. He has regularly killed off characters who threatened to become troublesome or

Two first editions of James Hadley Chase's works. Chase is one of the greatest contemporary detective novelists. His models have been William Faulkner, James M. Cain, and John Steinbeck.

James Hadley Chase. Only a few of his novels have been made into films, but No Orchids for Miss Blandish *has had two film versions.*

limiting; as he himself has said, how can one possibly create suspense if the reader knows from the outset that the hero will survive? Therefore, he explains, he kills the hero every so often, so that the reader can never be sure of what is coming. The private detective Dave Fenner, the ex-journalist who appears in *No Orchids for Miss Blandish*, appears in only one other novel, *Twelve Chinks and a Woman* (1940). The same is true for Vic Mallory, Mark Girland, Corrigan, and Don Micklem, all heroes of only two or three novels.

Chase wrote more than seventy novels, many under the pseudonyms Raymond Marshall, Ambrose Grant, and James L. Doherty. Among his most famous are: *Trusted Like a Fox* (1948), *The Flesh of the Orchid* (1948), *You Never Know with Women* (1949), *Tiger by the Tail* (1954), *Come Easy, Go Easy* (1960), *There Is a Hippy on the Highway* (1970), and *Do Me a Favor . . . Drop Dead!* (1976).

7 | THE FRENCH CONNECTION

The myths of the detective novel
satisfy the secret nostalgias of modern man who,
knowing himself to be fallen and limited,
dreams of one day becoming
an exceptional character, a hero.

Mircea Eliade

THE GREAT TURNING POINT IN THE 1930S

After World War I, the fashion for detective fiction spread in France and French-speaking countries. The fairly broad tradition which incorporated Arsène Lupin and Fantômas soon led to a taste for fantastic and sensational spy novels, full of mad scientists and "phantom robbers," as in *Le roi de l'abime* by Jean Petithuguenin, or for the repetition of earlier myths, such as the dilettante detective and avenger Lord Palmure, created by Frédéric Valade. Many authors, however, preferred to concentrate on political or social intrigues. It is enough to recall André Armandy's *Les loups-cerviers* and many other writers who are practically forgotten today.

Many French writers of the period followed the rules of the classic English detective novel unreservedly, in the wake of the tremendous success enjoyed by the English authors published by Hachette and then in such crime series as *Le masque*, started in 1927 by Albert Pigasse, and *L'Empreinte*, started in 1929 by Alexandre Ralli.

The great national turning point for the French detective novel took place during the 1930s, when, within a few months, a number of books were published which started the careers of such talented writers as Pierre Véry, Stanilas-André Steeman, Georges Simenon, and Claude Aveline. These were soon followed by works by Jean Bommart and Pierre Nord (who soon branched off into spy stories), Pierre Boileau (destined for a great career in collaboration with Narcejac), Noël Vindry, and Jacques Decrest. Some of these authors became

The trademarks of two of the most important series of detective novels published in France—Le Masque founded in 1927 by Albert Pigasse, which has published more than 1,600 titles, and Alexandre Ralli's L'Empreinte.

known to the public through the Prix du Roman d'Aventures, established by Albert Pigasse, the greatest of many French prizes for criminal fiction.

Most of these authors, while accepting the strict discipline of the classic mystery novel, consciously sought to free themselves from the rules laid down by Van Dine. In fact, while the English detective novel is all too often a rather thin affair, concentrating principally on the dismantling of the mechanism of the crime and the various alibis, French detective fiction comes closer to the pure novel. The authors took great care with their language and characters, making them all, including the victim, both physically and psychologically complete. This care can also be seen in the tendency to place the exceptional event—the crime—in an everyday setting: if not a village, then the neighborhood rather than big-city atmosphere of Paris or the provinces.

Perhaps the most representative of this new school is Pierre Véry (1900–1960), who won the first Prix du Roman d'Aventures with his *Testament de Sir Basil Crookes* (1930), a novel of the English classic type. Between 1930 and 1949, Véry published twenty-eight mystery novels, as he called them. He wrote that his dream was to reform criminal fiction, making it humorous and poetic. This, he said, explained his decision to write a series of mystery novels, some forty or so, after the model of Chesterton's masterpieces, where the characters are no longer puppets in the service of a mystery requiring a solution, but human beings struggling with reality.

In *Meurtre quai des Orfèvres, Monsieur Marcel des pompes funèbres*, and *L'assassinat du Père Noël* (all 1934), Véry created the typical French detective, Prosper Lepicq, a Parisian lawyer who has a very idiosyncratic method of getting clients: he discovers the criminals before the police do in order to secure their defense in court. Lepicq's ten adventures take place in a typical French village in Lorraine. A great deal of space is devoted to amusing details of everyday life, stirring records of old traditions, more like a fable or fantasy than a rigorously logical detective exposition. This tendency is most fully expressed in Véry's series of "country" novels whose protagonist is a strange detective, Goupi-Mains-Rouges, a sort of good-natured wizard, the head of a family-tribe of picturesque names.

Stanilas-André Steeman (1908–1970), a Belgian born in Liège, also came out with a puzzle novel of the English type: *Six hommes morts* (winner of the Prix du Roman d'Aventures in 1931). It was so English, in fact, as to closely resemble *Ten Little Indians* although it was written nearly ten years before Christie's masterpiece. This novel marks the first appearance of Inspector Wenceslas Vorobeïtchik, generally known as Wens. Monsieur Wens is a refined detective who, after a short time in the official police, sets up on his own. Tall and balding, with an air of refined elegance (Steeman's self-portrait, according to his wife), Wens declares himself to be a bad detective because he does not like to doubt other peoples' words. Unlike Sherlock Holmes and his followers, he always tries to guess and makes many mistakes, although in the end he always manages to hit the right answer.

It is interesting to note that, before Wens, Steeman had created the pipe-smoking Aimé Malaise, a calm and subtle investigator in the style of Maigret. This character appeared a year before Simenon published the first novel featuring his famous commissioner. In his last books Steeman moved away from pure criminal fiction toward fantasy novels. In pointing out his great concern for adapting tone, style, and character to the situation described in the book, Jean Cocteau called him the "Fregoli of the detective novel."

AVELINE: THE RIGHT TO DISTRACTION

In 1932 a famous novelist and essayist, Claude Aveline (the pseudonym of Claude Avtzin, b. 1901) published, to amuse himself, a lively detective novel: *The Double Death of Frederick Belot (La double mort de Frédéric Belot)*. It was in many ways a curious book: it was the first time that a French author of standing turned to detective writing, and while chronologically it was the first of a set of five detective novels to be written over a forty-year period, logically it belonged at the end of the series. The other books in the series are *Voiture 7, place 15, (Carriage 7, Seat 15)*, 1937; *Le jet d'eau (The Fountain at Marlieux)*, 1947; *L'abonne de la ligne U (The Passenger on the U)*, 1947; *L'oeil du Chat (The Cat's Eye)*, 1970. (Arranged in order of their action they are: 1, *The Passenger*; 2, *Carriage 7*; 3, *The Fountain*; 4, *The Cat's Eye*; and 5, *The Double Death*.)

Aveline develops his argument from a precise concept: "There is no prohibition against the belief that we can encompass the problem in human terms, as a living issue . . . I believe that life sets itself to prove to us that everything is possible and that the craziest imagination has less scope than destiny. What is important to me is that every act and every thought should be justified by the character of the person to whom the

Claude Aveline, alias Avtzin, novelist and disciple of Anatole France, dedicated himself to criminal fiction. His first detective novel, The Passenger on the U, *was published in 1947. Aveline wrote his first detective novel when he was thirty as a challenge, based on his love for detective fiction.*

author allots them" ("A Double Note on the Detective Novel," p. 194, *The Double Death of Frederick Belot*, 1949). When a critic asked him how he could pass from detective novels to serious, psychological novels, Aveline replied that he never made any distinction between the two. Psychology, he said, was an indispensable element of criminal fiction; without it, criminal fiction would deteriorate into a game that although perfectly constructed, would lack soul. In the same way, the problem, the dramatic starting point which leads the reader to ask himself "What is going to happen?" (a question which we also ask ourselves when reading Proust or Dostoevsky), is indispensable to the so-called psychological novel which, otherwise, would be no more than a stylized dissertation. As for the form, Aveline argued, why should it be ignored in one case and not in the other? Edgar Allan Poe wrote his essays, poems, and his *Tales of Mystery and the Imagination* in one distinctive style. As Aveline said a hundred times and never tired of saying, inferior literary genres do not exist.

The protagonist of *The Double Death* is the young Inspector Simon Rivière, "a tall, slight chap, clean shaven, with fine, well-cared-for hands . . . His looks had nothing of the inquisitor about them; on the contrary they were distant, distracted." The son of an inspector, Rivière joined the police thanks to two of his father's closest friends: Frederick Belot, his godfather, and Monsieur Picard, who became head of the Police Judiciaire. Belot had inexplicably rejected the job of head of police in favor of the largely sedentary job of

"Head of the Special Branch." This is not the only strange thing about Belot which surprises his friends; an inveterate bachelor, he has only recently met the pleasant Madame Deguise and is already talking of marrying her. One evening, Picard waits in vain for Belot in his office while on an important case and finally sends Rivière to look for him. The young man goes to Belot's house and finds him dying on the floor in the drawing room, his face bloody and a revolver lying beside him. Then, behind the curtain, he finds the dead body of another man. "And this man is Frederick Belot as well!" Rivière, faced with the two identical corpses, fears he has lost his reason. Which is the real Belot, his friend and godfather? From this incredible situation a story develops based on the theme of an exchange of characters, as we learn that Belot used a double when it was useful or might serve him well. Aveline used this theme of an exchange of personalities in other novels that feature Rivière (*Carriage 7, The Passenger on the U*), though on a more psychological level than the bizarre physical exchange in *The Double Death*.

The protagonist of *The Cat's Eye* is, instead, Commissioner Belot coming to grips with a complex case whose components range from passion to hate, from sordid interests to vendettas. (The cat's eye is a stone set in a ring found on the ring finger of a woman's severed hand.) Belot also solves the mystery in *The Fountain*, the haunting history of the Redoux family.

Claude Aveline's contribution to criminal fiction has been to rehabilitate the detective novel and make it part of the "cultivated" public's reading as a literary work. Aveline produced an interesting theory on the detective novel: "The detective novel is a novel which *begins again at the end*. If there is a type of novel made for being re-read then, contrary to the general view, it is this one. The reader has followed out an inquiry from inside the skin of the inquirer. He can now follow it again with the eyes, not of the author ... but of the criminal. The eyes, the heart and the guts of the criminal. In place of the movements of the future victor, we get the torments of the hunted creature, or his remorse. In the case of the 'ordinary' or 'literary' novel, the reader can muse only through his first reading ... With the detective novel, on the other hand, he becomes capable of evoking a new drama. He can create."

SIMENON AND MAIGRET

If in the whole of criminal fiction there is one author who escapes any influence or fashion, and has created a world which is worthy of standing next to Balzac's *Human Comedy* not only for the number of novels but also for their literary quality and humanity, it is Georges Simenon, a Belgian born in Liège, 1903, but French in culture and inspiration.

Simenon is the creator of an endless oeuvre which contains over four hundred novels (two hundred of which are signed Simenon, the remaining under twenty-three pseudonyms—starting with Georges Sim, under which, when only seventeen, he published his first popular novel, *Au pont des Arches*, following on with the various Gom Gut, Jean du Perry, Luc Dorsan, Christian Brüll, and many more). To these can be added over a thousand stories and some fifteen volumes of autobiography and memoirs, to which he has dedicated himself during the 1970s, after definitively ending the series of Maigret novels in 1973.

Maigret enjoys a love-hate relationship with his author, who more than once tried to get rid of him. He is the protagonist of one hundred and two adventures, novels, and stories, as well as the "autobiographical" works presumably written by him, such as *Les Mémoires de Maigret*. It is interesting that from the first book featuring Maigret, "The Strange Case of Peter the Lett" ("Pietr-le-Letton"), in *Inspector Maigret Investigates*, which was written in 1929 on board the cutter *Ostrogoth* moored in Holland, up to the fiftieth book in the series, the commissioner's name hardly ever appears in the titles, although afterward it became a "canonical" monogram.

As Simenon himself has said, the character of Maigret was born well before his first public appear-

Georges Simenon, one of the most popular writers of the century. With Maigret he has left a deeply human mark on criminal fiction. A 1970 study estimated that his books had sold 50 million copies, had been translated into twenty-seven languages, and had been read by four hundred million people. Simenon is very popular in Russia and is the only French detective novelist to meet with substantial success in the English-speaking world, particularly the United States.

ance. From the age of fourteen, Simenon wrote, he had wondered why a normal doctor might not play some intellectual role as well. A doctor who knows the patient, his age, physique, and potential and can advise him on which course to take in life. These thoughts led to the creation of Maigret; this is exactly what Maigret does, and this is why he had to study medicine for two or three years. For Simenon, Maigret is an arranger of destinies. A doctor plays a similar and more important role then a confessor, as the confessor's dogma makes him dangerous rather than health-giving. If one judges men according to principles based on dogma, Simenon writes, one cannot really do anything to help them.

There is no other fictional character who has such a well-established physical and psychological biography as Maigret. This is also due to an impressive number of movies and television films which have been shown throughout the world, in every language, nearly all of a very high level, particularly those featuring Jean Gabin and the Italian television series with Gino Cervi.

In "The Strange Case of Peter the Lett" we meet the Maigret we all know, the classic pipe in his mouth, the slow step. He is an impassive man, self-assured, silent, full of an infinite curiosity about people and things. His looks are, all in all, rather undistinguished, like a placid, stubborn farmer who has no time for urbane elegance even if he is always well dressed. By his fourth appearance, in *Le Charretier de la Providence* (1931—Simenon produced a Maigret novel a month) the commissioner's detective technique is well established: when asked for particular ideas or theories, he cannot provide any nor would he seek to discover clues,

The most famous television Maigrets gather around Simenon on the occasion of the unveiling of a statue of Maigret by the sculptor Pieter Dhondt in Delfzijl, the Netherlands, where Simenon wrote the first Maigret story. **Left to right:** *Rupert Davis of England, Simenon, Heinz Ruhmann of Germany, Gino Cervi of Italy, and Jan Teulings of the Netherlands. The sketch of Georges Simenon was made by Maurice de Vlaminck.*

strictly speaking. His method is to try to soak up the general atmosphere.

Maigret is already complete by this stage and all the details that are subsequently added—the marriage to "Madame Maigret," his slow rise through the Police Judiciaire, his independent spirit, and all those habits, manias, and characteristics that the author was to give him—these merely serve to fill out the portrait. Similarly, the recurring characters in Maigret's world and the famous atmosphere—Parisian or provincial—which is described by Simenon's masterly pen are all there in the earliest works.

Maigret is not a detective like the others; he owes nothing to Dupin, as Boileau and Narcejac have explained. They go on to say that reasoning and deduction are not his forte: Maigret does not try to explain; he tries, first and foremost, to understand. The crime interests him less than the criminal. Fundamentally, the critics argue, Maigret's membership in the Police Judiciaire is a convenience. Rather than a commissioner, he is more like a "weigher of souls." Boileau and Narcejac point out that his choice of clues is in itself revealing: fingerprints and forgotten objects do not matter for him; rather a gesture, a word, a glance, or a silence. The reader must ask himself just one question: if I had committed the crime, would I make that gesture? Would I use that word? And this assumes that the crime might have been committed by the reader, by any normal man or woman as the victim of one of those common passions which affect us all. For Maigret, solving the crime does not mean discovering the method of the murder, but living through the psychological crisis which provoked the drama.

Simenon himself has seen the development of the various characters, situations, and settings in Maigret's career as reflecting moments in his own life. One trait is certainly not common to both character and author: Maigret's dislike of any change, travel, or adventure. Simenon has lived and worked in Holland, France, America, and Switzerland without ever lapsing from his strict rules of work, or straying from a certain repeated way of writing his books. For example, he always sketches out the plot and characters in advance on a yellow envelope as that is how he began his first novel. There is a large bibliography on Simenon's method of work, which has been added to by the recently published, rather bitter memoirs of his first wife *(Un oiseau pour le chat*, 1978).

More than once, during the years, Simenon has tended to play down the value of his detective novels. He has said that a detective novel does not correspond to the personality of the author, and does not satisfy his need for artistic expression, but only his need for money. Serious criticism, however, after years of indifference, judges Simenon's work to be greater than any other in the field of criminal fiction. As the Italian critic Alberto del Monte has put it, Simenon started off with a certain craftsmanship which he perfected, refined, and renewed, bringing it to the threshold of poetry.

BOILEAU-NARCEJAC: THE THEORISTS OF THE DETECTIVE NOVEL

For about thirty years one of the most harmonious, refined and active couples in the history of criminal fiction has been the Boileau-Narcejac team. They have produced the most revolutionary detective novels of the last quarter century, in which the character of the detective—professional or amateur—has been suppressed in favor of a psychological study of the characters and an extreme tension, which grips the reader from the first pages of the book. It is often the victim himself who conducts the investigation. Some of the most famous suspense films have been made from their books: *Les diaboliques* (1954), directed by Clouzot, and Alfred Hitchcock's *Vertigo* (1958), to name just two. Finally, Boileau and Narcejac are among the most acute and precise theorists of criminal fiction and have written, together or individually, various critical works, from essays published in the highly respected *Pleiade Universal History of Literature*, to the recent *Une machine à lire: Le roman policier* (1975).

Pierre Boileau (b. 1906) started on his own in 1934, with the novel *La promenade de minuit*, followed by five more books, among which were *Le repos de Bacchus* (1938), which won the Prix du Roman d'Aventures that year, and *Six crimes sans assassin* (1939), later collected under the title *Chambres closes* (*Locked Rooms*). This collective title clearly indicates the type of detective novel written by Boileau: traditional English-style stories of suspense centered on the problem of a locked room, which calls for an infallible detective, here André Brunel. However, the theme underlying Brunel's investigation is not so much "who" or "why," as "how": it is, Boileau has written, the only question that can really fascinate the reader, the only one that can appear as a challenge to logic and thus create a close link between the detective novel and the fantasy novel.

Thomas Narcejac (left) and Pierre Boileau, the diabolical duo of French criminal fiction.

A teacher of philosophy, Thomas Narcejac (the pseudonym of Pierre Ayraud, b. 1908) started a few years later with some pastiches of Lupin, Poirot, and Holmes; a study, *Esthétique du roman policier*; a few novels: *L'assassin du minuit* (1946), and *La mort est du voyage*, which won him the Prix du Roman d'Aventures in 1948 and led to his meeting with Boileau. The two authors soon decided to work together. As an amusing saying of theirs goes, "Boileau is the skeleton, Narcejac, the meat"; the former has the idea, and the latter develops it.

Their first book, refused by nearly every publisher, nevertheless established itself as a masterpiece: *Celle qui n'etait plus* (*The Woman Who Was*, 1952). To date Boileau and Narcejac have published some twenty novels, among which are *The Living and the Dead* (*D'entre les morts*, 1954), *The Prisoner* (*Les Louves*, 1955), *"L'ingéniéur aimait trop les chiffres* (1960)

Maléfices (1961), Opération primevère (1973) and the latest, L'age bête (1978).

Passionate readers of Arsène Lupin, Boileau and Narcejac decided a few years ago to revive Leblanc's hero in a new series of adventures: La Justice d'Arsène Lupin and Le secret d'Eunerville (which won the Prix Mystère de la Critique).

SÉRIE NOIRE: VIOLENCE AND ANGER

Just as the appearance of detective novels in the English style conditioned French criminal fiction of the 1930s, so the birth in 1945 of the Série Noire, edited by Marcel Duhamel, brought about a fundamental renewal, importing the great American hard-boiled classics of Hammett and Chandler into France. The translations were full of slang and even harder than the originals. The detective novel became the accepted form to portray the violence and suffering of the times, the tragic inheritance of the war.

The program that Duhamel presents to his readers is very clear: no investigations à la Sherlock Holmes, no morality or good feelings. There are policemen, he wrote, more corrupt than the criminals they are hunting. The nice detective doesn't always solve his cases. Often there isn't even a mystery. Sometimes there isn't even a detective. But there is always action and violence, punch-ups and shoot-outs. The new heroes were, above all, those of Peter Cheyney and James Hadley Chase, who attracted a school of pedestrian imitators, although later there were some talented authors.

In fact, France can claim a significant precursor in this field: Léo Malet (b. 1909), journalist, friend of Bre-

Some of the most tortured films of the past thirty years have been made from the novels of Boileau and Narcejac, including Clouzot's Les Diaboliques and Hitchcock's Vertigo, which starred James Stewart and Kim Novak (above left). Above right: Narcejac's 1975 critical study on criminal fiction. Below: The mark of the Serie Noire, a series begun after the war which created a new type of detective novel. Sartre once noted that in a way he was leading a double life: he was still far more willing to read Serie Noire novels than Wittgenstein.

ton and the surrealists, poet and novelist, who in 1943 began publishing a series of detective novels under the collective title *Les nouveaux mystères de Paris*. The first book was called *120 rue de la gare*, and introduced the Bohemian detective Nestor Burma, cynical and unlucky, poor, but kind and carefree. His adventures continue in *Brouillard au Ponte Tolbiac* (1946) and some other novels that have the various quarters of Paris as their settings. These same settings were soon to provide the backdrop for an excellent and truly French series of *noire* novels. Their authors were not smooth professionals, but real "savage" writers who had come out of the lowest classes, such as Albert Simonin and Auguste Le Breton.

Albert Simonin (b. 1905) is also one of the first French authors to have published in the *Série Noire*: his *Touchez pas au grisbi* (1953), completely conceived and written in slang (so much so that a glossary of terms had to be added by the author), was number 148 in the series, with a preface by Pierre MacOrlan of the Académie Goncourt. *Grisbi*, an expansive picture of Parisian low-life, was filmed in the same year it was published, directed by Jacques Becker, with Jean Gabin, Jeanne Moreau, and Lino Ventura. Simonin continued with a notable series of novels which include *La cave se rebiffe* (1954), *Du mouroun pour les petits oiseaux* (1960), and the recent series which feature Le Hotu (*Le Hotu: Chronique de la vie d'un demi-sel*, 1973; *Hotu soit qui mal y pense*, 1973).

The work of José Giovanni (b. 1923) was also based on slang and violence and was taken up by the *Série Noire*. His first novel was *The Break* (*Le trou*, 1957), which was made into a film directed by Jacques Becker. Giovanni then wrote various novels based on prison life involving violence between convicts, escape plans, and punishments—before becoming a screenwriter, and one of the most highly esteemed film directors of recent years.

Other French writers in the *Série Noire* are Jean Amila (b. 1910), Jean-Pierre Bastid, Francis Ryck (one of the most original), Pierre Lesou, Pierre Siniac (b. 1928), Raf Vallet, and the youngest, Jean-Patrick Manchette (b. 1942), winner of the Grand Prix de Littérature policière in 1973 (his *Nada* [1972] and *Le petit bleu de la côte ouest* [1976] are both very good), and Alain Fournier (b. 1947), who has nearly always signed himself with the monogram A.D.G., the writer of cruel, satirical, and slangy works which are presented with an almost cinematographic style (*Les Panadeux*, 1971; *Cradoque's band*, 1972; *La buit des grand chiens malades*, 1975; *Le grand môme*, 1977).

LE BRETON, THE ANARCHIST OF DETECTIVE FICTION

The most authentic and prolific representative of the French "black" novel is Auguste Monfort (b. 1913, Lesteren, Brittany), known throughout the world of criminal fiction and low life under the pseudonym Le Breton.

A war orphan, Le Breton rebelled against the discipline of the orphanage and soon came to know the reformatory, falling into the underworld. He emerged after many years, when he started writing an autobiographical novel, *Les hauts murs* (1946), an evocation and denunciation of his years in the orphanage. It waited seven years before it found a willing publisher, but it was an immediate success. Today, nearly thirty years after it was first published, new editions are still coming out.

During the following years, Le Breton continued to recount the various threads of his terrible life experience in more autobiographical novels: *La loi des rues* (the reformatory), *Les jeunes voyous* (the first adventures in the Parisian underworld), *Malfrats and C.* (from crime to the resistance), and lastly *Monsieur Rififi* (which tells of his beginnings as a writer, his first successes, film work, his meetings with old friends of the underworld and the death of his greatly loved dog Rififi).

At the same time as his first autobiographical books, Le Breton also started writing low-life novels in

Auguste Le Breton is known all over the world as the creator of the term rififi *(brawl, fight, clash). The word has entered every language in the world, including Japanese, from his novel* Du rififi chez les hommes *(1953) and the 1955 film by Jules Dassin.*

Frédéric Dard, alias Sanantonio, is the most original and successful popular French author of the postwar period. As Dard, he has published and continues to publish some of the most sophisticated suspense novels of French criminal fiction; as Sanantonio, he has created a saga of over thirty thousand pages, which has broken all French publishers' sales records (over 600,000 copies a title). Shown here is the original jacket of one of the illustrated books in the Sanantonio series.

unembellished slang, on the advice of a journalist on the *Paris-Soir*, Marcel Sauvage. His first sample was *Du Rififi chez les hommes* (1953), the story of a dramatic raid on a jeweler's store which ends in a massacre because a band of blockheads stupidly tries to escape with the loot. The book immediately achieved a tremendous world-wide success, thanks also to the film *Rififi* which Jules Dassin made in 1955 (screenplay by Le Breton, who has always closely followed the fifteen films made from his books).

Le Breton has written some thirty novels, all successful, although all equally hard and aggressive, carrying an element of truth, a measure of rough sociological analysis, and a denunciation of the miseries of man. Later came the series on the Gang Fighters' Brigade, with the famous *Le clan des Siciliens*. Le Breton has recently started a new series of novels centered on the champion of the Gang Fighters' Brigade (*L'As et la marquise, L'As et la casse du siècle* . . .).

Le Breton is a real writer, the last great "poet of the underworld." His detective novels are not based on pure skill, dry and false, but provide a glimpse of a little-seen element of life. They recount stories that have actually happened, based on personal memoirs or those of a friend effectively mixed with the imagination.

All of Le Breton's books express a sense of nostalgia for the romantic underworld of the 1930s and 1940s, typified by a vigorously enforced code of honor, which was broken by the savage violence of the new generation of criminals. It is an inheritance from his years among what the middle-classes would call low-life. Le

Breton has kept from those dark years a sense of respect for and obedience to the rules of that class, of brotherhood and helping friends in need, and of silence. He displays great hatred for falsehood, cowardice, and authoritarianism, not to mention his hatred for spies, police informers, and for those who do not respect the underworld's code of honor. He often describes not the struggles between criminals and police but rather the violent struggles between the "true" gangsters, those with a sense of honor, and the "sharks," the roughs ready to do anything for "filthy lucre," including squealing, betraying their colleagues, and kidnapping wives and children.

Honor, respect for one's given word, for friendship, for hospitality, are qualities that might seem surprising in the pages of a book dealing with the underworld. For Le Breton, they represent the positive alternative to a blind violence which is not always caused by the delinquent. Such violence, he argues, is caused by an unjust society, elitist and hypocritical, which represses the unconventional and never lets it rise above the mud. In this, Le Breton considers himself and is considered by critics to be an anarchist in the world of the detective novel.

SANANTONIO, THE NEW RABELAIS

In 1965 the Centre de Sociologie des Faits Littéraires at Bordeaux University conducted a seminar on the Sanantonio phenomenon, attended by illustrious teachers from the Sorbonne and foreign universities. "Our researchers have shown that the popularity of the Sanantonio novels on all intellectual and educational levels, in all socio-professional categories, constitutes a unique phenomenon in the reading habits of the French." Twelve years later, on the publication of the ninety-second novel of the series featuring Police Commissioner Sanantonio, Jacques Cellard wrote on the front page of the authoritative *Le Monde*, "If Sanantonio didn't exist, would he have to be invented? Yes, without doubt."

Who is this Sanantonio who, in a series of a hundred and ten "scatalogical, ignoble, and absurd novelettes," as characterized by one of his detractors, has broken all sales records and won the largest number of the most prestigious literary prizes? Is he the "Rabelais of the twentieth century," as he has been described by critics, including some university scholars; or a "stercoraceous" author who wants to liberate himself with a redeeming fire or simply with a scornful silence, as part of the French intelligentsia maintains? An hour-long debate on French television in January 1978 resulted in a vote in favor of Sanantonio: "He is the greatest living French-speaking writer." And even more: "He has succeeded where Rabelais himself failed." Among this argument's most authoritative supporters is Bertrand Poirot-Delpech, literary critic for *Le Monde*, who a few months later, July 7, 1978, wrote a long, provocative article in Sanantonio's bizarre, slangy style, arguing strongly in favor of Sanantonio's work, and attacking those intellectual snobs who shy away from it on account of its popularity and end up supporting other work which is all too obviously rubbish. Jean Cocteau called Sanantonio a "left-handed writer," arguing that he had created a whole new language.

Sanantonio first appeared in December 1950 with *Laisse tomber la fille*. The author signed the books with the name of the protagonist, saving his own, Frédéric Dard (b. 1921) for more serious works. The novel is written in a relaxed, direct style, in imitation of Peter Cheyney's works. From this, his first appearance, Commissioner Sanantonio always maintained a certain resemblance to the hero of American detective novels: he is handsome, manly, a lady-killer, sharp, easy-going and, above all, very lucky. He is very soon surrounded by a believable human, literary, and philosophical universe.

The human world is born with the creation of a series of fixed characters which include Inspector Bérurier and his wife Berthe, Inspector Pinaud, "the Old Man" (head of the Paris police, to whom Sanantonio, Berù, and Pinaud are accountable), Félicie, Sanantonio's mother (who acts as a balancing force, a positive alternative to the stream of beautiful and fatal women scattered through the stories), and, finally, the

Antoine Sanantonio, police commissioner and central character in the series which bears his name. The illustration is from Henri Desclez's studio, which produced a comic strip edition of some of the detective's adventures.

little Marie-Marie, Bérurier's niece, a character in the style of Queneau's Zazie.

Together with Sanantonio, and more in evidence than he in the last novels is Bérurier (called Berù, Mammoth, Fats, Guts, Slob—all the characters in these novels have a long list of strange nicknames). Despite his greed, his profound ignorance, and his blockheadedness, Berù is gifted with a healthy animal sense, a sound popular instinct, a love of life, and courage and dedication, which make him the most realistic character in the whole series. A medievalist, Professor Paul Burguière, has compared him to the protagonist of a *chanson de geste*, the famous Rénard, a good giant who is primitive, simple, and unattractive, but who kills all his enemies with his enormous club and triumphs in the name of justice.

One of the most important aspects in the work of Sanantonio is their literary-linguistic quality: his novels consist of a continuous stream of new words, puns, and disguised literary quotes which constantly flash past the reader, who is steadily and directly involved, abused, and provoked, but also helped. It is exactly this inexhaustible creativity which has made Sanantonio's novels so difficult to translate, although it has enabled Sanantonio to receive the sincere recognition of President Pompidou of France for his services in enriching the French language through his writing.

Although acted out in an epic or fantastic tone, Sanantonio generally conducts his investigations under the rules of a good policeman; at times, however, they slip into spycraft or end with a brilliant, final surprise which is not totally justified.

The technique of the final surprise is one of the principal characteristics of the novels which Frédéric Dard has published under his own name. These establish him not only as one of the most refined crime writers in the world today but also, at the same time, a great novelist who deserves more than the simple title of crime writer. His works include *Toi le venin, Imitation au meutre, Delivrez-Nous du mal,* and *A San Pedro ou ailleurs,* to mention just a few. They are novels that mix nightmare and atmosphere with the psychological detective novel. Atmosphere is the essential component in Dard's works: a dark, tormented atmosphere, in which the psychologically contorted or corrupted characters move.

Frédéric Dard-Sanantonio is the main writer for *Fleuve Noir*, a publishing house specializing in French crime writing, set up after World War I by a young publisher of Italian origin, Armand De Caro. Among Sanantonio's many colleagues who should be mentioned are Michel Carnal (b. 1928), Pierre Nemours (b. 1920), Marc Arno, Claude Joste, M. G. Braun (the author of a series, Sam and Sally, recently adapted for television), Mario Ropp, Peter Randa, André Lay, G.-J. Arnaud, Roger Faller, Brice Pelman, Claude Rank, and Serge Laforest.

Among the most recent *Fleuve Noir* detective novelists, Serge Jacquemard has shown himself to be particularly good, writing strong, violent, and cruel novels centered around a killer, Shultz, who, in order to complete his missions, often has to carry out some professional detective work.

EMPHASIS ON THE VICTIM

French detective novels have always been characterized by a greater tension than Anglo-French ones, a more malicious imagination (to the detriment of the scientific quality of the solution), a taste for dramatic scenes which contradict the facts of the mystery without going so far as to betray the reader or cheat him too obviously. The style favors atmosphere rather than investigation, emphasizes the human contacts between the characters, and the psychology of the two great antagonists—the murderer and his victim—rather than the doings of the detective.

At times the story is told by the victim; more often, by the murderer. A casual murderer, with all the psychological traumas that would afflict any normal man after committing a murder, or a cynical, almost demonic being who has chosen crime to achieve his ends (wealth, revenge, or the suppression of witnesses). The latter is the type of protagonist in many of the novels of Hubert Monteilhet (b. 1928), who is one of the most significant writers in the Denoël suspense series (*Crime Club, Super Crime Club, Sueurs Froides*) and was the winner of the Grand Prix de Littérature policière in 1960 for his *The Praying Mantises* (*Les mantes religieuses*).

Monteilhet's cloaked characters are Vera Canova, who wants to achieve wealth and freedom through crime (she kills her husband and his son from a previous marriage), and Béatrice Magny, the wife of Vera's lover. Discovering the two lovers' evil plans, Béatrice cruelly blackmails them, toying with them before finally leading them to suicide, while she, in her turn, is killed by an avalanche of snow. A true Greek tragedy in which the central protagonist is Fate.

The next novels, *Return from the Ashes* (*Le retour des cendres*, 1961) and *Les pavés du diable* (1964), con-

tain even more elements of Greek tragedy. In the first, a very rich French-Jewish woman doctor, deported by the Nazis, returns to Paris at the time of the Liberation. Her husband, who thought her dead, comes across her by chance and finds her "so similar to his poor wife" that he "adopts" her. He wants her to play the role of the presumably dead wife and so recoup her large fortune. The doctor does not disclose her identity because she wants to find out what sort of a man she had married. She finds out that it was he who denounced her to the Nazis, and that he is now the lover of her daughter by a previous marriage. Despite this, she loves him and reveals her identity to him. In the final act, she is gassed to death by her jealous daughter, who then commits suicide. The husband is arrested for his crime during the occupation. The second novel centers on the crimes uncovered by the investigations of a sociology professor into the sex life of a small French town, using a tape recorder in the confessional in church!

Monteilhet constructs his suspense stories with a flexible time scheme, moving back and forth, using statements, letters, and conversations of people who are already dead. Among his other noteworthy novels are *Non-sens* (1971), *Dead Copy* (*Mourir à Francfort*, 1975) and *Esprit es-tu là?* (1977).

Also under the Denoël mark is Sébastien Japrisot (the pseudonym of Jean-Baptiste Rossi, b. 1931), the author of refined novels built upon complicated machinations in the style of William Irish, in which the victim is often also the culprit: *The 10.30 from Marseille* (*Compartiment tueurs*, 1962), *Trap for Cinderella* (*Piège pour Cendrillon*, 1962), *The Lady in the Car with Glasses and a Gun* (*La dame dans l'auto avec des lunettes et un fusil*, 1966). All these novels have been made into films by, respectively, Costa Gravas, Andre Cayatte, and Anatole Litvak.

8 | A REPORT ON THE CURRENT SCENE

by Edward D. Hoch

Mickey Spillane in the 1950s. By this time he had made a name for himself with his violent, action-packed writing, which was to open up a new field for the American hard-boiled novel.

MICKEY SPILLANE AND THE PRIVATE EYE

In 1947, Mickey Spillane published his first Mike Hammer detective novel, *I, the Jury*. It was to become the best-selling mystery of all time, with total sales in the United States alone of over six million copies, and Spillane's next five novels were close behind it in popularity. Most of these sales were in paperback (*I, the Jury* sold only seven thousand copies in its hardbound edition), and most were to male readers. Decades later, when Gothics and historical romances were to dominate the paperback racks, publishers would still be trying to recapture the magic Spillane formula that lured male readers into the bookstore.

Mickey Spillane was born in Brooklyn in 1918 and grew up in Elizabeth, New Jersey. In 1935 he began writing for slick and pulp magazines and comic books. After serving with the Air Force in World War II he returned to writing and created the toughest of all private detectives, Mike Hammer. (Is it possible the name Hammer was subconsciously suggested to the author by its similarity to the name Hammett?)

The public enthusiasm for Mike Hammer and Spillane's other characters was rarely shared by the critics, who often condemned the brutality of the books and Hammer's inclination to serve as jury and executioner. It was the same sort of reception that greeted the novels of James Hadley Chase in England. But Spillane's readers did not care much about the opinion of the critics. They identified with Mike Hammer—and certainly the first to identify with him was Mickey Spillane himself, who played Hammer in one of several films made from the books during the height of their popularity (*The Girl Hunters*, 1963).

Despite the books' negative aspects, Spillane's work remains a milestone in the history of detective fiction and the private-eye novel. He was one of the first mystery writers to realize the importance of cinematic movement in his novels, and there is no denying that his style is gripping and realistic. It continues and strengthens a tradition born in the early pulps.

Mike Hammer has appeared in eleven novels to date. Following *I, the Jury*, some of the others are *The Big Kill* (1951), *One Lonely Night* (1951), *Kiss Me, Deadly* (1952), and *Survival . . . Zero!* (1970). Other Spillane novels have dealt with Tiger Mann, a secret agent who fights the Russians.

Of the many other private-eye contemporaries of Mike Hammer, some deserve special mention in this section. One is Mike Shayne, who appears in the novels and stories of Brett Halliday, the pseudonym of American writer Davis Dresser (1940–1977). Halliday's first published novel, and the first book about Shayne, was *Dividend on Death* (1939). It was followed by more than sixty-five others, as well as a number of short stories. Shayne also stars in some three hundred novelettes which have appeared monthly in *Mike Shayne's Mystery Magazine*, but for the most part these have been ghostwritten by other writers using Halliday's name.

Mike Shayne is a red-haired Miami private detective whose wife died in 1943, after which he temporarily relocated in New Orleans. His secretary Lucy Hamilton, reporter Timothy Rourke, and detective chief Will Gentry often figure in his investigations. Perhaps the best of the Shayne novels is one that takes him to the Kentucky coal fields and a miners' strike—*A Taste for Violence* (1949).

Less popular, although certainly worth reading are the adventures of New York private eye Peter Cham-

Mickey Spillane is a self-proclaimed anitifeminist. In his books the women are usually nude and lying on their backs. When, rarely, a woman has a positive character almost as admirable as a man's, Spillane takes his revenge by having her sadistically maltreated. However, when he comes across a woman whose figure in a tight skirt reminds him—to put it in his own words—of a curving mountain road, things change. Spillane's wife Sherry (left, with him) is one of those women. In fact, Sherry, the married woman with the beauty-queen figure, appears on the jacket of one of her husband's books, showing all her mountain curves (right).

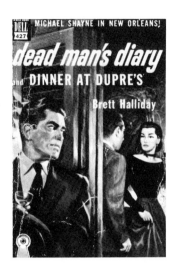

Brett Halliday (right) *led, at least for a few years, a romantic life. After leaving school early, he traveled through the southern states and Mexico working in oil fields. Eventually he went to college and graduated with a degree in civil engineering. Unable to find work because of the depression, he decided to try out detective-story writing. After some initial failures he was successful in creating the detective Mike Shayne. The cover of one of his early books is shown here.*

bers, recorded in the novels and stories of Henry Kane. Born in New York in 1918, Kane published his first novel about Chambers, *A Halo for Nobody*, in 1947. Others include *A Corpse for Christmas* (1951), *Death of a Dastard* (1963), and *Unholy Trio* (1967). The mystery puzzles in Kane's books are generally more complex than those in the average private-eye novel. A 1955 book, *Too French and Too Deadly*, also published as *The Narrowing Lust*, has Chambers solving a locked room mystery.

Kane has also published three novels about Inspector McGregor of the New York police, who retires to become a private detective: *The Midnight Man* (1965), *Conceal and Disguise* (1966), and *Laughter in the Alehouse* (1968).

Michael Avallone, born in New York in 1924, has written some thirty novels about private eye Ed Noon, beginning with *The Spitting Image* (1953). And Bart Spicer, born in Virginia in 1918, wrote seven novels about Carney Wilde before abandoning him. Best of the Wilde books are *The Dark Light* (1949) and *Blues for the Prince* (1950).

Before considering some other private-eye writers, let's look at another important facet of the modern mystery novel—the police procedural.

The first edition of one of Henry Kane's novels. Kane's most popular character is Peter Chambers, a young, handsome private detective who likes women, jazz, good food, and drink.

A novel by HENRY KANE

DECISION

THE POLICE PROCEDURAL

Perhaps it was a reaction to the tough private eyes who dealt out their own brand of justice. Perhaps it was merely a desire for more law and order in our society. Whatever the root cause, the advent of the police procedural novel in the years after World War II was to be one of the most important aspects of the contemporary whodunit.

Some critics date the police procedural from Lawrence Treat's *V as in Victim* (1945), about the hardworking but human detectives Mitch Taylor, Jubb Freeman, and their associates. Treat, a New York native born in 1903, continued to write about Taylor and Freeman in a series of "alphabetized" novels and short stories, but he denies he had any intention of creating a new form of detective fiction. It seems more likely that the real impetus for the police procedural came from the tremendous success in 1949 of Jack Webb's radio and television series "Dragnet" and Sidney Kingsley's Broadway play *Detective Story*. In the years that followed, the main practitioners of the form were J. J. Marric in Britain and Ed McBain in the United States.

It's interesting to note that Marric and McBain were both pseudonyms of writers already well established under their own names. Marric was really John Creasey (1908–1973), the most prolific writer in the history of crime fiction. Under a record number of twenty-eight pseudonyms (mainly Marric, M. E. Cooke, Michael Halliday, Kyle Hunt, Peter Manton, Anthony Morton, Gordon Ashe, Norman Deane, Jeremy York, Robert Caine Frazer, Margaret Cooke, Elise Fecamps, Henry St. John Cooper, Tex Riley, William K. Reilly, and Patrick Gill) he published some 560 novels, and for each pseudonym he was able to develop a different writing style.

Often compared to Edgar Wallace because of his vast output and the "thriller" quality of much of his work, Creasey wrote novels about Chief Inspector Roger West of Scotland Yard under his own name. De-

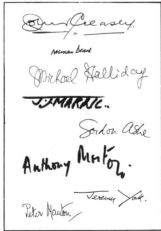

John Creasey is the most prolific novelist in detective fiction, perhaps even in all of literature. He wrote over five hundred books which have been published under twenty-eight names—some shown here as the signatures used by Creasey on his contracts.

Despite Creasey's immense list of books, it was not until 1955 that his fame spread beyond England, with the creation of Inspector Gideon of Scotland Yard.

spite their success in Britain they were not well received abroad. Other characters, like Creasey's Toff and Anthony Morton's Baron, seemed too closely based upon thief-detectives like Arsène Lupin and The Saint. It was not until publication of the first J. J. Marric book, *Gideon's Day* in 1955, that both critics and readers really took notice of Creasey.

Commander George Gideon of Scotland Yard, a large slow-moving police detective who often must tackle several developing cases at one time, went on to appear in twenty more books, notably *Gideon's Fire* (1961). The British actor Jack Hawkins played Gideon in the 1958 film *Gideon of Scotland Yard*, and a television series was shown in England during the 1960s. As in the books, the film versions show Gideon's family and their problems, contrasting them with the daily work at Scotland Yard.

The typical Gideon novel features one important case which serves as a centerpiece, but the reader and Gideon are distracted by other cases, isolated or related, of more or less importance. While on the trail of a murderer, Gideon may have to deal with a wife beating, a petty theft, a body in the Thames, and so forth. A similiar multiple case technique has been used successfully in this country by Dell Shannon in her novels about Lieutenant Luis Mendoza of the Los Angeles Police Department. (Shannon, too, is a pseudonym, for mystery writer Elizabeth Linington, born in Aurora, Illinois, 1921.)

Like Creasey, the American writer Evan Hunter was well established as the author of *The Blackboard Jungle* (1954) and other novels when he used the Ed McBain pseudonym in the first of his 87th Precinct novels, *Cop Hater*, in 1956. He had also published other novels and stories under the pseudonyms Curt Cannon, Hunt Collins, and Richard Marsten, often in the magazine *Manhunt*, but it was as Ed McBain that he was to become most widely known. Born in New York in 1926, Hunter worked for a prominent literary agent before turning his talents to full-time writing.

Long-suffering and hardworking, the detectives of the 87th Precinct work around the clock. They are a mixed lot—Steve Carella, an Italian-American whose beautiful wife Teddy is a deaf-mute; Meyer Meyer, who is Jewish; handsome Cotton Hawes; Lieutenant Peter Byrnes; Andy Parker; Arthur Brown, who is black; and Bert Kling, youngest member of the squad. McBain has stated it was his intention to kill off Steve Carella in an early book, but Carella survived to become the leading character of the series.

The 87th Precinct novels (and three novelettes collected as *The Empty Hours*, 1962) are set in an imaginary city that bears a striking resemblance to New York. The section called Isola in the books seems like Manhattan seen from a different angle, and Calm's Point and Riverhead could well be Staten Island and the Bronx. The city lives in these pages, with details of summer heat and winter cold forming striking vignettes in the midst of murder investigations.

Several of the 87th Precinct novels have been made into movies in the United States, Japan, France, and Canada, sometimes with the names of the characters changed. An American television series had a thirty-week run during 1961, and recently a pilot film for a possible new series was being written.

All thirty-four of Ed McBain's books about the people of the 87th Precinct are worth reading. In addi-

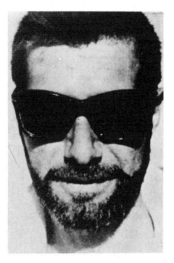

Evan Hunter (left) *published his novels about the 87th Precinct under the pseudonym Ed McBain.* Below: *Yul Brynner appeared in a film made from a McBain novel in 1972.*

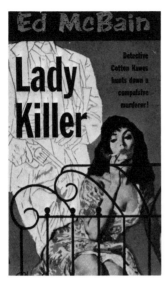

The original jacket for one of McBain's books.

tion to those already mentioned, some others are *The Con Man* (1957), *Killer's Choice* (1957), *Killer's Wedge* (1959), *King's Ransom* (1959), *Ten Plus One* (1963) and *Fuzz* (1968).

Among other authors who excel at the police procedural are two who have written about the Amsterdam police. Nicholas Freeling, born in London in 1927, wrote ten novels about Inspector Van der Valk before the inspector met an untimely end in the final book. Now he has begun a series about Van der Valk's widow. The best of the first series is *The King of the Rainy Country* (1966). Janwillem van de Wetering also writes about members of the Amsterdam Police Force. Born in the Netherlands in 1931, he now lives in the United States.

Two American authors of police novels should also be mentioned. Hillary Waugh, born in New Haven in 1920, is the author of *Last Seen Wearing . . .* (1952), which was highly regarded by several critics. And perhaps the most authentic police novels of all are those of Joseph Wambaugh. Born in East Pittsburgh, Pennsylvania, in 1937, Wambaugh was a detective sergeant with the Los Angeles Police Department before becoming a full-time writer in 1974. Four of his novels have been made into feature films and another, *The Blue Knight* (1972), became a television series. The Wambaugh novels, however, are not detective stories or whodunits in the strict sense of the terms.

ETHNIC DETECTIVES

Nearly all policemen and private detectives in mystery fiction have been white. During the 1920s and 1930s Oriental sleuths like Charlie Chan and Mr. Moto were made popular through the pages of *The Saturday Evening Post* and the books and films in which they appeared, but this was to some extent a reaction against the "yellow peril" image of Fu Manchu and other villainous Oriental characters. The only black detective of the period, Octavus Roy Cohen's private eye Florian Slappy, was little more than a caricature.

All this began to change in the mid-1960s with the debut of George Baxt's black homosexual detective Pharaoh Love in *A Queer Kind of Death* (1966) and more importantly with the first recorded case of John Ball's Virgil Tibbs a year earlier. Ball was born in Schenectady, New York, in 1911 and had written a number of juvenile novels before creating the black detective Virgil Tibbs in 1965's memorable *In the Heat of the Night*. The book won the MWA Edgar Award, and a film version went on to win the Academy Award for best picture of the year in 1968.

Virgil Tibbs is a shrewd, southern-born police detective on the Pasadena, California, Homicide Squad. On a return trip home he becomes a murder suspect simply because he is a black stranger passing through the town. Finally he solves the case and wins the reluctant admiration of the bigoted local police chief. Tibbs went on to star in several more books and films, but none of them achieved quite the popular success of his first case.

Another black detective, John Shaft, appeared for the first time in Ernest Tidyman's 1970 novel *Shaft*, which also became a successful motion picture. A tough private eye who seemed to be patterned after Mike Hammer, Shaft starred in seven novels before the author retired him. Tidyman, born in Cleveland in 1928, is also well known as the author of the popular screenplay *The French Connection* (1971).

Both John Ball and Ernest Tidyman are white authors writing about black detectives. The outstanding black mystery writer is undoubtedly Chester Himes, whose fast and violent novels about Coffin Ed Johnson and Grave Digger Jones have been appearing here since 1959. Born in Jefferson City, Missouri, in 1909, Himes has spent much of his life in France, and all his novels about black detectives Johnson and Jones were first published in Paris. Two of the earliest books were *The Crazy Kill* and *The Real Cool Killers*, both of which appeared in France in 1958.

Another ethnic detective who achieved great popularity in the 1960s and 1970s was Rabbi David Small, star of seven novels by Harry Kemelman beginning with *Friday the Rabbi Slept Late* (1964) and continuing

From his first appearance in 1966, John Ball's Virgil Tibbs quickly established himself as the best black detective in criminal fiction. Played on screen by Sidney Poitier, he soon achieved worldwide popularity. Poitier is shown here in a scene from In the Heat of the Night *(1967), with Rod Steiger. Shown also is an original jacket of one of the Virgil Tibbs stories.*

Chester Himes's and Ernest Tidyman's black detectives are more violent than Virgil Tibbs, and their adventures, for the most part, tend toward the exaggerated and extravagant. Below: *This is an illustration for Tidyman's* Shaft.

through each day of the week. Kemelman, a Boston native born in 1908, won the MWA Edgar for his first book about Rabbi Small. Jewish customs and lore form an important part of the best-selling series.

Even rarer than black and Jewish detectives have been American Indian sleuths. Although Manly Wade Wellman won first prize in an *Ellery Queen's Mystery Magazine* contest in 1946 with a short story about Indian detective David Return, the character appeared in only one other tale. It remained for Tony Hillerman, an Oklahoman born in 1925, to create the first really popular American Indian detective in Lieutenant Joe Leaphorn of the Navaho police, whose beat is a huge Arizona reservation. Two of the books, *Dance Hall of the Dead* (1973) and *Listening Woman* (1978), have been winners of the MWA Edgar Award for best novel of the year.

WOMEN MYSTERY WRITERS

Although women mystery readers have traditionally outnumbered men by about three-to-one according to

FROM SHERLOCK HOLMES TO JAMES BOND

After World War II, the spy novel developed from the detective novel to take its place as an independent genre.

Spies and traitors have always existed in literature, the despised figure who sells himself or betrays his country out of greed, a desire for revenge, or some kind of idealism. As characters, spies were usually so unappealing that they rarely were the main character of significant literary works.

There is, however, a legitimate detective tradition for the spy novel. Conan Doyle and Maurice Leblanc both involve Sherlock Holmes and Arsène Lupin in patriotic spy plots and were imitated a few years later by Agatha Christie. But John Buchan stands out among the innovators in the genre. His best-known book, *The Thirty-Nine Steps*, has been filmed by various directors, including Alfred Hitchcock. Richard Hannay, the spy who is featured in most of Buchan's novels, started the classic English spy tradition in which an obscure character is forced, practically against his will, to become the unknown hero in a game in which he is only a pawn; a tradition which was to be continued in the works of Eric Ambler, Somerset Maugham, Graham Greene, and John Le Carré, writers who in fact stand outside the limitations of the detective-spy genre and merit a place in the literary history of the twentieth century.

The spy novel boom came into its own after World War II. It reflected, perhaps even more closely than the detective novel, the tensions of the Cold War, when people were living between two opposed forces balanced on the edge of destruction. In such an atmosphere the spy is called upon to fight a continuing underground struggle, in place of that more conventional warfare which could now only lead to world destruction.

In such a climate the spy novel takes on the role of a chronicle, recording the problems and pressures felt by contemporary society. It is by reflecting these problems and pressures that the spy story enters the literary tradition as an independent genre like the detective novel.

Sean Connery originated the role of Ian Fleming's James Bond in such films as Dr. No *and* Goldfinger.

some publishers' figures, not all women mystery writers were as willing to admit their sex as were Anna Katharine Green, Agatha Christie, Dorothy L. Sayers, and Mignon G. Eberhart. The names Anthony Gilbert and M. V. Heberden hide the identities of women writers, and to this day the mysteries of British writer Elizabeth X. Ferrars are published in the United States as by E. X. Ferrars. (Things are changing, though. Early in 1981 an American publisher began reissuing the mysteries of John Stephen Strange under her real name, Dorothy S. Tillett.)

One writer who uses initials instead of her first name has never made any secret of the fact that she is a woman. P. D. James was born Phyllis Dorothy James in Oxford, England, in 1920. She published the first of seven novels about Commander Adam Dalgliesh of Scotland Yard in 1962, and since then, in the words of the *Times Literary Supplement*, "she has revitalized a genre considered by many thriller readers to be past its prime." The *TLS* considered *Shroud for a Nightingale* (1971) the best of the Dalgliesh books, while other critics prefer *An Unsuitable Job for a Woman* (1972). In this book Dalgliesh makes only a brief appearance, and the leading character is a woman private detective named Cordelia Gray.

In 1980 P. D. James tried something completely different—a suspense novel without Adam Dalgliesh. *Innocent Blood* was a hit with critics and the public alike and became an immediate best seller. It tells of an eighteen-year-old adopted girl who discovers her natural mother is a convicted murderess about to be released from prison.

James's Commander Dalgliesh has often been compared to an earlier Scotland Yard sleuth, Josephine Tey's Inspector Alan Grant. Tey's real name was Elizabeth Mackintosh (1897–1952), and between 1929 and the time of her death she wrote eight memorable mysteries, six of them about Grant. By general agreement the best of these are *The Franchise Affair* (1948), in which Grant appears only briefly, and *The Daughter of Time* (1951), in which Grant solves a historical mystery involving Richard III while confined to a hospital bed.

Another British writer who has achieved great popularity is Ruth Rendell. Born in London in 1930, she has published some twenty novels and two collections of short stories since 1964. Her work is almost equally divided between detective stories about Detective Chief Inspector Reginald Wexford and stories of psychological suspense. The division even extends to her short stories—*The Fallen Curtain* (1976) is a col-

Since the beginning of detective fiction there have been many important women writers of detective fiction and many important women fictional detectives. Anna K. Green, shown here, coined the term "detective story," and the greatest detective novelist of the twentieth-century was Agatha Christie. An important contemporary writer is Doris Miles Disney, an American novelist of the English school. Below: The cover of one of her novels.

lection of suspense tales including the Edgar-winning title story, and *Means of Evil* (1979) is a collection of Wexford mysteries. Notable among Rendell's novels are *The Best Man to Die* (1969) and *A Sleeping Life* (1978), both about Wexford, and the suspense novels *One Across, Two Down* (1971) and *A Demon in My View* (1976).

Among other contemporary British writers mention should be made of Christianna Brand, born in Malaya in 1907, whose highly regarded novels *Green for Danger* (1944) and *Fog of Doubt* (1952) are among those she wrote about Inspector Cockrill. Celia Fremlin, born in Kent in 1914, has written a dozen suspense novels and short story collections. E. X. Ferrars, mentioned earlier, is the pseudonym of Morna Brown, born in Burma in 1907. She is the author of nearly fifty novels, including *Always Say Die* (1956), *Furnished for Murder* (1957), *The Busy Body* (1962), *The Small World of Murder* (1973), *Alive and Dead* (1974), and *Blood Flies Upwards* (1976).

The list of contemporary American women active in the mystery field is led by Margaret Millar, the wife of Ross Macdonald. Born in Canada in 1915, she has lived with her husband in California since the end of World War II. To date she has published eighteen novels, notably *Wall of Eyes* (1943), *The Iron Gates* (1945), the Edgar-winning *Beast in View* (1955), *An Air That Kills* (1957), *How Like an Angel* (1962), *Beyond This Point Are Monsters* (1970), and *Ask for Me Tomorrow* (1976).

Dorothy Salisbury Davis, a Chicago native born in 1916, is best known for her suspense novel *A Gentle Murderer* (1951), in which a priest must track down a killer who confessed to him before the man kills again. She has written sixteen mystery and suspense novels since 1949, as well as two books outside these genres, and has published a dozen memorable short stories.

A number of women writers produced scores of good

Left to right: *First editions of works by Stanton Forbes, Dorothy Uhnak, and Rae Foley.*

detective novels during their lifetime without ever quite achieving wide popular success. Typical of these was Doris Miles Disney (1907–1976), who published forty-six novels before her death. Especially worth remembering are the eight novels about insurance investigator Jeff DiMarco, who stars in *Dark Road* (1946), *Straw Man* (1951), and *The Chandler Policy* (1971). Other Disney titles include *A Compound for Death* (1943), *Room for Murder* (1955), *Unappointed Rounds* (1956), *The Departure of Mr. Gaudette* (1964), *The Hospitality of the House* (1964), *Do Not Fold, Spindle or Mutilate* (1970), and *Three's a Crowd* (1971).

Other writers with a long list of books include Rae Foley, pseudonym of Elinore Denniston (1900–1978), who also wrote as Dennis Allan. Her novels numbered nearly fifty in all, including *Death and Mr. Potter* (1955), *The Shelton Conspiracy* (1967), *One O'Clock at the Gotham* (1974), and *The Barclay Place* (1975). Helen Nielsen, who was born in Illinois in 1918, has published nearly twenty books, including *The Severed Key* (1973) and *The Brink of Murder* (1976). Ursula Curtiss, born in Yonkers, New York, in 1923, is the daughter of mystery writer Helen Reilly. Her nineteen novels include *Don't Open the Door* (1968) and *The Birthday Gift* (1975).

Some women writers are known primarily for a single book. Vera Caspary, a Chicago native born in 1904, wrote a great deal, but her name is forever linked to *Laura*, published in 1943 and filmed the following year. Helen Eustis, born in Cincinnati in 1916, received the MWA Edgar Award for her 1946 novel *The Horizontal Man* but wrote little thereafter. Lucille

Fletcher, born in Brooklyn in 1912, is remembered for *Sorry, Wrong Number* (1948), based on her radio play. Her later novels include *The Girl in Cabin B-54* (1968) and *Eighty Dollars to Stamford* (1975). Patricia Highsmith, born in Texas in 1921, is usually identified as the author of *Strangers on a Train* (1950), despite an impressive body of novels and short stories that followed this debut.

Other women deserving of mention are Dorothy B. Hughes, born in Kansas City in 1904, who wrote *Ride the Pink Horse* (1946) and other fine novels; Helen McCloy, born in New York in 1904, whose novels and stories about psychiatrist Dr. Basil Willing include *Through a Glass Darkly* (1950); Patricia McGerr, born in Nebraska in 1917, whose first novel, *Pick Your Victim* (1946), had a completely new twist; and Lillian de la Torre, a New York native born in 1902, best known for her short stories in which Dr. Sam Johnson solves mysteries against a background of eighteenth-century London. Emma Lathen, pseudonym of Mary Latis and Martha Hennissart, writes novels about banker sleuth John Putnam Thatcher, notably *Accounting for Murder* (1964). And Stanton Forbes has published some forty novels, under her own name and as De Forbes and Tobias Wells.

Two newer women writers are former policewoman Dorothy Uhnak, author of *The Ledger* (1970), *Law and Order* (1973), and *The Investigation* (1977), and Mary Higgins Clark, author of three best-selling suspense novels including *The Cradle Will Fall* (1980).

ROSS MACDONALD

There's little doubt that the leading mystery writer of this generation, in terms of importance to the genre, is Ross Macdonald, the pseudonym of Californian Kenneth Millar. Educated in Canada, where he met his wife, Margaret Millar, he has often been drawn back to childhood roots in his writing, especially in the recurring theme of a father search.

Born in 1915, Kenneth Millar was twenty-nine years old when his wife's success with mystery novels encouraged him to publish his own first novel, *The Dark Tunnel* (1944), a mystery-espionage tale set against a background of World War II. He published three more novels under his own name, notably the tough *Blue City* (1947), before adopting the pseudonym John Macdonald, which he later changed to Ross Macdonald to avoid confusion with John D. MacDonald.

The first Macdonald novel, *The Moving Target*

(1949), introduced private eye Lew Archer, who seems a direct descendant of Hammett's Spade and Chandler's Marlowe. (In fact Sam Spade's murdered partner in *The Maltese Falcon* was named Archer.) Archer is more sensitive and far less violent than Spillane's Mike Hammer of the same period; although both are private detectives, they are worlds apart. Archer follows a strict ethical code and rarely becomes involved personally with the women in his books. His own marriage was broken by a total dedication to his work, and he seems at times a lonely man.

The plots of the Ross Macdonald novels have grown more complex over time. Often they involve a murder or disappearance many years in the past, sometimes a crime that was witnessed and half-remembered by a small child now grown to adulthood. There is an intertwining of family relationships that can sometimes baffle the casual reader, but everything becomes clear in the end.

All eighteen of the Lew Archer novels are worth reading. In addition to *The Moving Target*, the best of them are probably *The Drowning Pool* (1950), *The Ivory Grin* (1952), *The Galton Case* (1959), *The Chill* (1964), *The Far Side of the Dollar* (1965), *The Goodbye*

After establishing himself under his own name, Kenneth Millar (opposite) *decided to change his image as a detective novelist and created the character of Lew Archer under the pseudonym of Ross Macdonald. Below: An illustration by Ferenc Pinter for* The Seven Labours of Lew Archer *(1966, U.S. title:* The Name Is Archer*). Lew Archer has been played on screen by Paul Newman, where his name, for screen reasons, was changed to Lew Harper.*

Look (1969), *The Underground Man* (1971), and *The Blue Hammer* (1976). Archer also appears in nine short stories collected as *Lew Archer, Private Investigator* (1977). Even though they are very good, they lack the exceptional quality of the best novels.

WESTLAKE, MACDONALD, AND THE AMERICAN MODERNS

The popular novels of Donald E. Westlake perhaps best exemplify the twin strains of tough realism and wild humor that are the hallmarks of the modern American mystery-crime novel. Born in New York in 1933, Westlake worked for a literary agency before turning to writing himself. After several short story sales he published his first novel, *The Mercenaries*, in 1960. He is a prolific writer and has published more than fifty novels in the past twenty years, many of them under the pseudonyms Richard Stark and Tucker Coe.

The early novels under his own name—books like *361* (1962) and *Pity Him Afterwards* (1964)—showed Westlake to be a talented follower of the hard-boiled school. Then in 1967 came a big change, with *God Save the Mark*, which introduced humor to the Westlake mysteries. The book won the MWA Edgar Award, and subsequent novels featured characters like the inept thief Dortmunder. The Dortmunder books—*The Hot Rock* (1970), *Bank Shot* (1972), and *Jimmy the Kid* (1974)—attracted attention in Hollywood, and the first two were made into successful films. Other Westlake books like *Cops and Robbers* (1972) and *Dancing Aztecs* (1976) also managed to blend crime with comedy.

Westlake's versatility was further demonstrated in 1963, with the first of the Richard Stark books, *The Hunter*. Its protagonist, Parker, is completely emotionless, as cold and calculating and "stark" as possible. Although planned for only one book, Parker proved so popular that he reappeared in nearly twenty others, including *The Outfit* (1963), *The Score* (1964), *Slayground* (1971), *Plunder Squad* (1972), and *Butcher's Moon* (1974).

Under the pseudonym Tucker Coe, Westlake has also written five novels about detective Mitch Tobin, including *Kinds of Love, Kinds of Death* (1966), *Murder Among Children* (1968), and *Don't Lie to Me* (1972).

Even more popular than Westlake have been the Travis McGee novels of John D. MacDonald. Born in Pennsylvania in 1916, MacDonald wrote under several pseudonyms for the pulps and other magazines before

The first edition of Millar's The Three Roads.

Robert Redford (left) *and George Segal in Donald E. Westlake's* The Hot Rock, *directed by Peter Yates.*

publishing his first novel in 1950. He is the author of nearly seventy books, including *The Executioners* (1958) and *A Key to the Suite* (1962), but his greatest fame rests with the nineteen novels about Travis McGee.

Half detective, half romantic musketeer, McGee lives on a houseboat in Florida and makes a living recovering stolen or lost funds. Often he goes to the aid

Three Westlake books, published under various names—Richard Stark, Tucker Coe, and Donald E. Westlake.

of an old friend or a damsel in distress. The novels, all with a color in their titles, proceed from *The Deep Blue Goodbye* (1964) to *Free Fall in Crimson* (1981).

Another writer who could be classed with the American moderns is Brian Garfield, born in New York in 1939. Author of numerous western novels starting in 1960, Garfield soon turned to the mystery-suspense story. His best-known novels are *Death Wish* (1972) and *Hopscotch* (1975). The latter won the MWA Edgar Award and was successfully filmed in 1980. Garfield has also published a number of short spy stories.

Hardly a modern in the sense that he is new to mystery writing, Hugh Pentecost still deserves mention in this section. Pentecost is the pseudonym of Judson Philips, who was born in Mssachusetts in 1903. Under his own name and the Pentecost pseudonym, he has published a steady stream of detective novels since 1936, now numbering more than eighty. His mysteries continue to appear, sometimes as often as four times a year. The most popular have been the Pentecost novels about hotel manager Pierre Chambrun and artist John Jericho.

An even more prolific writer is Aaron Marc Stein. Born in New York in 1906, Stein has published more than a hundred novels under his own name and the pseudonyms George Bagby and Hampton Stone. Both Pentecost and Stein have received the Grand Master Award from Mystery Writers of America.

The school of tough realism that best exemplifies one strain of the American modern tradition can be seen in the work of three Boston area writers. George V. Higgins, born in 1939, published the highly successful novel *The Friends of Eddie Coyle* in 1971 and has followed it with several other books, all written in tough, taut, highly realistic dialogue. Robert B. Parker, born in 1932, created Boston private eye Spenser in *The Godwulf Manuscript* (1973) and won the MWA Edgar for a later Spenser book, *Promised Land* (1976). Gregory Mcdonald, born in 1937, won Edgars for his first two novels, *Fletch* (1974) and *Confess, Fletch* (1976), both about an investigative reporter.

The wealth of new mystery writing talent in the Boston area is balanced across the country by San Francisco area writers Bill Pronzini and Joe Gores. Pronzini, born in 1943, has published nearly two hundred short stories and twenty novels. His nameless San Francisco private eye, in the grand tradition of Hammett's Continental Op, appeared in *The Snatch* (1971) and *Blowback* (1977), among other novels and stories. Some of Pronzini's books, notably *Snowbound* (1974) and *Games* (1976), are taut suspense thrillers,

The American writer John D. MacDonald, who created Travis McGee, an unusual figure halfway between a private detective and a romantic musketeer who specializes in recouping mislaid funds.

but *The Running of Beasts* (1976), written in collaboration with Barry N. Malzberg, is a brooding psychological mystery. Pronzini has also published four novels under the pseudonym Jack Foxx.

Joe Gores, born in Minnesota in 1931, has published several novels and stories about Dan Kearney Associates, a team of auto repossessors. He is best known for his first novel, *A Time of Predators* (1969), which was an MWA Edgar winner, and *Hammett* (1975), in which Dashiell Hammett functions as the detective against a background of San Francisco in 1928.

Among other well-known American writers, Robert L. Fish is unique in having specialized in two entirely different types of mystery writing. His novels are often about Captain José da Silva of the Rio de Janeiro police, while his short stories are likely to be outrageous Sherlockian parodies about the inept Schlock Homes. His first novel about da Silva, *The Fugitive* (1962) was an MWA Edgar winner. Fish, born in Cleveland in 1912, also wrote novels as Robert L. Pike; one of the Pike books was made into the popular motion picture *Bullitt* (1968).

Stanley Ellin, a New Yorker born in 1916, is best known for his three dozen excellent short stories beginning with the award winner "The Specialty of the House," but he has also published twelve fine novels, including the 1958 Edgar winner, *The Eighth Circle*. Jack Ritchie, born in 1922, specializes in offbeat mystery short stories but has yet to publish a novel. Another excellent short story writer, Robert Bloch, is a Chicago native born in 1918. He has also published nearly twenty novels and is best known as the author of *Psycho* (1959), on which the Hitchcock film was based.

Some other American writers deserve brief mention. Known for his popular scientific books and his science fiction, Isaac Asimov, who was born in the Soviet Union in 1920, has also written several volumes of detective short stories and a few novels, most recently *Murder at the A.B.A.* (1976). New York attorney Harold Q. Masur has written nine novels about lawyer detective Scott Jordan. The late Lawrence G. Blochman (1900–1975) wrote a novel and two books of stories about pathologist Dr. Daniel Webster Coffee. Thomas Chastain writes about New York's Inspector Max Kauffman. Lawrence Block has published several novels about burglar-detective Bernie Rhodenbarr, notably *The Burglar Who Liked to Quote Kipling* (1979). And newcomer William L. DeAndrea has the distinction of winning the MWA Edgar for each of his first two books, *Killed in the Ratings* (1978) and *The Hog Murders* (1979).

DICK FRANCIS AND THE BRITISH MODERNS

Of the British mystery writers of the past two decades, certainly Dick Francis has made the greatest impact, on both critics and the public. Born in 1920, Francis was a steeplechase jockey before turning to thriller writing in 1962 with *Dead Cert*, the first of nineteen mystery-suspense novels and a handful of short stories set against a background of British horse racing.

Francis has used a series character in only two books. Injured jockey Sid Halley becomes a private detective specializing in racing crimes. The rest of Francis's heroes have been jockeys, trainers, racing reporters, and other hangers-on at a typical British track. Every phase of racing, from breeding the horses to gambling on the outcome, has provided plot material for Francis. All the novels are good, but special note should be made of *For Kicks* (1963); *Forfeit* (1969), winner of the MWA Edgar; *Enquiry* (1969), a favorite of Ross Macdonald; and *Whip Hand* (1979), winner of the Crime Writers' Association Gold Dagger Award. Francis's most recent book is *Reflex* (1981).

Peter Dickinson is another of the newer British writers much admired by critics on both sides of the Atlantic. Born in Zambia in 1927, he published his first novel in 1968. Since then he has written a dozen mystery novels and an equal number of juvenile books. Of the mysteries *The Glass-sided Ants' Nest* (1968) and *The Old English Peep Show* (1969) deserve special mention.

Peter Lovesey, born in Middlesex in 1936, writes Victorian mysteries about Sergeant Cribb and Constable Thackeray that admirably capture the flavor of the period. Notable among them are *Wobble to Death* (1970) and *Waxwork* (1978). Lionel Davidson, born in Yorkshire in 1922, has published seven novels, including the memorable *Night of Wenceslas* (1960), *The Menorah Men* (1966), and *The Chelsea Murders* (1978). H. R. F. Keating, born in Sussex in 1926, has written a dozen novels about Inspector Ganesh Ghote of the Bombay police, beginning with *The Perfect Murder* (1964).

A long-time popular British writer is Michael Gilbert, born in Lincolnshire in 1912. Since 1947 he has published twenty novels and four collections of short stories, as well as doing a great deal of writing for

British television. Notable among his novels are *Smallbone Deceased* (1950), one of several about Inspector Hazelrigg, and *Blood and Judgement* (1959). His short story volume *Game Without Rules* (1967) is one of the finest collections of short spy tales ever published.

Among British writers whose work veers between mystery and thriller, Andrew Garve deserves special mention. Garve is the pseudonym of Paul Winterton, who was born in Leicester in 1908. He first published some mysteries under the name Roger Bax, then switched to Garve with *No Tears for Hilda* in 1950, followed a year later by *Fontego's Folly*. Detection is often lacking in Garve's books, which are usually suspense novels with exotic settings—a cave in *A Hole in the Ground* (1952) and a lighthouse in *The Sea Monks* (1963), to name just two.

Frederick Forsyth is another writer whose books are more thrillers than mysteries. Born in Kent in 1938, Forsyth won the MWA Edgar Award for his first novel, *The Day of the Jackal* (1971), which does indeed contain elements of detection in its assassination plot. Like Forsyth, Alistair MacLean is a thriller writer who sometimes uses elements of mystery in his books. Born in Glasgow in 1922, MacLean has published some thirty books to date, eight of them under the pseudonym Ian Stuart.

THE SPY NOVELISTS

Studies of the whodunit often omit novels of espionage and intrigue entirely, but I think this is a mistake. Spy novels sometimes *are* whodunits, with the identity of the spy or traitor revealed only at the very end, as in Eric Ambler's *Epitaph for a Spy* (1938), Len Deighton's *The Ipcress File* (1962), and John le Carré's *Tinker, Tailor, Soldier, Spy* (1974). Certainly they deserve mention here, as do their most famous creators. I am not the first to suggest that some of the best fiction writing coming out of Britain today can be found in spy and intrigue novels.

Why the British should be more adept at spy novels than the Americans is not something to be considered here, but it has been true for generations. The modern espionage novel has its roots in books like Joseph Conrad's *The Secret Agent* (1906), John Buchan's *The Thirty-nine Steps* (1915), E. Phillips Oppenheim's *The Great Impersonation* (1920), and W. Somerset Maugham's *Ashenden* (1928). All four authors were British, although Conrad, of course, was born in Poland.

It was in the 1930s, with Graham Greene and Eric Ambler, that today's spy novel really came of age. It would be hard to overestimate the influence of Graham Greene on modern writing in general and the novel of intrigue in particular. Born in Hertfordshire in 1904, Greene published his first novel in 1929. All of his twenty-three novels and numerous short stories contain elements of mystery or suspense, even though many have been published as mainstream fiction. Of special interest in a discussion of the spy novel are *Orient Express* (1932), *The Confidential Agent* (1939), *The Ministry of Fear* (1943), *The Third Man* (1950), *The Quiet American* (1955), *Our Man in Havana* (1958), and *The Human Factor* (1978). They represent not only the highest achievements of the espionage novel but also some of the finest fiction of our times.

Eric Ambler, born in London in 1909, has rarely written about the professional spy. His characters are more often businessmen or journalists caught up through circumstances in intrigues they barely understand. The best of these are probably *A Coffin for Dimitrios* (1939), *Journey into Fear* (1940), *Judgement on Deltchev* (1951), *The Schirmer Inheritance* (1953), *Passage of Arms* (1959), and *The Light of Day* (1962), although a dozen others are almost as good.

During the early days of World War II, two other espionage writers appeared on the scene. Manning Coles, a pseudonym of Adelaide Manning and Cyril Coles, wrote twenty-five novels about Tommy Hambledon of British Intelligence, notably *Drink to Yesterday* and *A Toast to Tomorrow* (both 1940). And Scottish-American writer Helen MacInnes has written seventeen spy novels, without a series character, beginning with *Above Suspicion* (1941) and *Assignment in Brittany* (1942). Her popularity is unvarying, with *The Hidden Target* (1980) on American best-seller lists.

The 1950s brought Ian Fleming's James Bond, and because of him for many years the spy novel was not quite the same. Fleming (1908–1964), a native of London, created Agent 007, with a license to kill from British Intelligence, and some of the violence and sex of Spillane moved over into the espionage novel. Bond was a superhero, quite unlike the characters of Greene or Ambler, and the books and films about him were immensely popular in Britain and the United States. The best of the dozen Bond novels are probably *Casino Royale* (1954), *From Russia, With Love* (1957), *Doctor No* (1958), and *Goldfinger* (1959).

The spy novel might never have recovered from James Bond had it not been for John le Carré, the pseudonym of David Cornwell, who was born in Dorset in 1931. Le Carré's first two novels about British agent George Smiley went almost unnoticed. But his third book, *The Spy Who Came in from the Cold* (1963), won both the CWA Gold Dagger and MWA Edgar and hit the best-seller lists as well. In recent years le Carré has completed a highly successful trilogy about George Smiley: *Tinker, Tailor, Soldier, Spy* (1974), *The Honourable Schoolboy* (1977), and *Smiley's People* (1980).

The basic sadness and loneliness of George Smiley prompted a whole new wave of unglamorous secret agents, going about their business with mixed emotions, often betrayed by their own side. Len Deighton, a London native born in 1929, wrote a series of witty, well-crafted novels that carefully detailed the workings and morality of the world of espionage. His nameless hero, called Harry Palmer in the film versions, was at his best in *The Ipcress File* (1962), *Funeral in Berlin* (1964), and *Yesterday's Spy* (1975). Adam Hall, pseudonym of crime writer Elleston Trevor, created British secret agent Quiller and won the MWA Edgar with *The Quiller Memorandum* (1965).

The spy novel has been given a whole new life.

THE MYSTERY FANS

Until now we have spoken of mystery writers and their characters. A closing word should be said about those who read mysteries and their influence on the marketplace. The past few years have seen a score of mystery bookstores open in large cities. Small publishers like The Mysterious Press have begun producing the sort of books—mainly short story collections—from which most general publishers shy away. Library publishers like Gregg Press and Arno Press have begun reprinting classic out-of-print mysteries. And general publishers like Harper & Row, Dell, Scribner's, and others have stepped up their programs of mystery reprinting. More than that, an increasing number of scholarly works have been published about the mystery field. Jacques Barzun and Wendell Hertig Taylor's *A Catalogue of Crime*, Allen J. Hubin's *The Bibliography of Crime Fiction 1749–1975*, John M. Reilly's *Twentieth-Century Crime and Mystery Writers*, and Chris Steinbrunner and Otto Penzler's *Encyclopedia of Mystery and Detection* have preserved and enlarged our knowledge of mysteries and the people who write them.

The fans themselves are organizing. They hold the Bouchercon Convention, named for the late *New York Times* critic Anthony Boucher, in a different American

THE MASTER OF SUSPENSE

Crime movies are to a large degree synonymous with Alfred Hitchcock. However, this important director, who was born in London in 1899 and died in 1980, not only championed criminal fiction through his films but also through anthologies and a magazine which bear his name. These are his major crime movies.

1940: *Rebecca*, from the book by Daphne du Maurier, starring Laurence Olivier, Joan Fontaine, and George Sanders.

1941: *Suspicion*, from a Francis Iles book, starring Cary Grant and Joan Fontaine.

1946: *Notorious*, based on Hitchcock's own story. Starring Ingrid Bergman.

1947: *The Paradine Case*, from Robert Hitchens's book, starring Gregory Peck, Anne Todd, and Charles Laughton.

1948: *Rope*, from Patrick Hamilton's drama, starring James Stewart, John Dall, and Joan Chandler.

1951: *Strangers on a Train*, based on Patricia Highsmith's book with Farley Granger and Ruth Roman.

1954: *Dial M for Murder*, based on Frederick Knott's play, with Ray Milland and Grace Kelly.

1954: *Rear Window*, based on a Cornell Woolrich story, with Grace Kelly, James Stewart, and Raymond Burr.

1955: *To Catch a Thief*, from David Dodge's book, with Cary Grant, Grace Kelly, and Jessie Royce Landis.

1955: *The Man Who Knew Too Much*, script by Charles Bennet and D. B. Wyndham-Lewis, starring James Stewart, Doris Day, and Daniel Gélin.

1958: *Vertigo*, taken from the book by Boileau and Narcejac, starring James Stewart and Kim Novak.

1959: *North by Northwest*, script by Ernest Lehman, with Cary Grant, Eva Marie Saint, and James Mason.

1960: *Psycho*, from Robert Bloch's novel, starring Anthony Perkins, Janet Leigh, and Martin Balsam.

1966: *Torn Curtain*, script by Brian Moore, with Paul Newman, Julie Andrews, and Lila Kedrova.

1971: *Frenzy*, based on A. Labern's novel, starring Jon Finch, Alec McCowen, and Barry Foster.

1976: *Family Plot*, based on a Victor Canning novel, with Karen Black and Barbara Harris.

From left to right, Doris Day and James Stewart in a scene from The Man Who Knew Too Much; *the cover of an anthology of crime stories edited under Hitchcock's name, and Anthony Perkins in a scene from* Psycho.

Interest in the well-plotted, neatly crafted mystery has led to several new paperback lines devoted to the classics. The new editions sleekly re-created the style of these whodunits, as shown by the covers of these Harper & Row Library titles.

city every year. And the long-active Baker Street Irregulars, dedicated to the memory of Sherlock Holmes, have been joined in recent years by the Wolfe Pack (admirers of Rex Stout's Nero Wolfe) and the G. K. Chesterton Society. These groups are more than mere fan organizations. The Wolfe Pack gives an annual award to a mystery writer, and the Chesterton Society recently discovered and reprinted an unknown Father Brown story written by Chesterton in collaboration with an obscure magazine publisher.

Even though some publishers now are cutting back on their mystery lists or merging them with mainstream fiction, it seems clear that the mystery is in no danger of dying. Other publishers are taking up the slack, encouraging new writers while they reprint old masters. Interest in the classic mystery—the whodunit—is on the rise once more, and if you can't find that old classic at your corner drugstore, chances are there's a mystery bookshop or public library within reach of your home.

Whodunit? All of us—every author and every fan who is keeping the mystery alive.

9 | WHO'S WHO IN WHODUNITS

Aarons, Edward Sidney (1916–1975). American writer of mystery and spy stories.

Abbott, Pat and Jean. Investigators. A couple created by Frances Crane.

Abner, Uncle. Detective created by Melville Davisson Post.

Allain-Souvestre (Marcel Allain (1885–1970) and Pierre Souvestre (1974–1914). One of the most famous partnerships in French crime fiction. Together they wrote a series of novels around the character of Fantômas and his great enemies, the policeman Juve and the journalist Fandor.

Alleyn, Roderick. Scotland Yard inspector created by Ngaio Marsh.

Allingham, Margery (1904–1966). English writer of mystery stories. Creator of Albert Campion.

Ambler, Eric (b. 1909). English writer of spy stories, who often ventured into detective fiction.

Anderson, Frederick Irving (1877–1947). American writer and journalist well-known in the 1920s for his stories involving the New York policeman Parr; the cunning criminal Godahl; and the writer Oliver Armiston.

Appleby, John. Scotland Yard inspector, later commissioner of London's metropolitan police, in a long series of novels and stories by Michael Innes.

Archer, Lew. The direct descendant of Sam Spade and Philip Marlowe; created by Ross Macdonald.

Armstrong, Charlotte (1905–1969). American poet, dramatist, and writer of mystery stories.

Asimov, Isaac (b. 1912). American science-fiction writer, author of traditional thrillers and detective stories published in *Ellery Queen's Mystery Magazine*.

Aveline, Claude. Pseudonym of Claude Avtzin (b. 1901). Well-known French author and essay writer, who has concentrated on thrillers, producing a series of five detective novels published between 1932 and 1970. One of the great theorists and apologists of the genre.

Bailey, Henry Christopher (1878–1961). English author; creator of Reggie Fortune.

Ball, John (b. 1911). American writer, creator of Virgil Tibbs. In 1965 he won an Edgar.

Ballinger, Bill (1912–1980). American thriller writer and screen and television scriptwriter.

Barr, Robert (1850–1912). English novelist and humorist; creator of the French detective Eugène Valmont.

Beck, Martin. Swedish commissioner of police in the novels of Sjöwall and Wahlöö.

Beeding, Francis. Pseudonym for the two English writers of thrillers and spy stories John Leslie Palmer (1885–1944) and Hillary Aidan St. George Saunders (1898–1951).

Bellairs, George. Pseudonym of Harold Blundell (b. 1902), author of some forty thrillers centering on Inspector Little John of Scotland Yard.

Bencolin, Henri. French police head created by John Dickson Carr. Works as a private investigator to supplement his salary.

Benson, Ben (1920–1959). American writer well-known for his series of novels dedicated to the various state police departments.

Bentley, E. C. (1875–1956). English lawyer and journalist; creator of Philip Trent.

Berkeley, Anthony. Pseudonym of Anthony Berkeley Cox (1893–1970), an English satirical journalist and author of mystery stories and humorous novels. Under the name Francis Iles he wrote critical essays on the thriller, as well as three suspense novels.

Biggers, Earl Derr (1884–1933). American author and playwright; creator of the exotic detective Charlie Chan.

Bioy-Casares, Adolfo (b. 1914). Well-known Argentinian writer, author of thrillers, and collaborator of Jorge Luis Borges.

Black Mask. The most important American pulp magazine, published 1920–1951; it launched the hard-boiled school of mystery writing.

Blake, Nicholas. Pseudonym of English poet laureate, novelist, and critic Cecil Day Lewis (1904–1972). Nicholas Blake wrote twenty detective novels.

Bloch, Robert (b. 1917). American author famous for having written *Psycho*, from which Alfred Hitchcock made the film of that name with Anthony Perkins.

Boileau, Pierre (b. 1906). French author of several novels dealing with locked-room problems. Since 1951 has been collaborator of Thomas Narcejac.

Boileau-Narcejac. One of the best-known partnerships in modern French psychological thrillers. Also writers of important essays on thrillers.

Bonaparte, Inspector Napoleon. Half-caste Australian detective created by Arthur W. Upfield.

Bond, James. Famed British Agent 007 in a series of thrillers by Ian Fleming.

Borges, Jorge Luis (b. 1899). Internationally famous Argentinian poet, storyteller, and critic. Fascinated by thriller techniques, he has written in this genre both independently and with Bioy-Casares, with whom he has edited anthologies and series of detective novels. Pseudonyms: Bustos Domecq and Suarez Lynch.

Boucher, Anthony. Pseudonym of William Anthony Parker White (1911–1968), American mystery and science-fiction writer and literary critic.

Bramah, Ernest. Pseudonym of the English writer Ernest Bramah Smith (1868–1942), creator of Max Carrados.

Brand, Christianna. Pseudonym of the English writer Mary Christianna Lewis (b. 1907), creator of Inspector Cockrill.

Brown, Father. Priest-detective created by G. K. Chesterton. Ellery Queen has described him as one of the three best fictional detectives. One of the first to stress the importance of psychological factors in crime detection.

Brown, Fredric (1906–1972). Writer of short science-fiction stories and some successful thrillers. *The Fabulous Clipjoint* won an Edgar for First Novel in 1948.

Buchan, John (1875–1940). Scottish diplomat, publisher, journalist, lawyer, and writer of historical, adventure, and spy novels; also talent scout—he discovered E. C. Bentley and got his works published.

Bucket. Police inspector created by Charles Dickens in *Bleak House*.

Burnett, W. R. (b. 1899). American writer, one of the originators of the hard-boiled school. Works of his were made into the films *Little Caesar* and *Asphalt Jungle*. MWA Grand Master award, 1979.

Burton, Miles. *See* Rhode, John.

Cain, James M. (1892–1977). American writer and author of *The Postman Always Rings Twice* (1934), which represented a turning-point in detective fiction, thanks partly to three film adaptations: Tay Garnett's (with Lana Turner), Luchino Visconti's (*Ossessione*, 1943) and Bob Rafelson's (with Jack Nicholson and Jessica Lange).

Campion, Albert. Aristocratic investigator created by Margery Allingham.

Canning, Victor (b. 1911). English government official and author of novels with international backgrounds.

Čapek, Karel (1890–1938). Czech writer, fond of detective fiction, who wrote suspense stories collected under the title *Tales from Two Pockets*.

Carr, John Dickson (1906–1977). American writer all of whose works follow the classic English thriller tradition. He specialized in locked-room murders. Also wrote under the names Carter Dickson and Carr Dickson.

Carrados, Max. Crime fiction's first blind investigator; created by E. Bramah.

Carter, Nick. Investigator, then spy, in a series of adventures written by a group of authors in collaboration under a common pseudonym.

Casey, Flashgun. Amateur investigator and photo-reporter created by George Harmon Coxe.

Caspary, Vera (b. 1899). American author of mystery stories and writer for film, television, and stage.

Chambrun, Pierre. Amateur investigator and manager of one of New York's smartest hotels. Created by Hugh Pentecost.

Chan, Charlie. Police inspector in Honolulu—the most famous exotic investigator in detective fiction. Created by Earl Derr Biggers. Charlie Chan's film career is one of the most prolific in the thriller world.

Chandler, Raymond (1888–1959). One of the best-known and most important American mystery writers. His thrillers, with Philip Marlowe as the protagonist, expose the violence of a society in crisis.

Charles, Nick and Nora. Husband and wife detective team created by Dashiell Hammett. Their great popularity is due in part to the *Thin Man* movies, starring William Powell and Myrna Loy.

Charteris, Leslie (b. 1907). Born in Singapore, a naturalized American. Creator of The Saint.

Chase, James Hadley. Pseudonym of the English writer René Raymond (b. 1906); head of the "new" violent novel school.

Chesterton, G. K. (1874-1936). English journalist, poet, critic, and writer; creator of Father Brown.

Cheyney, Peter (1896–1951). Ex-private investigator, English journalist and novelist, and creator of Lemmy Caution.

Christie, Agatha (1890–1976). English author considered the twentieth century's greatest and most popular thriller writer; creator of Hercule Poirot and Miss Marple.

Cockrill. Kent police inspector created by Christianna Brand.

Coe, Tucker. See Westlake, Donald E.

Cole, G. D. H. George Douglas Howard Cole (1889–1959) who with his wife Margaret Isabel Postgate Cole (b. 1893) had an important influence in both style and construction on the development of the detective novel.

Collins, Wilkie (1824–1889). A celebrated writer considered by critics as the father of the English detective story.

Connington, J. J. Pseudonym of Alfred Walter Stewart

(1880–1947), an English scientist and writer of thrillers featuring Sir Clinton Driffield.

Continental Op, The. Nameless private eye, employed by San Francisco's Continental Detective Agency. Created by Dashiell Hammett.

Cool, Bertha, and Donald Lam. Characters created by Erle Stanley Gardner under the pseudonym A. A. Fair—owners of a detective agency. Bertha Cool, at 286 pounds, is the female counterpart of Nero Wolfe. Donald Lam is a lawyer who has been barred from practice and who, before teaming up with Bertha Cool, was often in trouble with the police.

Coxe, George Harmon (b. 1901). American scriptwriter and author of mystery stories. His overall work made him an MWA Grand Master in 1963.

Crane, Frances (b. 1896). American author of mystery stories; famous for having created the globe-trotting investigators Pat and Jean Abbott.

Creasey, John (1908–1973). English writer held to be the most prolific in the world, with over five hundred novels to his credit written under his own name and twenty-eight pseudonyms. The pseudonyms include J. J. Marric, who created Commander Gideon of Scotland Yard.

Crime Writers' Association. Organization of professional British crime writers founded in 1953 by John Creasey and Nigel Morland.

Crispin, Edmund. Pseudonym of the English musician and writer Robert Bruce Montgomery (1921–1978), who has a reputation for thinking up disconcerting plots, liberally sprinkled with humor.

Crofts, Freeman Wills (1879–1957). Irish engineer and writer of detective novels. He introduced real police methods into the novel.

Crook, Arthur. Attorney-detective created by Anthony Gilbert.

Cuff Sergeant at Scotland Yard. The detective in Wilkie Collins's *The Moonstone*.

Curtiss, Ursula (b. 1923). American writer of suspense stories. Many of her novels are about children or girls in danger.

Dannay, Frederic. See Queen, Ellery.

Dard, Frédéric (b. 1921). One of the most prolific and successful French thriller writers, author of some thirty psychological and situation novels, subtle and often macabre in tone. He has written American-style novels of violence under the names Kaputt and L'Ange Noir. Famous especially under the pseudonym Sanantonio (cf.).

Da Silva, José. A Brazilian investigator created by R. L.

Fish. Has a degree in criminology, and was a policeman in Rio de Janeiro for fifteen years before rising to the rank of captain.

Davis, Dorothy Salisbury (b. 1916). American author of suspense novels and short stories, notably "A Gentle Murderer" (1951).

Davis, Mildred. American author of numerous suspense novels. Winner of the Edgar award in 1948.

Dawlish, Patrick. A character created by Gordon Ashe (alias John Creasey).

Dee, Judge. Hero of numerous mysteries inspired by the life of a seventh-century Chinese judge; researched and written by Robert Van Gulik.

Deighton, Len (b. 1929). British author of espionage thrillers.

De la Torre, Lillian (b. 1902). American playwright and short-story writer, author of a long series of mysteries in which Dr. Sam Johnson is a detective in an authentic historical setting.

Deming, Richard (b. 1915). Author of classic detective novels. Also writes under the name Max Franklin.

Department of Dead Ends. Scotland Yard Department created by British author Roy Vickers.

Department of Queer Complaints. Scotland Yard department specializing in impossible crimes; created by Carter Dickson (John Dickson Carr).

Detection Club. The first important organization of mystery writers, founded in London in 1928 by Anthony Berkeley. Its first president was G. K. Chesterton.

Devine, D. M. (b. 1920). Scottish writer, author of psychological thrillers and suspense novels.

Dewey, Thomas B. (b. 1915). American writer of private-eye stories and novels, some under the pseudonym Tom Brandt.

Dickens, Charles (1812–1870). One of the giants of world literature, whose work on several occasions verges on the thriller style.

Dimarco, Jefferson. Investigator for an insurance company featured in several novels by Doris Miles Disney.

Disney, Doris Miles (1907–1977). American novelist with an excellent narrative sense.

Disney, Dorothy Cameron (b. 1903). American writer of mystery novels, acclaimed for the atmosphere created and for the construction of the plots.

Doyle, Sir Arthur Conan (1859–1930). Scottish doctor and writer, creator of Sherlock Holmes, and author of historical novels.

Drew, Nancy. Created by Carolyn Keene. The most famous heroine in thrillers for children.

Drummond, Bulldog. Created by H. C. McNeile. Former army captain, and committed "protector" of his nation.

On the author's death the series was continued by Gerard Fairlie.

Duluth, Iris and Peter. Famous couple created by Patrick Quentin. He is a stage director and producer; she, an actress.

Du Maurier, Daphne (b. 1907). Well-known English popular novelist, author of several "romantic" thrillers thick with suspense. MWA Grand Master award, 1977.

Dupin, Auguste. Edgar Allan Poe's famous cavalier—the prototype of all the great detectives in crime fiction.

Durbridge, Francis (b. 1912). English writer of mystery novels, plays, and radio and television plays. His best-known character is Paul Temple.

Dürrenmatt, Friedrich (b. 1921). German-Swiss writer—one of the most highly regarded writers in contemporary literature. Author of three detective novels, each profoundly human, with Inspector Barlach as the hero.

Eberhart, Mignon G. (b. 1899). American writer of over fifty thrillers, creator of one of the most famous nurse-investigators: Sarah Keate.

87th Precinct. Fictional big-city police precinct in a series of novels by Ed McBain.

Ellery Queen's Mystery Magazine. The world's leading magazine of mystery, detection, and crime stories; edited since its founding in 1941 by Frederic Dannay.

Ellin, Stanley (b. 1916). American writer well-known for his thriller and horror stories. Twice winner of the Edgar Award, in 1954 and 1956, for the best short story of the year. In 1958 he won the same prize for best novel, and in 1975 received the French Grand Prix de Littérature policière.

Eustis, Helen (b. 1916). American writer known also for her excellent thriller *The Horizontal Man*, winner of the Edgar First Novel award in 1947.

Fair, A. A. Pseudonym of Erle Stanley Gardner.

Fairlie, Gerard. See Drummond, Bulldog.

Fantômas. Gothic hero of a cycle of novels by the Allain-Souvestre team.

Fell, Dr. Gideon. One of the most eccentric investigators in crime fiction. Created by John Dickson Carr. Always involved in apparently supernatural "cases" which in the end he unravels brilliantly.

Ferrars, Elizabeth. Pseudonym of Morna Doris Brown (b. 1907), a notable English writer, acclaimed for her ability to create rounded human characters. Published in U.S. as "E. X. Ferrars."

Fischer, Bruno (b. 1908). Writer of German origin, who went to America when very young. Translated into twelve languages.

Fish, Robert L. (1912–1981). American writer known above all for his parodies of Sherlock Holmes. Was the author of a popular series of novels with the Brazilian captain José Da Silva as the hero. Under the name Robert L. Pike he produced novels and short stories with the police as heroes.

Fleming, Ian (1908–1964). British novelist, creator of James Bond.

Fletcher, J. S. (1863–1935). English writer who set stories in the provinces rather than the big cities.

Fletcher, Lucille. American writer, dramatist, screen and TV scriptwriter, and author of excellent suspense novels.

Forbes, Stanton. Pseudonym of De Loris Stanton Forbes (b. 1923). American journalist and author of mystery novels.

Ford, Leslie. Pseudonym of Zenith Jones Brown (b. 1898). American author whose works abound in different themes, atmosphere, and characters. She has also written under the names of David Frome and Brenda Conrad.

Fortune, Reggie. Surgeon often called in by Scotland Yard. Created by H. C. Bailey.

Four Just Men, The. Created by Edgar Wallace. An association that deals with cases outside the power of the law.

Francis, Dick (b. 1920). Former Welsh jockey who writes suspense novels set against a background of British horse racing. MWA Edgar winner in 1969 for *Forfeit*.

Freeman, R. Austin (1862–1943). English doctor and writer, father of the scientific thriller, and creator of John Thorndyke. Also wrote under the name Clifford Ashdown.

French, Joseph. Scotland Yard inspector created by Freeman Wills Crofts.

Fu Manchu, Dr. One of the most famous "sinister Orientals," out to take over the world, using every foul means. Created by Sax Rohmer.

Futrelle, Jacques (1875–1912). American writer, one of the first exponents of the scientific thriller, and creator of the Thinking Machine.

Gaboriau, Emile (1832–1873). Successor to Edgar Allan Poe, and creator of the French thriller. Among his most famous characters are Père Tabaret and Lecoq.

Gardner, Erle Stanley (1889–1970). One of the most famous American detective story writers, creator of the "devil's advocate" Perry Mason. Under the name A. A. Fair he wrote several novels featuring Bertha Cool and Donald Lam as the heroes.

Garfield, Brian (b. 1939). American writer of suspense novels and short stories. MWA Edgar winner in 1975 for "Hopscotch," from which he also coproduced the 1980 film version.

Garve, Andrew. Pseudonym of the English writer Paul Winterton (b. 1908), author of numerous detective and spy novels.

Gault, William Campbell (b. 1910). American writer of hundreds of short stories and many novels, winner of the Edgar First Novel award in 1952.

Gethryn, Anthony. One of the cleverest amateur sleuths; created by Philip MacDonald.

Ghote, Inspector. Bombay police inspector created by British author H. R. F. Keating (b. 1926).

Gibson, Walter B. (b. 1897). American magician and writer of detective novels with The Shadow as their hero.

Gideon, George. Scotland Yard superintendent created by John Creasey under the pseudonym J. J. Marric. One of the first policemen to be seen at home as well as at work. The novels in which he appears are slices of everyday life at Scotland Yard.

Gilbert, Anthony. Pseudonym of Lucy Beatrice Malleson (1899–1973), English writer of mystery novels and short stories.

Gilbert, Michael (b. 1912). English lawyer and author of detective novels which reveal considerable knowledge of law, situations of war, and life in general. He has also written an essay on the thriller.

Godey, John. Pseudonym of the American author Morton Freedgood (b. 1912), PR man for various leading film companies, and writer of thrillers which often contain a strong vein of humor.

Goodis, David (1917–1967). American thriller writer. His heroes are disenchanted drunkards, desperate men, burning up their last resources of strength in action.

Goodwin, Archie. Right-hand man and general dogsbody to the investigator Nero Wolfe, created by Rex Stout.

Gould, Chester (b. 1900). American designer, creator of the first comic-strip thriller, with Dick Tracy as hero.

Green, Anna Katherine (1846–1935). American author, inventor of the term "detective story."

Greene, Graham (b. 1904). Famous English writer of novels dealing with espionage, as well as some good suspense novels.

Gribble, Leonard Reginald (b. 1908). One of the most prolific English writers, creator of Superintendent Slade, and others, of Scotland Yard.

Gryce, Ebenezer. Police detective, hero of numerous novels by Anna K. Green.

Hall, Adam. Pseudonym of Elleston Trevor (b. 1920). English novelist, known especially for his spy books, but with a reputation also as a thriller writer. Films have been made of many of his novels, including *The Quiller Memorandum* with George Segal, Alec Guinness, Max von Sydow, and Senta Berger.

Halliday, Brett. Pseudonym of Davis Dresser (1904–1977), the American writer known for his creation of Michael Shayne. He wrote dozens of short stories of all sorts, under different pseudonyms, for popular magazines.

Hambledon, Tommy. British secret agent created by Manning Coles.

Hamilton, Bruce (b. 1900). English playwright and historical and political writer, who has also written excellent detective novels.

Hamilton, Patrick (1904–1962). English writer of plays and tales of mystery.

Hammer, Mike. One of the best-known and toughest modern private detectives; created by Mickey Spillane.

Hammett, Dashiell (1894–1961). American writer, instigator of the hard-boiled school.

Hanaud, Gabriel. Inspector of the Sûreté, created by A. E. W. Mason.

Hannay, Richard. Character created by John Buchan.

Hare, Cyril. Pseudonym of Alfred Alexander Gordon Clark (1900–1958), English lawyer and judge, and author of detective novels which draw on his own legal experience.

Harrington, Joseph (b. 1903). American journalist and writer, known for the realism of his detective novels based on real-life murders.

Harris, Herbert (b. 1911). The most prolific English short story writer: 3,500 published in twenty-six countries, and translated into nineteen languages.

Hart, Frances Noyes (1890–1943). American author, known chiefly for her first novel *The Bellamy Case*.

Heard, H. F. (1889–1971). British author who wrote several novels about Mr. Mycroft, a detective resembling Sherlock Holmes.

Helm, Matt. Hero of a series of thrillers by American writer Donald Hamilton (b. 1916).

Hewitt, Martin. A character of Arthur Morrison's. One of the earliest and most popular detectives to follow in the footsteps of Sherlock Holmes.

Heyer, Georgette (1902–1974). English author of historical romances and period mystery novels along classic lines.

Higgins, George V. (b. 1939). American writer of crime novels, notably *The Friends of Eddie Coyle* (1972).

Highsmith, Patricia (b. 1921). American writer of short stories and suspense novels, notably *Strangers on a Train*.

Himes, Chester (b. 1909). American writer of "black" novels set mainly in Harlem.

Hitchcock, Alfred (1899–1980). English film director, considered a master of spine-chilling techniques. The best thriller films have come from him.

Hitchens, Dolores (1908–1973). American poet, teacher, and writer of good detective novels as D. B. Olsen, or as Hitchens, Dolan Birkley, or Noel Burke.

Hoch, Edward D. (b. 1930). American short story writer and 1967 MWA Edgar winner. During the past decade, the most frequent contributor to *Ellery Queen's Mystery Magazine*.

Holmes, Sherlock. The greatest detective in crime fiction. Created by Sir Arthur Conan Doyle. He was born on January 6, 1854, of a modest family, in Yorkshire. His early years are shrouded in mystery. He was probably educated at either Oxford or Cambridge, interrupting his studies and moving to London to pursue other disciplines, which enabled him to become a consultant investigator. His first case dates from 1877. In autumn 1879 he went to America with the Abbott Touring Company, an acting company, performing mostly Shakespeare. A few months after returning to Britain he met Watson and began the career that was to stretch over four novels and fifty-six short stories.

Hornung, E. W. (1866–1921). Sir Arthur Conan Doyle's brother-in-law, and creator of Raffles, the gentleman thief.

Hughes, Dorothy B. (b. 1904). American mystery writer and literary critic. MWA Grand Master award, 1977. Author of *Ride the Pink Horse* (1946).

Hull, Richard. Pseudonym of Richard Sampson (1896–1973), British mystery writer best known for *The Murder of My Aunt* (1934).

Hume, Fergus (1859–1932). New Zealand author of the best-selling nineteenth-century thriller *The Mystery of a Hansom Cab*.

Hunter, Evan. See McBain, Ed.

Iles, Francis. See Berkeley, Anthony.

Innes, Michael. Pseudonym of Jones Innes MacKintosh Stewart (b. 1906). English novelist well-known for his work outside the field of thrillers—novels and biographies of Rudyard Kipling and Joseph Conrad—but under his pseudonym he wrote several classic-style detective novels.

Irish, William. See Woolrich, Cornell.

James, P. D. (b. 1920). British mystery writer, creator of Chief Superintendent Adam Dalgliesh and author of the best-selling suspense novel *Innocent Blood* (1980).

Japrisot, Sébastien (b. 1931). Pseudonym of the French writer Jean-Baptiste Rossi, author of sophisticated psychological thrillers.

Kane, Frank. American writer of thrillers and novels of violence. Creator of Johnny Liddell.

Kane, Henry (b. 1918). American lawyer and writer, and one of the best exponents of the hard-boiled novel.

Keene, Carolyn. Pseudonym first of Edward L. Stratemeyer, then of his daughter Harriet S. Adams. American author of one of the most famous children's thriller series, with heroine Nancy Drew.

Keene, Day. American writer of stories of violence.

Kemelman, Harry (b. 1908). American university teacher and writer, known for his detective novels with Rabbi David Small as their central character.

Kendrick, Baynard (1894–1977). American writer, a founder and first president of Mystery Writers of America, and Grand Master winner for his complete works in 1966.

Kennedy, Craig. One of the earliest scientific detectives; created by Arthur B. Reeve.

King, C. Daly (1895–1963). American psychologist and writer of brilliant, lively detective stories.

King, Rufus (1893–1966). American writer known for the tension he creates in his novels. Creator of the French-Canadian lieutenant Valcour.

Knott, Frederick M. P. (b. 1918). English writer (born in China), known for his stage work, from which Hitchcock derived *Dial M for Murder*.

Knox, Ronald A. (1888–1957). English priest and writer of detective stories. Author of a thriller manual.

Lacy, Ed. Pseudonym of the American author Len Zinberg (1911–1968), winner of the 1957 Edgar award for best novel with *Room to Swing*.

Lady Molly of Scotland Yard. One of the first woman detectives, created by Baroness Emmuska Orczy.

Lane, Drury. Former Shakespearean actor and amateur detective in a four-novel cycle written by Ellery Queen under the pseudonym Barnaby Ross.

Latimer, Jonathan (b. 1906). Hard-boiled American novelist and film scriptwriter.

Leblanc, Maurice (1864–1941). French journalist and novelist, creator of Arsène Lupin.

Le Breton, Auguste (b. 1913). Author of *Rififi* and poet of the French underworld through a long series of novels in the violent style. Author of two excellent illustrated dictionaries of argot.

Le Carré, John. Pseudonym of David Cornwell (b. 1931), best-selling British author of espionage novels. Widely known for *The Spy Who Came in from the Cold* (1963) and *Tinker, Tailor, Soldier, Spy* (1974).

Lecoq. Chief investigator in the novels of Gaboriau, and direct descendant of Auguste Dupin.

Lee, Manfred B. See Queen, Ellery.

Le Fanu, Joseph Sheridan (1814–1873). Irish writer of tales of mystery and the supernatural.

Leroux, Gaston (1868–1927). One of the most famous French thriller writers, author of *The Mystery of the Yellow Room*.

Levin, Ira (b. 1929). American novelist and playwright, best known for *A Kiss Before Dying* (1953) and *Rosemary's Baby*, from which Roman Polanski made the film starring Mia Farrow.

Lockridge, Frances. See Lockridge, Richard.

Lockridge, Richard (b. 1898). American novelist and theater critic. Creator, together with his wife Frances, of one of the most famous investigator couples in crime fiction, Mr. and Mrs. North.

London, Jack (1876–1916). Famous American author who wrote a thriller about a crime syndicate, completed after his death by Robert L. Fish.

Ludlum, Robert (b. 1927). Best-selling American author of suspense and intrigue novels.

Lupin, Arsène. The "gentleman-thief" in a series of novels by Leblanc (continued recently by Boileau and Narcejac) and endless movies and television films.

Lone Wolf. A Lupin-type figure created by the American novelist L. J. Vance.

Lustgarten, Edgar (1907–1978). English criminologist and writer of novels based on real-life events.

McBain, Ed. Pseudonym of Evan Hunter (b. 1926), famous for his novels about the 87th precinct. Under his real name he has written novels about juvenile violence. He also wrote the script for Alfred Hitchcock's *The Birds*.

McCloy, Helen (b. 1904). American writer of mystery novels and short stories. She was the first woman president of the Mystery Writers of America.

McCoy, Horace (1897–1955). The "enfant terrible" of the American "black" novel, who "shoots words like bullets" (*Time*). Hollywood scriptwriter, author of *No Pockets in a Shroud* (1948).

MacDonald, John D. (b. 1916). American mystery writer. 1971 Grand Master winner for his complete works. Creator of Travis McGee.

MacDonald, Philip (b. 1896). Anglo-American writer of detective novels and short stories. Creator of the amateur private eye Anthony Gethryn.

Macdonald, Ross. Pseudonym of Kenneth Millar (b. 1915). American mystery writer. After writing a few novels under his own name, he adopted the pseudonym to avoid confusion with his wife Margaret, also a writer of detective novels. Ross Macdonald's private detective hero is Lew Archer.

McGee, Travis. Character midway between detective and thief, created by John D. MacDonald.

McGivern, William P. (b. 1924). American mystery writer and film scriptwriter, whose hard-boiled novels are often condemnations of a corrupt police force. MWA president, 1980.

McGuire, Paul (b. 1903). Australian diplomat. Author of detective novels with excellent story lines.

MacInnes, Helen (b. 1907). American writer of Scottish origin. Writer of atmospheric thrillers.

McKee, Christopher. Inspector in the New York Metropolitan Police, created by Helen Reilly.

McMullen, Mary (b. 1920). Daughter of Helen Reilly, and sister of Ursula Curtiss. Winner of the Edgar First Novel award in 1952.

McNeile, H. C. (1888–1937). English professional soldier who wrote various novels under the name "Sapper." The best known is the Bulldog Drummond series.

MacShane, Mark. (b. 1930). Australian author of parapsychological detective novels.

Maigret, Jules. The most famous police commissioner in crime fiction. He figures in over a hundred stories by Simenon, and in dozens of films and TV films from all over the world.

Malet, Léo (b. 1909). Great precursor of the modern French thriller, author of a series of light-hearted Paris novels centering on the character Nestor Burma.

Malone, John J. Chicago lawyer, slightly too fond of the bottle, created by Craig Rice.

March, Colonel. Chief of Scotland Yard's Department D-3, created by John Dickson Carr under the name Carter Dickson.

Marlowe, Philip. One of the best-known private detectives in crime fiction. A hard man, but basically a romantic figure in pursuit of justice. Author: Raymond Chandler.

Marple, Jane. The most famous woman detective in crime fiction; created by Agatha Christie.

Marquand, John P. (1893–1960). American writer of spy-based thrillers. Creator of Mr. Moto.

Marric, J. J. See Creasey, John.

Marsh, Ngaio (b. 1899). New Zealand author, whose detective novels often take place in theater or art circles, and regularly feature superintendent Roderick Alleyn. 1978 Grand Master for her complete works.

Martineau, Harry. English police inspector, created by Maurice Procter.

Mason, A. E. W. (1865–1948). English thriller writer. His main character was the French detective Hanaud.

Mason, Perry. The most famous lawyer in crime fiction. Author: Erle Stanley Gardner.

Mason, Randolph. Unscrupulous American lawyer, created by Melville Davisson Post.

Masterson, Whit. See Miller, Wade.

Matsumoto, Seicho. Japanese writer of detective novels with social overtones. Author of many best sellers.

Mayo, Asey. Cape Cod sleuth in the novels of Phoebe Atwood Taylor (1909–1976).

Mendoza, Luis. Los Angeles police lieutenant in the novels of Dell Shannon.

Merrion, Desmond. English secret agent during World War I—at the end of which he becomes a private investigator. Created by Miles Burton.

Merrivale, Sir Henry. Character involved in numerous locked-room murders, created by John Dickson Carr, under the pseudonym Carter Dickson.

Millar, Kenneth. See Macdonald, Ross.

Millar, Margaret (b. 1915). Canadian-American writer, wife of Ross Macdonald. Many of her novels are set in California, and develop out of the California "freak scene." She won the Edgar award in 1956.

Miller, Wade. Pseudonym for Robert Wade (b. 1920) and Bill Miller (1920–1961), one of the many successful partnerships in crime fiction. They also produced novels of violence under the name Whit Masterson. Robert Wade has written two novels under his own name, and several more as Whit Masterson.

Monteilhet, Hubert (b. 1928). One of the most sophisticated exponents of the French psychological thriller.

Moriarty, Professor James. One of the first "evil geniuses" of English crime fiction; created by Conan Doyle.

Morimura, Seiichi. The most prolific Japanese writer of detective stories.

Morland, Nigel (b. 1905). English journalist and writer of detective novels, who has also used the pseudonyms Mary Dane, John Donovan, Norman Forrest, Roger Carnett, Neal Shepherd, and Vincent McCall.

Morrison, Arthur (1863–1945). English journalist and writer of short stories featuring the famous detective Martin Hewitt as hero.

Morton, Anthony. Pseudonym under which John Creasey created the Baron.

Moto, Mr. Hero of the novels of J. P. Marquand.

Mulligan, Patrick. A lawyer with few scruples, created by Baroness Emmuska Orczy.

Murdock, Kent. Boston's highest-paid photographer and amateur sleuth, created by George Harmon Coxe.

Mystery Writers of America (MWA) Writers' organization founded in New York in 1945. Awards annual Edgars—ceramic busts of Edgar Allan Poe—for best novel, first novel, short story, and so on, plus a Grand Master award for lifetime achievement.

Narcejac, Thomas. Pseudonym of Pierre Ayraud (b. 1908), theoretician and historian of the detective novel. Author, together with Pierre Boileau, of numerous suspense stories.

Natsuki, Shizuko. "Leading Lady" among the small handful of female Japanese thriller writers.

Nielsen, Helen (b. 1918). American writer of psychological detective novels and TV filmscripts.

North, Mr. and Mrs. One of the most famous couples in detective fiction; created by Frances and Richard Lockridge.

O'Breen, Fergus. Irish private investigator, who works alone in his own Los Angeles agency. Author: Anthony Boucher.

Old Man in the Corner, The. Detective created by Baroness Orczy.

Oppenheim, E. Phillips (1866–1946). English mystery writer, author of novels with cosmopolitan settings.

Orczy, Emmuska (1865–1947). Baroness of Hungarian extraction and English by adoption, famous as the creator of various characters: the Scarlet Pimpernel, the "old man in the corner," Lady Molly of Scotland Yard, and Patrick Mulligan.

Ozaki, Milton. American thriller writer. Also uses the pseudonym Robert O. Saber.

Palmer, Stuart (1905–1968). American writer and scriptwriter. Author of humorous thrillers with heroes Hildegard Withers and Oscar Piper.

Parker, Robert B. (b. 1932). American author of novels about Boston private eye Spenser. Winner of MWA Edgar award in 1976.

Parodi, don Isidro. Buenos Aires barber, wrongly found guilty of murder, who without leaving his cell solves six crimes. Hero of the detective stories written by Borges and Bioy-Casares under the name Bustos Domecq; published in the U.S. for the first time in 1981.

Patrick Q. See Quentin, Patrick.

Pentecost, Hugh. See Philips, Judson.

Perowne, Barry. Pseudonym of Philip Atkey (b. 1908). English writer best known as the man who continued the Raffles series.

Philips, Judson (b. 1903). American mystery writer (pseudonym, Hugh Pentecost), creator of the amateur investigator Pierre Chambrun. 1972 MWA Grand Master.

Phillpotts, Eden (1862–1960). English novelist, poet, and playwright, author of some remarkable detective novels.

Poe, Edgar Allan (1809–1849). One of America's greatest writers and poets, inventor of the thriller and the characteristic thriller "situations": the amateur detective, the narrator, the mystery of the locked room, etc.

Poirot, Hercule. Belgian detective created by Agatha Christie. One of the most famous investigators in crime fiction.

Pons, Solar. Detective in a lengthy series of Sherlock Holmes pastiches by American author August Derleth (1909–1971).

Ponson du Terrail (1829–1871). Pseudonym of Vicomte Pierre Alexis de Ponson, prolific French *feuilleton* writer, creator of the evil genius Rocambole, prototype of every kind of villain in popular crime fiction.

Poole, John. Scotland Yard's youngest inspector in the novels of Henry Wade.

Post, Melville Davisson (1871–1930). American lawyer and writer, creator of Uncle Abner.

Potts, Jean (b. 1910). American mystery writer and author of remarkable short stories. 1954 winner of the Edgar First Novel award.

Priestley, Dr. Lancelot. A John Rhode character.

Procter, Maurice (1906–1973). One of the first English writers to describe adventures of the official police, in a series of novels with hero Harry Martineau.

Queen, Ellery. Pseudonym of Frederic Dannay (b. 1905) and Manfred B. Lee (1905–1971). The most famous, highly esteemed, and highly honored partnership in American thriller fiction. The two also worked under the name Barnaby Ross. Ellery Queen is also one of the most famous detectives in crime fiction, a thriller writer who helps his father, Police Inspector Richard Queen, on difficult cases.

Quentin, Patrick. Pseudonym for one of the most complicated thriller-writing "firms," consisting of four writers: Richard Wilson Webb, Martha Mott Kelly, Mary Louise Aswell, and Hugh Callingham Wheeler. Other pseudonyms: Q. Patrick and Jonathan Stagge.

Raffles. Gentleman-thief created by E. W. Hornung. On Hornung's death the Raffles stories were continued by Barry Perowne.

Rampo, Edogawa. Pseudonym of Hirai Taro, one of the fathers of modern Japanese detective writing. The pseudonym is a phonetic transcription of Poe's name.

Rawson, Clayton (1906–1971). American author of four detective novels and several short stories about The Great Merlini, a magician sleuth.

Reeder, Mister J. G. Assistant to the Attorney General in London, created by Edgar Wallace.

Reeve, Arthur B. (1880–1936). Lawyer and journalist, creator of the "American Sherlock Holmes," Craig Kennedy.

Reilly, Helen (1891–1962). Well-known writer of detective novels featuring the Manhattan homicide squad.

Rendell, Ruth. First-rate British writer of detective novels and stories.

Rhode, John. Pseudonym of Cecil John Charles Street (1884–1964), English mystery writer, and creator of Lancelot Priestley.

Rice, Craig. Pseudonym of the American mystery writer and film scriptwriter Ann Randolph (1908–1957).

Rinehart, Mary Roberts (1876–1958). American author, whose novels feature a heroine who lands herself in trouble.

Robbe-Grillet, Alain (b. 1922). Main exponent of the French "nouveau roman." His *Erasers* is "also" a detective novel relating to the Oedipus myth.

Rocambole. Feuilleton character created by Ponson du Terrail. An evil genius who turns to good.

Rohmer, Sax. Pseudonym of Arthur Henry Sarsfield Ward (1883–1959), English novelist, creator of Dr. Fu Manchu.

Roos, Kelly. Pseudonym of the American thriller writers Audrey Kelley and William Roos.

Ross, Barnaby. See Queen, Ellery.

Rouletabille. Nickname of Joseph Josephin, the young journalist and amateur sleuth hero of a succession of novels by Leroux.

Runyon, Damon (1884–1946). Journalist and writer of humorous short stories. Best-known for *Guys and Dolls*.

Saint, The. Nickname of Simon Templar, a character created by Leslie Charteris.

Sanantonio. Pseudonym under which Frédéric Dard (cf.) began publishing a saga of over 30,000 pages about certain members of a mythical Paris police force and its associates (1950). The saga has a Rabelaisian richness of linguistic invention, pastiche, and word play. Sanantonio is also the name of the Paris police commissioner, hero of the novels by "Sanantonio."

Sano, Yoh. Japanese journalist and writer. One of the best postwar thriller-writers in terms of style and technique.

Sasazawa, Saho. Japanese writer of hard-boiled thrillers.

Sayers, Dorothy L. (1893-1957). English writer and poet, author of a series of detective novels with hero Lord Peter Wimsey.

Selby, Doug. District Attorney in the "D.A." books by Erle Stanley Gardner.

Shadow, The. Main character in the stories and radio plays of Leslie Charteris.

Shannon, Dell. Best-known pseudonym of Elizabeth Linington (b. 1921), who also writes as Linington, Anne Blaisdell, Leslie Egan, and Egan O'Neill. As Shannon, she created detective Luis Mendoza.

Shayne, Mike. Miami private detective created by Brett Halliday.

Sheringham, Roger. Detective created by British writer Anthony Berkeley, best known from *The Poisoned Chocolates Case* (1929).

Silver, Maud. Famous woman detective created by Patricia Wentworth.

Simenon, Georges (1903). Creator of Commissioner Maigret, and the greatest French-language thriller writer (he was born in Belgium). His novels transcend the narrow confines of crime fiction.

Simonin, Albert (b. 1905). One of the best of the French "black" and argot novelists. Has also published a dictionary of argot.

Sjöwall, Maj. See Walöö, Per.

Small, Rabbi David. Hero of seven detective novels by Harry Kemelman, starting with *Friday the Rabbi Slept Late* (1964).

Smiley, George. Hero of several espionage novels by John le Carré.

Spade, Sam. Private investigator, created by Dashiell Hammett.

Spillane, Mickey (b. 1918). American hard-boiled novelist. Head of the postwar "sex and violence" school.

Stagge, Jonathan. See Quentin, Patrick.

Stark, Richard. See Westlake, Donald E.

Starrett, Vincent (1886–1974). American journalist, bibliophile, essayist, poet, and novelist, author of excellent detective novels and essays on Sherlock Holmes. 1957 Grand Master.

Steeman, Stanislas-André (1908–1970). A compatriot of Simenon's. Author of twenty-seven detective stories featuring Inspector Wens.

Stein, Aaron Marc (b. 1906). American author of more than a hundred detective novels. MWA Grand Master award, 1978.

Souvestre, Pierre (1874–1914). *See* Allain-Souvestre.

Stevenson, Robert Louis (1850–1894). Great Scottish novelist and poet, who with Dr. Jekyll and Mr. Hyde introduced the theme of the dual personality, which has been so successfully used in thrillers and horror stories.

Stone, Fleming. Character created by Carolyn Wells.

Stout, Rex (1886–1975). One of the most famous American thriller writers, best known for his creation of the Nero Wolfe–Archie Goodwin team.

Strange, Violet. A young New York socialite, one of the first female detectives in crime fiction, created by Anna K. Green.

Strangeways, Nigel. Amateur investigator. Author: Nicholas Blake.

Stribling, T. S. (1881–1965). American novelist and Pulitzer Prize winner who created Professor Henry Poggioli in a series of detective short stories.

Symons, Julian (b. 1912). English poet, biographer, criminologist, novelist, and critic, best known for his essays on the detective novel and for some well-turned thrillers.

Templar, Simon. See Saint, The.

Tey, Josephine. Pseudonym of Elizabeth Mackintosh (1896–1952), Scottish writer, author of detective novels, sometimes with historical backgrounds.

Thatcher, John Putnam. Banker-detective in the novels of Emma Lathen.

Thinking Machine, The. Character created by Jacques Futrelle. His real name is Augustus S. F. X. Van Dusen, and his most memorable appearance is in the short story "The Problem of Cell 13."

Thomas, Ross (b. 1926). American thriller writer, winner of the Edgar First Novel award in 1966.

Thompson, Jim (b. 1910). The most pessimistic of the American Gothic novelists.

Thorndyke, John. One of the first and most famous scientific investigators in detective fiction. Author: R. Austin Freeman.

Thursday, Max. Private investigator in San Diego, created by Wade Miller.

Tibbs, Virgil. Black policeman from Pasadena, created by John Ball.

Togawa, Masako. Japanese singer and writer of psychological thrillers.

Tracy, Dick. The first comic-strip "super-detective," created by Chester Gould.

Treat, Lawrence (b. 1903). American mystery writer generally credited with having originated the police procedural novel.

Trent, Philip. Painter and journalist turned amateur investigator for love of adventure. Created by E. C. Bentley.

Tutt, Mr. Lawyer-detective created by Arthur Train (1875–1945).

Twain, Mark. Pseudonym of Samuel Clemens (1835–1910), one of the giants of literature, who wrote some novels and short stories with humorous suspense or detective plots.

Uhnak, Dorothy (b. 1933). American policewoman and mystery writer. 1968 winner of the Edgar First Novel award with her novel *The Bait.*

Upfield, Arthur W. (1884–1964). British writer who spent much of his life in Australia. Creator of Inspector Napoleon Bonaparte.

Valcour. French-Canadian lieutenant created by the American writer Rufus King.

Valmont, Eugène. Character created by Robert Barr.

Vance, John Holbrook (b. 1920). American mystery and science fantasy writer. 1960 winner of the Edgar First Novel award with his novel *The Man in the Cage.*

Vance, Louis Joseph (1879–1933). Author of a series of novels in which the hero is The Lone Wolf.

Vance, Philo. The most foppish, elegant, and aristocratic amateur detective in American crime fiction. Invented by S. S. Van Dine.

Van der Valk, Inspector. Amsterdam police inspector who starred in ten novels by Nicholas Freeling (b. 1927).

Van de Wetering, Janwillem (b. 1931). Native of the Netherlands who has written several novels about the Amsterdam police force.

Van Dine, S. S. Pseudonym of Willard Huntington Wright (1888–1939). Journalist and art critic, well known as the creator of Philo Vance and as the author of the "double decalogue" of the detective novel.

Van Dusen, Augustus S. F. X. See Thinking Machine, The.

Van Gulick, Robert (1910–1967). Dutch diplomat and

sinologist, transcriber (in part inventor) of the Judge Dee cases.

Véry, Pierre. Pseudonym of Pierre Toussaint Juge (1900–1960), one of the most original French thriller writers. His detectives: Prosper Lepicq and Goupi-Mains-Rouges.

Vickers, Roy (1889–1965). English thriller writer, whose best stories center on the Department of Dead Ends.

Vidocq, Eugène François (1775–1857). Ex-galley slave, founder and head of the Sûreté. Author of famous *Mémoires*.

Wade, Henry. Pseudonym of Sir Henry Lancelot Aubrey-Fletcher (1887–1969), an English writer of detective novels, creator of Inspector John Poole.

Wade, Robert. See Miller, Wade.

Wahlöö, Per (1926–1975). Swedish novelist, journalist, and radio and TV scriptwriter. Co-authored with his wife, poetess Maj Sjöwall, a series of novels whose protagonist is Martin Beck.

Wallace, Edgar (1875-1932). English novelist best known for his numerous detective novels. He has the distinction of having spread the thriller throughout the world.

Wallas. The special agent in Alain Robbe-Grillet's *Erasers*—he solves the (in fact non-existent) murder by himself killing the presumed victim.

Walsh, Thomas (b. 1908). American novelist and short story writer, MWA Edgar winner, 1951 and 1978. MWA president, 1981.

Wambaugh, Joseph (b. 1937). Former detective sergeant, author of several novels about the Los Angeles police department.

Watson, Dr. John H. Biographer and right-hand man of Sherlock Holmes, created by Sir Arthur Conan Doyle.

Waugh, Hillary (b. 1920). American mystery writer. Among the first to use the police as protagonists.

Wells, Carolyn (1870?–1942). Prolific American author of novels with hero Fleming Stone, investigator.

Wens. Inspector, hero of Steeman's novels.

Wentworth, Patricia. Pseudonym of the English historical novelist and mystery writer Dora Amy Elles Dillon Turnbull (1878–1961).

West, Roger. Scotland Yard's youngest Chief Superintendent, created by the prolific English writer John Creasey.

Westlake, Donald E. (b. 1933). American writer of basically humorous detective novels, and also of hard-boiled novels under the names Richard Stark and Tucker Coe.

White, Ethel Lina (1884–1944). English thriller writer, who became famous through the Hitchcock film *The Lady Vanishes*, adapted from one of her novels.

Williams, Charles (b. 1909). American author. Served in the navy before turning to writing. His detective novels are full of slang, black humor, and violence.

Willing, Dr. Basil. Psychologist-detective in the novels and short stories of Helen McCloy.

Wimsey, Lord Peter. Private investigator created by Dorothy L. Sayers.

Withers, Hildegarde. One of the most amusing woman detectives in crime fiction. Created by Stuart Palmer.

Wolfe, Nero. The most eccentric and most massive detective in the whole of crime fiction. A great gourmet, and passionately fond of growing orchids. Inventor: Rex Stout.

Woolrich, Cornell (1903–1968). American suspense writer, compared with Edgar Allan Poe because of his ability to create a terrifying atmosphere. Has also written excellent novels under the name William Irish.

Zadig. One of crime fiction's prototype detectives—hero of a short novel by Voltaire.

Zaleski, Prince. Bizarre detective in four short stories by M. P. Shiel (1865–1947).

Zangwill, Israel (1864–1926). Well-known English novelist, author of a novel in which the first locked-room murder occurs.

The famous "mechanical" puzzle, von Kempelen's automatic chess player (drawing by Alberto Martini). In his essay "Maelzel's Chess-Player," Poe solves the mystery: According to him there was a dwarf hidden inside the automaton. Poe maintains, however, that police investigations are closer to draughts than to chess, in which "nine times out of ten it is not the most skillful player who wins, but the player who concentrates hardest."

INDEX

PHOTO CREDITS

We would like to thank the following for permission to use illustrative material: Foto Mori; Jean Arlaud; British Museum; British Library; London Museum; Musée de la Prefecture, Paris; Philadelphia Board of Trustees of Drexel Institute of Technology; The New-York Historical Society; Jupiter Books, London: Bodleian Library, Oxford; Roger Viollet; Foto Freeman; Sherlock Holmes Society, London; Express News and Feature Service, London; New York Public Library; Scholastic Magazine, Inc., New York; Cyrus Cuneo, Chatto and Windus; Mitchell Library, Sidney; Max Parrish, London; Max Duperray; NBC, New York; Lord's Gallery, London; Thomson Newspapers, Ltd., London; Popperfoto; Mander and Mitchens Theatre Collection, London; C. A. Pearson Ltd., London; Marty Norman; *Redbook* Magazine; Pinkerton's Inc.; Chicago *Tribune* — New York News Syndicate; King Features Syndicate; The Condé Nast Publications, Inc.; Jill Krementz; Associated Press; Bibliothèques de la Ville de Paris; Mercure de France; Giancolombo; Jerry Bauer; S.P.A.D.E.M., Paris; Martin Monestier; Carlo Rossi Fantonetti; Fleuve Noir; Peter Stackpole; Giacomino Foto; Azienda Soggiorno Cattolica; Roma's Press Photo; Giorgio Lotti; Adriano Alecchi; Biblioteca Civica, Milan; Archivio Fotographico Mondadori. We would like to extend particular thanks to the editorial staff of Giallo Mondadori for the material they so kindly made available and to the following publishers for the use of covers or illustrations: Feltrinelli, Garzanti, Longanesi, Rizzoli, Rusconi, Ace Books, Bantam, Black Mask, Bobbs-Merrill, Christian Bourgois Editeur, Collins, Crime Club, Dell, Denoël, Dodd Mead & Company, Fleuve Noir, La Bruyère, Morrow, Pan Books, Penguin Books, Pocket Books Inc., Random House, Selection, Scribner's, Simon and Schuster, Torquil. We apologize if we have unintentionally omitted or cited erroneously any sources or photographic agencies.